Mark Bles is well qualified insurgency. Educated at Sandhurst and Oxford, he has served in the Royal Green Jackets and 22 Special Air Service Regiment. After leaving the regular army, he worked for several years as a kidnap negotiator, which experience he drew upon to write his acclaimed first book **The Kidnap Business.**

# Child At War

## Mark Bles

WARNER BOOKS

A *Warner* Book

First published in Great Britain by Hodder & Stoughton 1989
Published by Sphere Books Ltd 1990
Reprinted 1991
Reprinted by Warner Books 1992
Reprinted 1993, 1995

Printed in England by Clays Ltd, St Ives plc

ISBN 0 7515 0460 2

Warner Books
A Division of
Little, Brown and Company (UK)
Brettenham House
Lancaster Place
London WC2E 7EN

# CONTENTS

# Acknowledgments

This book would not have been possible without the complete commitment of Hortense to tell her story. She held back no details, however personal or painful. Sitting with her husband Syd, I listened fascinated for many hours while she brought to life the people and events of long ago. She showed a most impressive memory for their names, addresses and dates. So many times I asked myself the question she voiced about the winter of 1944–5 in Ravensbrück concentration camp: 'Really, sometimes I don't know how we survived.' We are lucky she did. Her story is an inspiration to all young people and I am fortunate to have made two such good friends.

Her family in Belgium were extremely helpful, particularly her sister Julia Rottie and her husband Fernand, with whom I stayed in Pleinstraat. It was a strange sensation to sit in the same house where Hortense's story took place, to bicycle on Julia's old-fashioned machine round the same streets where Hortense had bicycled under the Nazi swastika and the eyes of the Gestapo. My special thanks are also due to Pierre Hermans with whom I spent several agreeable days while he showed me round places located in the story and gave me a detailed insight into the Resistance.

Many people were good enough to give up their time in interviews, with correspondence and in other ways and I would particularly like to thank Douglas Arseneau; Art de Breyne; Elmer Dungey; Philip van Meerbeek for giving me a film; Danny Boon; Lisa Daman; Paulette Berges for putting me in prison; Directors of Prisons M. Vanakker and Luce Mertens for letting me out; Art Bowlby DFM; Joan Hermans-van den Wyngaerden; Freddi Desiron; Georges; Guillaume Vanderstappen; Professor M.R.D. Foot for assistance in my research; Paddy Sproule for giving me a telephone number and Elizabeth Harrison for giving me another; Jean Vanwelkenhausen and Jose Gotovitch of the CREHSGM in Brussels; Eddy and Mieke Rottie; Ralph Patton; C. Barette; Annette Pauporte-Eekman; M. Leroux; Jane Fish; Jan-Erik Mattsson; Jayne Richards; Stanislaus and Arlette Ciechanowski, and many others.

Finally my thanks to my wife Rebecca for her support and patient hours of reading the manuscript as the book developed.

M.B.

*To Hortense*

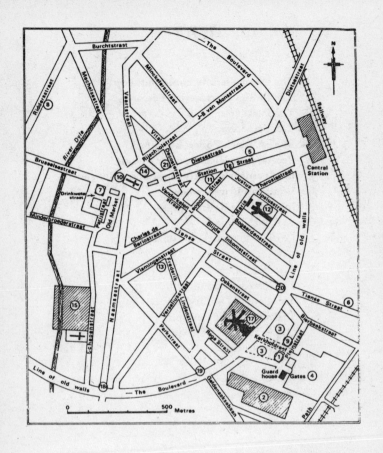

# THE CENTRE OF LOUVAIN

# KEY

1. The Daman family home and shop
2. The Philips Engineering Factory
3. The Park
4. The Cemetery
5. SS and 'Black Police' building
6. Professor de Vleeschauwer's house
7. Jan Sprenger's family home and tailor shop
8. Louis van Brussel's house
9. Josephine de Roost's house
10. St Peter's Church
11. Gestapo Interrogation Building
12. The Little Prison
13. The Monastery
14. The Kommandantur
15. The Convent of the Great Begijnhof
16. The Statue of Justo Lipsio
17. Central Prison in Louvain
18. Naamsepoort
19. Parkpoort
20. Tiensepoort
21. SS and Gestapo Headquarters

# 1

# Known Unto God

'While fighting for victory the German soldier will observe the rules of chivalrous warfare. Cruelties and senseless destruction are below his standard.' Rule 1 of the German Soldier's Ten Commandments printed in every soldier's paybook.

In the autumn of 1942 Hitler's armies dominated Europe from the Caucasus to Spain and imposed a crushing misery on the countries they had conquered. On the world stage the tide was about to change with momentous Allied successes at Stalingrad and El Alamein. However day to day life under the Nazi regime did not change. Allied victories were a boost to morale but offered no more than a glimmer of hope to those who fought in the Underground. The brutal consequences of choosing to resist hung over them and their families until the end of the war.

That autumn Hortense Daman was helping her mother serve in the small grocery shop at the top of a line of terraced houses in Pleinstraat, in the town of Louvain near Brussels. She was just sixteen years old, an attractive and vivacious girl with striking long blonde-auburn hair. She reached over the display in the shop window to adjust a card advertising Vigor soap and instinctively glanced up the street to check the German sentries. Since the invasion two years before they had occupied the guardhouse of the huge Philips factory which towered over Pleinstraat and the Louvain cemetery opposite her mother's shop.

The factory was quiet so she looked in the other direction down the line of closely terraced houses which curved slightly towards the Tiensepoort gate into the town. There were ragged gaps showing the bomb damage of May 1940 when a number of houses had been destroyed. The rubble had been cleared but the Germans had ordered that no new houses were to be built until after the war. Low in the sky the pale October sun shone through the gaps on to the cobbled road. The street was empty. Then she saw the superintendent of the cemetery turn quickly out of the cul-de-sac which led off Pleinstraat to the cemetery buildings and begin walking along the pavement towards the shop. Two years of war and working for François in the Underground had made her both keenly observant of people and deeply suspicious. Something in the superintendent's manner caught her attention. She watched him look nervously towards the German guardhouse and duck quickly into the shop.

'Good morning, Madame Daman,' he said to her mother, and smiled briefly at Hortense.

Her mother was serving a woman at the counter and Hortense saw an opportunity to signal that something was wrong. She moved from behind the counter and, standing so that the superintendent could not see, looked across the back of the woman being served and lifted her eyebrows in an almost imperceptible expression of surprise.

Stephanie Daman showed no reaction. She was a tall, impressive woman of forty-eight with strong principles. Running a grocery shop in times of severe rationing gave her considerable responsibility for the community, and she often tried to improve the rations of her neighbours with little extras. Smiling encouragement, she adjusted the woman's ration book rather favourably and handed her a parcel over the counter.

'Thank you so much,' the woman said warmly after checking her book, and left the shop.

'Goodbye,' Stephanie called after her and turned to the superintendent who was standing awkwardly in the corner by the counter. She had had time to think. She had learned to respect Hortense's judgment in the last two years and, looking at the man, it was clear to her that he was worried about something. She knew he was not closely involved with the Resistance, so she would be careful.

'Well, Monsieur le Superintendent, what can I get for you?'

'Nothing. I don't want to buy anything, thank you,' he replied in a rush and seeing her puzzled expression added, 'Madame Daman, you know me well, and I must honestly tell you something's badly wrong.'

Stephanie Daman had indeed known the superintendent for years. In addition to groceries she ran a flower business from the shop, supplying funeral wreaths and cut flowers for people visiting the cemetery. She had standing orders from richer families, in Brussels as well as in Louvain, to put fresh flowers on their family graves every week, and went herself to the big Kreer Market in Brussels to buy flowers. Each year on 1 November everybody visited their relations' graves in honour of the feasts of All Saints and All Souls and the Daman family worked hard providing masses of flowers for them. Before the war the cemetery had been covered in flowers on that day. Since the Occupation not so many came; but yes, Stephanie knew the superintendent well.

'What's the matter?'

He looked sharply out of the window towards the factory gatehouse. Sometimes the German soldiers came over the road to buy goods from the Daman shop, but the street was quiet.

'Listen,' his voice dropped to a whisper. 'The Germans telephoned from Vital Decosterstraat and ordered me to close the cemetery gates first thing this morning. They gave no reason and warned me not to breathe a word to anyone.'

There was a moment of silence in the shop. Stephanie watched the man's face closely. Then she said quietly, 'Hortense, shut the shop for a few minutes.'

She knew the cemetery was never closed during the day, but more important, Vital Decosterstraat meant the Gestapo and the Belgian SS were involved. They had taken over a fine Flemish merchant's house on the corner of Vital Decosterstraat and Diestsestraat in the centre of Louvain. She felt the superintendent's sympathies were with the Resistance but the conversation had taken a dangerous turn.

When the door was closed Hortense followed her mother and the superintendent into the kitchen at the back, which with the shop formed the ground floor of the little house. This was a homely place, the centre of the Damans' family life. On one side, steep wooden stairs led up to the bedrooms, and on the other stood a large cast-iron stove, constantly alight, warming the room against the cold outside. A large dresser filled with cups and saucers covered the end wall. The three sat at the wooden table in the middle of the room and the superintendent told his story.

'I was suspicious at once. They ordered me to keep out of the way, but I saw them arrive not long after their call.' He hesitated, looking at Hortense, wondering if he should continue with Madame Daman's young daughter listening.

'Go on,' Stephanie said. Hortense had learned a great deal about life in the two years of the Occupation, especially working for François. Stephanie knew her commitment to the Underground, but she never asked for details. She believed these things had to be done

4

and she trusted her son to look after his sister, her middle daughter. The thought of the risks they both ran tore at her soul but she took the sanguine view that Hortense was safer working with her blessing than doing something foolish on her own. Schoolfriends of Hortense's had been arrested bragging about 'fighting the Nazis' or scribbling graffiti on the wall, and youth was no defence against the Gestapo. In this kind of war the consequences of parental intransigence could be disastrous.

'I watched them from a distance through the trees, and I'm sure they buried someone.'

'So?'

'Madame Daman, it was not just that they had no priest with them, though God knows that's bad enough, but the Gestapo have never done this before. As I think you know, the poor devils they execute in prison are buried inside the walls in the prison plot. This is most irregular. Afterwards they told me I could open the gates, and when they'd gone I looked for the grave. I found it eventually against the wall on the far side.'

'With the poor?' Hortense asked.

'Exactly. It's sandy ground, easy to dig and the grave's unmarked. No one but me would notice it.' The superintendent glanced momentarily at the door, as if he feared someone might burst in and find him telling his story. He went on, 'Don't you see? The Germans aren't irregular people. It means they had something to hide. The burial was supposed to be a secret.'

'Why?' Hortense asked.

'That's what really worries me,' the superintendent whispered hoarsely. 'Madame Daman, I thought maybe you might know what to do.'

Stephanie paused a moment before replying, aware that Hortense and the superintendent were both looking at her. This much involved, the superintendent could hardly be making up the story. As for the poor wretch who had been buried by the SS, there was only one answer.

'We must see he gets a proper burial. And the sooner the better.'

The superintendent left the shop much relieved that the matter was in someone else's hands. He had no idea the Daman family was involved in the Resistance, but the corner shop was a centre to the community and to everybody living between the Boulevard, which ran along the walls on their side of Louvain and the big cemetery, Madame Daman was a great source of support. He knew she would think of something.

Stephanie told Hortense to mind the shop, put on her coat and hat and went out. There were arrangements to be made.

Later on, by chance it seemed to Hortense, her brother François slipped into the shop. He never told anyone where he would be or when he would come home. He worked on the simple but excellent security principle that the fewer people who knew where he was the better his chances of survival.

'Hallo, Brae,' Hortense said in surprise, using the nickname only she called him. 'It's lovely to see you!'

When she had a moment of privacy she joined him in the kitchen and told him about the strange burial in the cemetery. Their mother came back soon after and explained what she had been doing. He listened carefully, and then left to make some final preparations.

During the evening François returned with two friends, men also in the Resistance. Like François, they had refused to present themselves for deportation to work in the Third Reich and were on the run. Visits like these were commonplace in the Daman household, and Stephanie was always ready to give them something to eat. Often the meagre potato soup and bread was the only meal they had in the day. Being on the run meant no home, no family and no ration book. There were over two thousand young men in these circumstances in the Louvain area alone and they depended on the support of people like the Damans who were prepared to run the risk. Many of them came to look on the warm kitchen behind the corner shop in Pleinstraat as their home and on Hortense's mother as their own.

As usual the conversation in the kitchen was lively and cheerful, in spite of the cold and unfriendly atmosphere in the streets. All talking stopped shortly before midnight when there was a soft knock at the door. In a moment the priest, sombre in his black cassock and cloak, stood in the shop.

'Thank you for coming, father,' François said, naturally assuming control of the situation. He turned to the others in the kitchen. 'We'll go now.'

The two young men who had come with him nodded. Hortense put on her coat and stood with her mother. They quietly slipped through the front door and François led them down Pleinstraat in the safety of complete darkness. Not a light showed in the blackout. Nevertheless they clung to the walls of the houses in case the guard in the factory a hundred yards away saw their silhouettes hurrying down the street opposite him. Hortense thought it unlikely. She knew two of the soldiers, Karl and Paul. All the guards for static posts like the Philips electrical factory were older men, veterans of the Great War. Guard duty is a dull task at the best of times, and these men hated living in a hostile environment. They were homesick for Germany, the comforts of their homes and their hausfraus. Hortense was sure that keeping an eye on Pleinstraat on a cold night on the off chance of catching a group of grave robbers would neither occur nor appeal to them.

They turned off Pleinstraat and found the superintendent waiting for them by the cemetery gate. He let them in and they moved into deep shadow under the plane trees where Hortense was surprised to find Dr Breunigs waiting, a pathologist who lived in Maria Theresiastraat.

François and the two young men disappeared into the dark and came back in a few minutes carrying long-handled shovels.

Under François's directions they fell in one behind another and followed the superintendent across the cemetery. Grotesque memorial sculptures, marble crosses and angels rose out of the shadows as they passed along tree-lined avenues between the graves. One of the young men marched behind Hortense and she was glad not to be the last in the group. The superintendent stopped them against the wall farthest from the cemetery gates and the Daman shop. This was the part where the poor were buried, where few graves had headstones. Most were marked by simple wooden crosses but in this corner there were no more than a few bare hummocks. Hortense saw the glow of a small posy of Michaelmas daisies. They huddled round as the superintendent pointed to a pale scar in the dark sandy surface where the soil had been disturbed.

'Let's get on with it,' François snapped at the two men. 'We've not much time and God knows what we'll find.'

The priest muttered something she could not catch. She stood fascinated by the grim sight of her brother and his friends digging up a grave in the middle of the night while a priest, a doctor and her mother stood by watching. They did not have long to wait. Hortense knew at once when the blade of a shovel struck flesh.

'Bastards,' exclaimed the young man holding the shovel. 'They barely covered him with enough earth to keep out the rain.' He carefully scraped the sand from the shape in the hole and exclaimed, 'There's no winding sheet.'

The priest was now murmuring prayers continuously.

François knelt down and cupped his hands round a torch, shielding the light from shining anywhere but in the hole. 'He's wearing some sort of uniform.'

They did not take long to clear the remaining soil from the corpse in the grave. François and the two men wrapped it in a sheet they had brought and lifted it over one man's shoulder. Under threatening clouds the sinister-looking group followed the superintendent back along the paths between the graves to the administrative offices by the gate, to the mortuary, a tall brick building with a steep roof typical of turn-of-the-century architecture. The superintendent, under instructions, had carefully blacked out the high neo-Gothic windows, and while François posted one of the young men outside to act as a lookout and guard, the man carrying the corpse over his shoulder passed through the door and the others followed.

Once everyone was inside the superintendent closed the heavy door and lit several paraffin lamps. In the centre of a yellow circle of light the men laid out the dead man on a raised slab. Dr Breunigs took off his jacket, rolled up his sleeves and stepped over to the body.

Hortense found a place to perch on a table near the slab from which she could see every move the doctor made. He looked round the little group and began to remove the sheet they had wrapped round the corpse. They all stared in complete silence, even François, who was constantly turning to listen for a warning from the sentry outside. The only sound was the gentle spattering of sand falling from the sheet to the stone floor. No one was ready for what they saw, least of all Hortense. Dr Breunigs swore fiercely, though he had many years experience in pathology.

'I'm sorry, father,' he muttered, but the priest was transfixed. He never heard the blasphemy.

The body was that of a young man, no older than François's two friends and little older than Hortense, clad in the blue uniform of a Royal Air Force pilot. The pilot's wings were still visible, a small silver beacon on a ripped, filthy and bloodstained jacket. More than this it was the face that held their attention. The skin was puffed and particles of sand stuck to innumerable cuts and bruises.

The nose was flattened and the lips smashed, drawn back over broken teeth and gums which were stained ochre with dried blood. And the pilot had been blinded. Both the eyes were burst in their sockets, collapsed and glued with sand.

After a long moment Dr Breunigs dropped the sheet. Breathing hard, he set to stripping the body of its clothes. He found this easier than he expected and noted the limbs moved loosely, like the arms and legs of a rag doll. As he worked he saw that the flesh was swollen and mottled darkly with bruising. The colour was particularly intense round bone joints. He felt sick.

'There's hardly a bone not broken,' he stated.

'Must have been a dreadful crash,' the priest muttered.

'No, father. Not in his plane. They broke his bones. The Gestapo broke his bones deliberately, one after the other,' Dr Breunigs went on, relentlessly building up a picture of the young man's ordeal. 'Some of these bruises are older than others. They seem to have taken their time. Frankly they don't appear to have missed much out. Difficult to say at what stage they blinded him.'

Hortense watched in a vacuum of emotion, too shocked to feel sick, at once pitying, appalled and fascinated. It occurred to her that there were few places where the body was the dull white colour she expected to see in a corpse. When Dr Breunigs turned the dead man over she noticed outbreaks of what appeared to be sores scattered about his back where the sand had coagulated with the raw flesh.

The pathologist peered at them for a moment and his words coldly disabused her of this mild explanation. 'These marks are cigarette burns,' he said in a matter of fact voice, as if to an assistant taking notes for the police at an official post mortem.

François took his eyes off the pathologist and looked round the circle of faces. They were lit yellow by the dome of light over the slab in the centre of the room, stark splashes of colour against the deep shadows and uncertain shapes veiling the walls behind them. His mother's expression was inscrutable but he felt sure she was thinking of the pilot's own mother and father, thinking of them perhaps lying sleepless in their beds that night somewhere in England wondering what had happened to their son. The shock was easier to read in Hortense's young face but it impressed him how coolly she was taking it. In some ways she was more grown up than her sixteen years suggested, and more determined. He wondered again if he should have refused to let her witness this. Now at least she would really know the penalties of being caught.

'Hurry up,' François said rather abruptly. The pathologist, his hands filthy with blood and sand, looked up but said nothing. François's thin face showed no emotion but he added less severely, 'I'm sorry, Dr Breunigs. But please be as quick as you can now. We've still got to bury him and cover up the traces. We must be finished long before people in the street start getting up.'

The doctor turned back to the corpse. 'There's not much more I can do,' he said flatly. 'A young man of perhaps nineteen years, probably a pilot, but there is no identification. Cause of death? Medically, probably heart failure due to massive shock and fluid loss. In reality, you can see for yourselves what these swine have done.' He gestured helplessly at the dead man. 'What kind of information could they possibly have wanted to make them do this?'

'I don't know,' François said quietly, but he had already decided to send every particular in a coded message to London, by radio. Whoever he was, bomber pilot, agent of Special Operations Executive (SOE) or MI6, his operational headquarters had to be told. But all he said was, 'Thanks, Dr Breunigs. Let's clean him up. We can't put him to rest in this state.'

Once the pilot had been washed the men dressed him again and wrapped him in the sheet. François slipped out to check with the sentry, and the soft breath of fresh air through the door lifted the stale depression that had settled over the little group. They seemed to shake themselves and wake up. The pilot was dead but their own life went on. At a sign from François gentle hands moved swiftly to lift the shrouded body over the shoulder of one young man, and everyone was conscious of the uselessness of their sympathy to atone for the last brutal hours of the young British pilot.

It was still dark outside with no sign of dawn, and the superintendent led the way to another part of the cemetery where they had prepared a decent grave. Now the priest walked close to the young pilot, as though fearful the young man's soul might escape without that final comfort of absolution which had been denied him by the SS at his death. His murmured prayers were lost in the wind rustling the dead autumn leaves on the paths.

The air was cold and Hortense shivered. She stood close to her mother and watched the men lower the body into the narrow trench. She listened to the priest and fervently joined in the whispered responses. All the time she was filled with the magnitude of the pilot's sacrifice. Perhaps she was too young really to appreciate the terror he had suffered before dying, too ignorant of men's depravity to guess how long the Gestapo had tortured their victim before his spirit left him. But she was old enough to know what she had witnessed and to be filled with a storm of pity and outrage.

As she watched Hortense was reminded of the contacts and friends she had made working for François. Like the two men filling the grave, they were all older than herself though some were not twenty years of age. Like the unknown pilot. They fought in the vanguard of a battle with no front line, out of uniform, against an enemy which cruelly abused the Geneva Conventions and had all the odds in its favour. Hortense felt close to them through her brother, and their commitment could not have been more intense than hers. She had bent her head against the miseries of the Occupation like someone walking into the driving rain. Rationing, shortages and the constant presence of German troops had to be endured, but more than that it was the arrests, the imprisonments without trial and deaths like this one which had forged her hatred of the oppression and rape of her country. This scene in the cold graveyard in the autumn of 1942 plunged that burning hatred into the icy waters of a shocking personal experience which hardened it for ever.

The people she knew in the Underground were Belgians. They fought the oppression of their own country. That night Hortense was forcibly struck with the fact that this young man came from another country. Leaving his own family and home, he had come to join her fight for her people. Hortense was never an enthusiastic student at school, but she had always been interested in the history of her country and fascinated by the alliance between England and Belgium. She had listened to the story of the British army's victory against superior French odds defending Brussels itself at Waterloo, and to accounts of the hundreds of thousands of young men who gave their lives fighting in mud-filled trenches in the Great War to rescue Belgium from German occupation. Always, it seemed to her, the English came to help and her heart had gone out to them. Now more soldiers, sailors and airmen were dying in the fight against the second German occupation, dying for her freedom.

As they turned and walked slowly out of the cemetery, the sacrifice of all these young men seemed to be focused in the appalling death of this one British pilot they had just buried. Her sorrow, her fierce national pride and her certain knowledge that justice must be righted bound her irrevocably to repay his death. Now, as never before, she was committed to resistance, whatever the consequences.

The pilot was never identified. His mother and father never knew what had happened to their son, which was perhaps a good thing, but they never even knew which grave to visit. There is a little comfort in the words of Kemal Ataturk on the memorial to the dead at Gallipoli: 'You, the mothers who sent your sons from far away countries, wipe away your tears, your sons are lying in our bosom and are in peace.' After the liberation the British War Graves Commission arranged for his body to be disinterred and re-buried in the official War Cemetery, a couple of miles south of the Louvain cemetery where he was laid on that dark night in the autumn of 1942. There in a beautifully kept place under tall beech trees on the edge of Heverlee woods he is finally at peace with hundreds of others who made the ultimate sacrifice, his square marble gravestone marked simply with the phrase, 'Known unto God.'

# 2

# The Blue Skies of 1940

'If there are territories anywhere which we have a right to reclaim, then it is these.' Adolf Hitler on Belgium and Northern France.

Perhaps it was a privilege for Hortense to have witnessed the full degradation of the Nazi regime in the cemetery. She was given the sort of brutal impetus to join the Resistance that was denied to most others. Her family was a natural focal point for the community, and her brother, a successful career soldier before the war, was closely involved with the Resistance. So Hortense Daman had the opportunity. But would anyone in her place have become as committed?

When Germany invaded Poland on 1 September 1939 Hortense was thirteen. Of course she was ignorant of the grand issues affecting Europe, but by May 1940 she knew that Belgium, which had declared itself neutral, was threatened by war. Everyone at her school in Louvain had been talking about it. François was a sergeant in the Belgian Artillery and she assumed he would know all the answers.

'Brae, do you think the Germans will attack us?' she asked him when he came home on leave in the spring of 1940, smartly dressed in uniform.

'I don't think so,' he replied carefully, unwilling to

15

dramatise the situation. At twenty-six he was twice her age then and conscious that his pretty fair-haired sister listened avidly to his every word. She was always asking about his life as a soldier and about the Belgian army. An athlete and accomplished horseman, he was popular with his officers who liked to see the regiment win at competitions, and he was a skilled mechanic. 'Paul-Henri Spaak, our Foreign Minister,' he added seeing her look puzzled, 'told us last year that we'll stay neutral. He said it was all agreed with Britain, France and Germany three years ago in 1937.'

'But we can't trust the Germans,' Hortense stated simply. 'They attacked Poland, didn't they?'

François pushed his chair back and stood up. He straightened the belt at his waist, took a cup and saucer from the dresser and poured himself some coffee from a pot on the hob. He glanced at his father. Neither of them believed Belgium could avoid war, and Jacques Daman, who was fifty that April, could remember the German occupation of Louvain during the Great War. He remembered Stationstraat where the Kaiser's soldiers had rounded up dozens of men and boys and shot them in the middle of the afternoon. As a reprisal. Everyone in Louvain knew someone who had been killed. He looked fondly at his daughter. She was not much younger than some of those boys.

'I hope Monsieur Hitler will think twice before attacking,' he said gently. 'The French and British have big armies and a lot of these new tanks.' It was inconceivable that the Germans would succeed in defeating the Allies, but it was a different matter whether they would be arrogant enough to attack in the first place.

Jacques Daman was a master shoemaker for the massive Bata shoe business, for which he had invented several new and important leather treatment processes, and he travelled to Brussels on the train every day to work in the leather factory. No one there believed the Germans would hold off. There had been too many rumours and the actions of the government told their own story, with special preparations for a food-rationing system, plans to remove the country's gold reserves in emergency and the order for general mobilisation months ago, in August 1939. It saddened him to think that Hortense and ten-year-old Julia, the two youngest of his three daughters, would be caught up in another war. He remembered what life had been like in the 1914–18 war with François and Bertha as children. His eldest daughter Bertha was a year younger than her brother. He fervently hoped events would turn out better than they had then.

It should have been a wonderful summer. The weather was brilliant and Hortense was beginning to enjoy life. She made friends easily though she was not a superficial girl, and was looking forward to spending long sunny hours at the canoe club on the Vaartdijk canal in the town. This was a popular place among the young people and Hortense loved the atmosphere and excitement of the races. With her fourteenth birthday coming up on 12 August she considered herself rather grown up and got on well with the older boys. For their part they were happy to have the company of such a pretty and vivacious girl. At weekends she joined them on trips along the canals, when she tried to make sure she was in the same party as Jan Sprengers. He was several years older, always at the centre of the fun and games and she had become very fond of him. She was sure he felt the same way about her though he had never made his feelings plain in so many words.

'Belgium's neutral,' she said to him during a chat about the possibility of war. 'Paul-Henri Spaak said so.'

They were sitting on the bank in the sun, watching the couples canoeing up and down on the glittering water. War seemed very remote.

'Who's Paul-Henri Spaak?' Jan asked, laughing, and enjoying the serious look in her wide blue eyes.

'Our Foreign Minister,' she retorted, pleased that she

17

remembered clearly what François had said. 'Even Germany agreed, but I think they'll attack all the same.' She had noticed her father's expression when they had been talking in the kitchen and afterwards pressed François to tell her what he really thought. Her brother was a private, almost intense person but he had always had a close relationship with Hortense, more so than with Julia and Bertha. Julia was too young and Bertha was married and living her own life elsewhere in Louvain.

'They'll get a bloody nose in any direction,' Jan said cheerfully, and they both laughed.

Like everyone at the time Jan was convinced the Maginot line in France was impregnable and that Belgium's eastern approaches were as surely guarded by the concrete fortress of Eban Emael which towered above the Albert Canal.

'Our boys're the best. I'm sure we'll win,' Hortense said fiercely, thinking of François and his friends in the Artillery with a rush of national pride. Jan Sprengers was a qualified tailor who worked in Parijsstraat close to the Old Market in Louvain where Hortense's mother bought groceries for the shop early in the morning. Jan's father had died before Hortense was born and his mother had run the tailoring shop most efficiently ever since.

Occasionally Hortense would go to market with her mother when she would take the opportunity to see Jan before bringing the vegetables back to Pleinstraat in the front pannier and on the back of her bicycle. Apart from that, she felt it her duty to make herself useful in the grocery shop, even though Stephanie Daman then employed several girls. They worked in the house and shop and carried the lunches over to the workers in the canteen of the Philips electrical factory. Hortense joined them when she could during the school lunch break.

At the start of May 1940 this job had been more interesting. A unit of Belgian conscripts had marched into the factory and been billeted there for some weeks.

Hortense liked to go over and talk to them, especially since François's regiment had cancelled all leave and he had not been home. On Friday, 10 May she and Julia were playing near the gates, in the little park that separated the factory from her parents' shop at the top of Pleinstraat. The street turned under trees to the Boulevard round the town walls on one side, and the entrance to the cemetery was on the other. Some of the soldiers were lying about on the grass enjoying the sun.

'My brother's a sergeant,' Hortense announced to one man, whom she called Big René because he was so tall. He was lying on his back, his arms folded behind his head.

'So he must be a career soldier, eh?' René replied, squinting up at the two girls. They all knew Madame Daman's two daughters. They were always around the shop, in and out of the factory or playing in the park.

'Yes, of course.'

The group of conscripts laughed good-humouredly.

She was proud of these young men and it surprised her to see how badly fitted out they were compared to François. René wore battledress trousers so small that they looked like shorts on his massive frame, and none of their jackets seemed to be the right size.

They all heard the sound of aircraft at the same time. Everyone looked up, shading their eyes. The blue sky over the trees was empty.

'There's a lot coming over,' said René knowledgeably, his face expressionless.

The distant sound of aircraft gradually increased. For several minutes the sky remained the same, cloudless, unspoilt.

'There they are!'

One, two, then a wide stream of small dark arrows came into view, passing overhead from the east, filling the sky with harsh noise. None of the soldiers said a word.

'Are they ours?' Hortense asked, brushing her hair from her face and peering up. She was unsure what

19

Belgian planes should look like and upset by the soldiers' lack of spirit.

The big man shook his head. 'Luftwaffe,' was all he said.

Hortense stared up unbelieving. How could German planes be allowed to cross into Belgium? She saw one plane tilt and begin to fall. The drone of its engine increased to a deafening scream as it plummeted earthwards, directly towards them it seemed. Others tumbled and followed after it.

Hortense laughed and clapped her hands, shouting happily, 'We've got them! Our boys've hit them. They're crashing. Look! Julia, look!'

Several younger soldiers were laughing too, but most were silent, thoroughly alarmed by the shrieking roar. Stolidly, René noted that there had been no anti-aircraft fire.

Hortense saw the planes had odd gull-shaped wings. The howl of falling aircraft became unbearable. Just as she expected the leading plane to plunge somewhere into the factory it swooped away in a great black arc. She let her hands fall to her side and watched, crushed with disappointment, only dully aware of the broken black and white crosses on the tail, her first sight of the Nazi swastika. The first explosions rocked the air.

Immediately the soldiers began to move. They ran doubled at the waist to protect themselves from shrapnel. The explosions came from all directions. The Luftwaffe Junkers JU87B-IS, always known as Stukas, were attacking various parts of Louvain, which was in a key position on the Wehrmacht's route to Brussels and the west.

Before Hortense and Julia understood what was happening René leaped up and grabbed them both, tucking one girl under each strong arm, and ran towards the Damans' shop. As he did so a stick of bombs fell on the other side of the house, somewhere down Pleinstraat, and the blast rushed up the street shaking the branches of the trees. He turned aside to find the nearest cover, dropped the sisters in a dip in the ground in the park and fell in next to them covering them with his arms as best he could.

The din of the Stukas and the roar of explosions seemed to Hortense to go on and on, while René did his best to protect them from pieces of shattered brick and mortar falling back to the ground. In fact the dive-bombers soon discharged their bombs and the terrifying attack was over. René picked himself up, lifted Julia into his arms and taking Hortense by the hand led them back to their parents' shop through curtains of dust hanging in the air. Stephanie Daman thanked him profusely while she hugged her daughters and wiped the dirt off their faces. She had been terrified for them when the raid started and she found they were out of the house.

Hugging her mother and little sister, Hortense turned to look at her home. The corner house had suffered slight damage. There were roof tiles missing and shattered panes in the windows, but they had been lucky. There was far worse down the street. Pleinstraat was filled with a cloud of grey dust which stung her eyes and made her cough. Hortense could see that several houses less than a hundred metres from the shop had been pulverised. Piles of broken stone and timber spilled across the cobbles, the junction with Bierbeekstraat at the bottom had been flattened and frightened people had started to emerge from wherever they had managed to hide in the first moments of panic. Some were crying, some struggling to shift debris and search for victims, and some just wandered about, dazed at the sudden destruction of their lives. Hortense was amazed to see people's personal belongings, books, saucepans and clothes strewn about. The incongruity of a single lace-up man's shoe lying on the cobbles in the middle of the road particularly surprised her and she wondered if she should have known who it belonged to.

Madame Daman hustled her children into the house and settled them in the kitchen, reassuring them and

trying to ignore the evidence of disaster. The whole house
had been roughly shaken. Tins and boxes had fallen off
shelves in the shop, plates lay broken on the floor where
they had tumbled from the dresser and dust was thick
everywhere. The girls she employed were in tears and
Stephanie sent them home in case their parents, mostly
farmers, were worried about them. She went outside
again to see if there was anything she could do to help
her neighbours. She wished Jacques was at home, but he
was in Brussels, working. She felt certain they would have
attacked the capital and prayed he would be all right.

She met her friend Josephine de Roost, who lived in a
little red-brick house fifty yards down on the corner of
Pleinstraat and Kerkhof Drive.

'Yours . . . ?'

'Still standing,' Josephine laughed. 'But there's already
talk of more attacks. The Boche won't stop now.'

The two women talked briefly. Someone came up
from Bierbeekstraat and said even the cellars had been
wrecked. As if to underline their fears, they heard the
drone of more planes overhead and strained to glimpse
them through the smoke hanging over the houses but they
could see nothing.

Stephanie realised that she had to move the girls. She
hated leaving their home, still more leaving with no word
from Jacques, but the little cellar under the kitchen floor
would offer no protection from bombs. She quickly made
up a parcel of food and told Hortense to fetch some extra
clothes and wrap them up. Then, while her daughters
were getting ready upstairs, she fetched the money she
and Jacques had put away in a hiding place in the kitchen,
under a secret panel on the top of the dresser. She
scribbled a note for Jacques while she called Hortense
and Julia and quickly ushered her little family out of the
house.

Still shocked by the speed and horror of the attack,
Hortense clutched a brown paper parcel and looked down

the street where she had been born. Beyond the black clouds of smoke rising off the roofs the sky was blue. The German attack had ripped the heart out of Pleinstraat. Life had suddenly changed. There would be no summer now.

The sound of aeroplanes was almost constant, but distant. Stephanie was badly worried that they would be caught in the streets in another attack and walked fast, making the girls run. She led them through the Parkpoort into the town to a monastery a few hundred metres away in Frederik Lintstraat. The Damans supplied groceries to many of the religious foundations in Louvain and she knew the monks there had a large stone cellar. She had decided to ask them for shelter. It seemed the safest place.

Several houses had been hit in Frederik Lintstraat.

'Stay here. Look after Julia,' Stephanie Daman warned Hortense.

Ahead she had noticed a little knot of people gathered where the monastery should have been. All she could see was rubble. She ran over to find out what had happened.

'It's no good,' she told Hortense when she returned in a few moments, shaking her head. 'We must find somewhere else.'

Hortense did not understand her mother's expression behind the dust on her face and Stephanie did not think there was any need to explain to the young girls what had happened. The monks had taken cover in the cellar and a 500 lb bomb had ploughed through the roof and exploded deep inside the building, crushing the cellar on top of them.

Pulling her daughters away, she hurried them to another monastery, the Benedictine, where they stayed for two days. To Hortense's immense relief her father found them there later in the afternoon. It had taken him hours getting home fifteen miles from his work in Brussels. He said the roads and trains were in chaos. He confirmed reports that the Germans had bombed cities in Holland,

Belgium, Luxembourg and France that morning and were said to be attacking along all frontiers.

Her grandparents joined them – not Jacques's parents, who were dead, but Stephanie's mother and father, Barbara and Pierre Vanden Eynde. All the grandchildren affectionately called Pierre 'Bompa'. Her eldest sister Bertha also joined them.

Bertha's husband Guillaume was fighting in the army, like François. There was no word from the front from either of them. The family listened to every news broadcast and heard nothing but the blandest assurances that the government had everything under control. Meanwhile rumours multiplied in the streets, and no one had any good news; Belgian divisions could not hold the frontier; the Germans had taken Maastricht; and German parachute troops had captured Eban Emael. Hortense did not believe this because Jan Sprengers had told her the fortress was garrisoned with 1200 men and supplied with food and munitions for weeks. However, whatever the radio and rumours said, Hortense began to realise the sickening truth that foreign soldiers, Germans, were marching into her country. Men and women were beginning to fill the roads westwards to escape the invasion and their panicked accounts left no room for doubt.

The French and British armies had not been allowed into Belgium in time to organise defences, because King Leopold III and his government had insisted on Belgian neutrality till the last. The Allied armies, several million French soldiers and over 200,000 British soldiers, camped along the Belgian-French border. As soon as the Germans attacked they began to rush forward to meet them, and their generals had chosen the river Dyle as the next line of resistance. The Belgians were defending the northern sector, the British were to hold Louvain, which straddles the Dyle, and the French were hurrying to take up positions to the south.

Jacques Daman was not privy to any of these grand but tardy strategies but he knew full well that his family would be caught in the middle of the battle. For weeks he and Stephanie had discussed what they should do if the Germans came. Now he could feel death and misery building up around him and it left him no choice.

'We must leave too.'

'Why?' Hortense asked, plainly upset. She resented the idea of leaving. It seemed too much like running away. She thought they should stay and stop the enemy somehow.

'To avoid the Boche,' her mother explained softly. She and Jacques had reluctantly decided to take the family westwards. Life had been difficult enough under German occupation in the Great War. They were both convinced this new clash of armies would etch another bitter line of trenches, mud and death across the countryside and would again divide Europe for years. This time they wanted to keep their children on the Allied side.

They became refugees.

On Sunday, 12 May Hortense left Louvain with her parents and family and joined the swelling numbers that blocked the roads to France. They took the road to Brussels pushing bicycles laden with parcels. Shocked by the sudden loss of her home and background, Hortense walked next to her mother and tried to settle down to the slow pace of the wagon-train which inched away from the German blitzkrieg.

She was surprised there were so many people. Everybody of all ages seemed to have brought as much as they could carry or push in carts of all shapes and sizes. The lucky ones had horse-drawn carts or buggies which had been piled with bedding, clothes, food, cooking utensils. Even chairs and cupboards were roped on. Others pushed wheel-barrows or bicycles and some staggered along with bulging suitcases. Among them were a few cars and lorries creeping along at walking pace, rarely able to overtake, their drivers leaning out of the windows, hands on horns, shouting furiously to people to clear the road. Hortense noticed a car abandoned and pushed off the road, its doors hanging open, and guessed it had run out of fuel. As she walked past she was disgusted to see the fittings inside had been plundered. The pace was slow but charged with a frightening undercurrent of panic, which occasionally burst to the surface in looting or savage fights.

Near Bertem, a small village about five kilometres west of Louvain where they stayed the first night, a group of men were shouting at a businessman in a car at the side of the road.

'What're they doing?' Hortense asked her mother, looking at the scene ahead.

'Spy! You're a German spy,' she heard them scream. Two of the men were yanking at the driver's door which suddenly flew open. Elated they grabbed the businessman inside, dragged him out and started to beat him up.

'They think he's giving information to the Germans,' her mother said quietly. She realised there was little she or Jacques could do to stop their daughters seeing such unpleasantness. She wondered sadly who had said war was supposed to bring out the finest characteristics of human nature, without knowing that the remark had been attributed to Germany's best known philosopher, Goethe, whose oak tree, once famous for shading the great man while he worked, was now at the centre of a place called Buchenwald, a concentration camp which by 1940 had been in existence for seven years.

'Is he really a traitor?' Hortense asked. The treatment seemed arbitrary, but she was in no doubt that it was wrong to help the Germans.

'I don't think so,' said her father. 'They're just frightened. I expect we'll be seeing more of that.' Jacques Daman was a mild man and he hated seeing his children exposed to such violence.

As he spoke, the man broke free and escaped across a ditch into the fields. Hortense watched the men shouting after him but they soon got tired. They turned back to the car, tore open his suitcases and divided his personal effects among themselves.

Hortense and her family were among thousands who fled before the German armies of Field Marshal Fedor von Bock and General von Runstedt. It was afterwards estimated that some seven million people stumbled over the cobbled roads of Belgium, France and the Low Countries to flee west. Over 50,000 Belgian registered cars were identified in the south of France later that summer.

The Damans were one family in many, their tragedy far from unique. In her home town Hortense was only one of 38,000 whose lives were disrupted and whose homes were destroyed. On 14 May, two days after the family left, British troops ordered the evacuation of the town and only 500 people stayed behind.

The chaos on the roads was made worse for the civilians by frequent convoys of army trucks, personnel carriers and artillery forcing their way past in the other direction, *en route* to the battlefront. Hortense was cheered by the English soldiers who stuck up their thumbs in encouragement and waved. Narrow as the tree-lined roads were, people made way as best they could.

The Stuka pilots did not leave them alone. They were attracted by the military convoys on the roads and unable, or unwilling, to tell the difference between soldiers and civilians. The more chaos, the more the Allies were hampered reaching the front. On the second day, still on the road to Brussels, Hortense watched three Stukas scream into the attack some way behind them. Some of the people near her ran for cover in the ditch, but even Hortense could see they were in no danger with the planes so far away. As soon as they left the road their place in the line of refugees closed up as though they had never been there. Walking backwards to keep up, she watched the frightening black planes dive vertically towards the tall poplar trees lining the road and heard the explosions in the distance. She remembered angrily what had happened to the houses in Pleinstraat and knew very well what devastation the bombs would wreak on the unprotected column of refugees.

Jacques Daman decided they must leave the main roads. He was afraid they would never reach France in time to escape, and progress was too slow. Often they had to stop altogether to allow military transport through. They had been joined by Bertha's mother-in-law, Madame Berges, and her daughter Marie-Louise. Jacques led the group on to secondary roads and they made their way south-west towards Mons, the best direction, he thought. They had to walk much of the way, but occasionally a farmer or merchant would give them a lift in a truck for a short distance. The whole country seemed to be travelling to the west.

As if mocking them, the weather held brilliantly for one fine day after another. Hortense found the journey very tiring. She was fit, for she had bicycled everywhere in Louvain and had begun to work more and more in the shop, but her boots, which her father had made for her, grew hot and the soles of her feet hurt. When they camped by the side of the road at night she was exhausted. Hortense was glad to be away from the selfish people shoving and pushing on the big roads, but now they were more or less on their own she noticed other things, in some ways more distressing. All too often they came across the dead, soldiers and civilians alike, lying at the side of the road, swollen to bursting point in the hot sun and covered with flies.

'Why doesn't anyone bury them?' Hortense asked her mother, shocked that families should not bury their own dead.

'No one has the time,' Stephanie replied. 'They're all too busy trying to escape.'

She and Jacques had brought up their family in a traditional Roman Catholic society. There were dissenting views elsewhere in the family and by agreement religion was not discussed in the Daman household. Stephanie pragmatically and staunchly supported the basic rules of decent social behaviour. She followed the instructions of her priest but played down what so often seemed to her to be pointless rules of dogma. This was a common attitude in Belgians at the time. Stephanie knew that Belgian Catholics were among the strongest and it saddened her to see how fast these social structures fell apart under pressure.

The frightful lowing of cows was almost worse. Still alive, the poor beasts stood motionless in agonies as no one had milked them for days. Even the farmers had fled. From time to time her father stopped the march, to rest the children and Hortense's grandparents and to milk the cows. They were all hungry and the milk was warm and delicious. Hortense wanted to milk a little from them all to ease their pain, but there was no time. She felt better when her mother pointed out that they were not the only people to tap this ready source of food.

After eight hot dusty and tiring days they reached Mons on 20 May and sheltered in the basement of a school. Hortense had never been so far from home before. They sat round on boxes rubbing their aching muscles and feet. Her mother shared out some bread and cheese, and they drank milk. Her father asked the schoolmaster for news of the fighting. The official reports had continued with vague assertions of Allied successes and they were all desperate to find out what had really been happening. He rightly assumed the schoolmaster had heard stories from considerable numbers of refugees in the past ten days.

'It's bad,' said the schoolmaster shortly and their spirits sank as they listened. In surprise they learned that the

German armoured divisions had infiltrated through the difficult mountain terrain of the Ardennes, had punched across the Meuse at Sedan avoiding the much-vaunted Maginot line altogether and that Brussels had fallen on Saturday, 18 May.

Hortense did not believe it until she looked at her father's face.

'That means they're in Louvain,' Jacques said.

'Must be,' the schoolmaster replied. 'Apparently the king is still holding out but the situation is terribly confused. The Germans seem to be everywhere.'

King Leopold was Commander in Chief of the army and had his general headquarters in Breendonk, which lay south of Antwerp. Breendonk was a concrete geometric-shaped fortress constructed in 1906, covered with earth and surrounded by a large moat, from which he had been trying to rally his soldiers. The Belgian troops had been fighting hard but were badly off-balance after the German strikes. By 20 May they were pressed into a defensive perimeter with their backs to the coast.

'What about around here?' Jacques asked, conscious that he had to steer the family round the battle.

'They've taken St Quentin, eighty kilometres away,' the school-master replied pessimistically. 'And I heard today some of their reconnaissance units have been seen in the country not far south of Mons.'

'We'll have to head north for a while,' Jacques Daman decided without enthusiasm. 'We'll try and find a way in a circle round the front by Lille and then head south-west.'

No one in the cellar knew that General Heinz Guderian's XIX Panzer Korps had driven into Abbeville on the French coast that same evening. The German blitzkrieg had swept in a wide arc from the Ardennes to the sea in ten days. The British Expeditionary Force, the French army and the Belgian army were surrounded. The Daman family was one tiny group caught in the net with their route to freedom irrevocably cut off.

# The Blue Skies of 1940

Hortense watched her father's face and saw the lines of tiredness and depression. As long as she could remember he had always been calm and gentle, a quiet strength in the family. She had never seen him so disturbed as in the last few days and this upset her more than the air raid, the damage to her home and the exhausting march.

They walked slowly towards Lille. Stephanie had her hands full looking after Julia, but even Julia was able to keep up better than her grandparents. The weather continued glorious. Hortense had become used to hearing the continual boom of artillery and the sharper snap of machine-gun fire in the distance. It was odd to hear the noise of war carried faintly but unmistakably in the hot air while she and her family walked in peace along leafy green lanes and across fields of yellow corn.

At the border into France they were suddenly confronted round a corner with a concrete pillbox and an emplacement of steel tank traps stuck in the ground, like dragon's teeth, blocking the road. They stopped in their tracks and Hortense stared at the black slits in the wall of the pillbox wondering who was behind, watching them from the darkness. Was it occupied by French soldiers? Or Germans?

Nothing stirred in the burning sun. Even the birds rested mute in the shade, too hot to sing. Hortense noticed that the distant rattle of war had ceased too and she found the stillness even more sinister. Frightened, she hurried over to her father and stood close to him as he sized up the situation and decided what to do.

He walked on and they all followed uncertainly. When they levelled with the emplacement they found the place deserted. The soldiers had gone. They stopped in a farm beyond the pillbox and found the farmer had disappeard with all his family and animals.

They dropped their motley possessions in the farmyard and slumped to the ground grateful of the chance of a rest. Hortense watched her grandparents sink down and push their legs out in front of them on the baked earth. It occurred to her that she had never heard them complaining.

Jacques Daman went off to look round the farm to find something to eat. He had been away some while and everyone but Hortense was dozing in the sun when he reappeared rather suddenly round a corner with his clothes covered with blood. Hortense was horrified to see her father hurt and ran across the yard to help him.

'It's all right, Hortense,' Jacques said, seeing the look on his daughter's face as she grabbed him and clung to his waist. 'I found a dovecote with some pigeons in it and I thought we could all do with some meat.' He smiled and held up four pigeons, their necks broken.

Hortense's fright turned to astonishment that her father could be so savage. She had never seen him do anything remotely violent as long as she could remember. She would never have believed he was capable of wringing the birds' necks but she understood he had only done it for his family.

They reached Lille on Wednesday, 29 May. It was immediately obvious to the adults that this was the end of the road. Hortense and Julia were too tired to care. There seemed to be endless crowds milling round them. The town was packed with refugees and soldiers, leaderless and lost.

The Allies were beaten. The evacuation from Dunkirk was in full swing, after Hitler had inexplicably refused to allow his generals to complete the annihilation of the British army on its retreat to the coast.

Jacques Daman decided to go into the centre of the town. On the way he tried to get water from the little stand-pipes in the streets and Hortense was shocked when the French refused to let them take any unless they paid one franc for every glass. She had become accustomed to her family's solidarity in the face of the upheaval, so it was a greater surprise to find there were others like them whose bile was directed more against their fellow-sufferers than against the Germans who had caused all the misery.

They passed the Cathedral of Notre Dame de la Treille on the way to the centre. It was surrounded by scaffolding to the top of the nave, but there was no roof. The vast Gothic building had been seriously damaged in the First Great War and was still unrepaired when overtaken by the Second War.

Jacques Daman called a halt to their trek in the main square, where they slipped to the ground in a huddled group among other refugees. There was a dull hubbub of noise all around them as everyone told their stories.

The crowd stirred in panic. 'The Germans are coming!' The cry rippled across the square. Many thought they would all be killed on the spot.

Hortense looked up and for the first time saw a German soldier close to. He was an officer of General Schmidt's 39th Panzer Korps, which had come through Louvain two weeks before, and his grey uniform was grimed with the dirt of battle. Behind him came a platoon of soldiers armed with the famous German MP40 Schmeisser machine pistol.

'All the Belgians must report to me,' he shouted at the crowd.

Hortense saw her father and mother looking worriedly at each other and became frightened. Were the people right? Were they all going to be killed?

'In Belgium the war is finished,' the officer continued, shouting at the reluctant mass of people. 'Your soldiers have surrendered and the fighting has stopped.'

Hortense listened appalled. The German went on to say that the king had given himself up and all Belgians were at peace with the Third Reich. What had happened to François? She thought of the dead soldiers they had passed, bodies bursting out of their khaki battledress, but such was her faith in her brother that she quickly put the idea out of her mind. She wondered when she would see him again.

'You have to go home,' the German was saying. 'All the Belgians must go home. Walloons on this side and Flemish here.'

The officer pointed his instructions and his soldiers began to carry out his orders, herding the dispirited mass of civilians into groups. They wanted to divide the French-speaking Walloon Belgians from the Flemish-speaking Belgians. The Damans who were Flemish were not the only ones who were instinctively suspicious, but there was nothing they could do. Hortense was surprised to see the soldiers well-behaved. They pushed, persuaded and cajoled the refugees with businesslike efficiency, and the milling families waited to see what would happen to them next.

The German plan was simple. Flanders was close to Germany and had historical and linguistic links with Germany. Nazi race theorists had concluded that the Flemish were worthy to become members of the Greater German Reich so the Germans wanted to persuade them that the occupation of Belgium was well-intentioned and in their interests.

'You'll get in these trucks,' the officer ordered, pointing at a line of lorries bouncing over the cobbled square towards them, and finished with a flourish, 'This transport will take you home.'

The French-speaking Walloons had to walk home, under guard.

The journey back to Louvain was quick by comparison with their long march out, but miserable, underlining as it did the pointlessness of their attempt to escape. Nearly four weeks after leaving their house, they were left at Tiensepoort and walked up Pleinstraat again, picking their way round the rubble of houses which had fallen over the road. Artillery fire during the short-lived defence of the town by the British Guards Brigade had caused more damage than the Stuka attack. The British withdrew in the night of 16 May and the Wehrmacht entered Louvain in the early hours of 17 May.

They stopped finally outside their house and for the last time dropped their few belongings in the dust. Hortense felt like a stranger looking at her home. No. 130 was cold and empty, the roof was falling in, and someone had nailed a few planks across the windows, sealing and blinding the house. The air of desolation was frightening.

'What are you lot doing?' A smartly uniformed, middle-aged German captain approached them across the square from the Philips factory.

The German army's staff work was immaculate. All the key points in occupied territories had been identified before the invasion and small guard forces were in position almost as soon as the infantry had fought through. The Philips electrical factory was one of those important points and German troops occupied the guardhouse from the morning of 17 May 1940 to the liberation in September 1944. Pleinstraat was literally under the eye of the invader throughout the war. For the Damans this stony surveillance was to have catastrophic consequences.

'This is my house,' Hortense's father muttered. Hortense cringed to hear the deep depression in his voice as he spoke. Her mother was staring at the house in a state of shock.

'Ah! The Damans,' said the officer, regarding them critically. He was obviously not impressed with either the house or their personal condition. 'I had your windows boarded up. There was a lot of looting,' he added, plainly disgusted that Belgians should loot from their own countrymen. 'You will stay here now. Remember, there is an old German saying, "*Was hilft laufen, wenn man nicht auf dem rechten Weg ist?*" which means "what's the point of running away if you're not on the right road?"' He looked round the group of expressionless Belgians for a moment and shrugged. 'Incidentally, I also arranged for your dog to be fed while you were away.'

Satisfied with this report, he turned on his heel and marched back across the little square under the trees to the factory guard room.

Jacques Daman unlocked the front door of his shop and they went inside. Nothing, not even the experiences of the last weeks, had prepared Hortense for what she saw. The house was derelict. Not a single item remained on the shelves, all but the biggest pieces of the furniture had gone and broken chair legs lay in thick dust on the floor. All the cushions, blankets, pictures, pans, ornaments, plates and cutlery had been stolen. The boards of the first floor were hanging down into the shop, as though smashed through by a huge foot stamping on to the house; the ceiling above had caved in and tiles lay round them on the ground floor where they had fallen from a gaping hole in the roof.

Hortense could not believe such devastation, but she was far more deeply wounded to see the effect on her parents. Her mother stood quite still and stared round, her eyes vacant and her face unnervingly devoid of expression. Her father sat on a pile of shattered bricks lying in the centre of the shop and gazed at the wreckage of his home with tears running down his cheeks.

After a long moment he found his voice and whispered, 'You can see the blue sky through the roof.'

# 3

# Occupation

'Belgium is to be administered by a Military Governor until further notice.' Adolf Hitler, appointing
General of the Infantry Baron Alexander von Falkenhausen as Militärbefehlshaber (Military Governor) of
Belgium and Northern France, 20 July 1940.

Jacques Daman found the family a small apartment
in the middle of Brussels in the Rue Sainte-Anne
near the Central railway station while their home was
being repaired. The summer Hortense and Jan Sprengers
had planned sitting in the sun at the canoe club was
certainly gone for ever. In Brussels she was separated
from her schoolfriends and suffered her parents' hurt
every day as she watched them struggle to cope with
the new circumstances. The upheaval could not have
been more dramatic, but there was little remarkable in
her case. She was one of thousands of children reeling
under the Occupation, too young to know more about it
than the stories they had heard from their parents about
the Great War.

Most people tried at once to patch over the disruptions
and re-establish some normality in their lives. The German authorities showed the flavour of their rule early on
with arrests and harsh sentences for minor offences. A
man who organised a peaceful gathering to remember

the 1914-18 Armistice Day was given ten years hard labour. It was safer not to be noticed, a course adopted by the vast majority, but the circumstances of Hortense Daman's life and character led her down a path of choices into dangerous ground.

Hortense watched the people return to Brussels, gradually filling the streets and trams again with life, albeit much subdued. The trains were started again quite quickly by the Germans but they were always packed, never on time and liable to military requisition as the Wehrmacht moved across the conquered territories settling Hitler's grip on Europe.

Eventually François came back from the fighting, as Hortense confidently expected him to do. He had been a prisoner of war and returned with Pierre van Goitsenhoeven and Jacques Gyssens, both cousins on his mother's side and close friends of the family. His wife Elisa and their little son Jacques joined the rest of the family in Brussels and he told them all of the chaos during those few days in May when they had tried to stem the German advance and then been caught in the shambles of retreat.

'In Cambrai the Germans made a whole column of British soldiers wear women's underwear on their heads,' he said, smiling ruefully, but the story enraged Hortense. 'And on the way back not long ago we heard reports of German soldiers exercising on the canals.'

'D'you think they'll invade England?' Jacques asked his son, recognising the significance of the troop movements.

'They're certainly preparing for it and making no secret of the build-up. It seems to be a matter of common speculation though I've heard some German soldiers are afraid of drowning in the Channel on the way over.'

Hortense smiled at this, but the same story would mean much more to her later on, at a time when the German invasion of England would be no more than a Nazi dream.

Unaware of the real issues, Hortense never believed the Germans would succeed in defeating Britain, but news that they were going to cross the Channel was as depressing to her as the sight of German troops in the streets. The soldiers were usually well-behaved but their grey uniforms, black swastikas and jackboots were a constant reminder of defeat.

In the autumn Hortense began school again and often took a route which passed the statue of Edith Cavell, the nurse arrested by the Germans in 1915 for helping British soldiers escape. She found that Edith Cavell had been born in England, and that the Belgians had erected the memorial to her after the war in recognition of her bravery helping to fight the German occupation. She also knew that German soldiers had tied her to a post on a grassy bank at the Tir National, the national shooting range in Brussels, and executed her by firing squad. She often stopped at the statue and looked up at the stone eyes under the carved nurse's cap wondering at the kind of person who could give her life for total strangers in a foreign country. One morning in September as she walked to school she saw a German officer standing in front of the statue. Edith Cavell's spirit of resistance to an earlier German occupation had taken on a new meaning in 1940, and it was quite usual to see Belgians leaving flowers at the foot of the statue where they lay until they faded away, a mute badge of protest against German force of arms. She was surprised to see the officer bend and lay his own flowers, red roses, among the others. She watched him closely as he stepped back and saluted. He looked up at the stone face above them but there was no question in his eyes. The Wehrmacht officer, her enemy, was saluting the young nurse's bravery and sacrifice. In her innocence Hortense admired a heroine, while the German officer, a professional soldier, recognised qualities which he knew from his own experience of battle were rare in such a degree.

The heroes of the past were evocative but Hortense had already noticed that her brother seemed to be involved in more solid opposition to the Occupation. François and their cousins had gone without hesitation to work for the Red Cross in offices in the Rue aux Laines. The street ran alongside the Palais de Justice not far from the apartment in the Rue Sainte-Anne. The Red Cross worked tirelessly to repatriate Belgian prisoners of war still held in Germany and organise the shattered lives of servicemen who had returned to find their homes broken and their families disappeared. Naturally this work attracted many soldiers and officers of the army who wanted to do what they could to mitigate the disasters of May 1940, and just as naturally they found common cause in the beginnings of resistance to the Germans.

François was a serious and responsible young man whose qualities were soon appreciated by men and women like General de Lattre, Colonel de Rait, the Comte d'Oultremont, Colonel and Madame Lascelles, the Comte de Line, Colonel de Reed, Madame d'Rait, Madame d'Naire, Colonel Roussel whose family owned the big Brussels newspaper *Le Soir*, and General van Overstraten who came from the village of Kortenberg where François used to ride in regimental competitions. Under cover of the Red Cross these and other officers formed La Légion Belge (the Belgian Legion) in July. Later, in 1944, the Legion became L'Armée Secrète (the Secret Army) and membership rose to over 54,000. These men, nearly all servicemen, were the self-appointed representatives in Belgium of the government-in-exile in London, with which they were in contact. They were the nucleus of the deposed Belgian establishment.

Of course the officers in this group had been men with influence. The Belgian army was an important political element and its Secret Service was staffed by army officers with well-established connections in other countries, particularly with the British MI6 in London.

Such connections became especially important under German occupation and were formalised in November 1940 by the Belgian government-in-exile, which reconstituted the Sûreté d'Etat, which became responsible for all clandestine action in occupied Belgium.

Civilian clothes sit uncomfortably on military shoulders. Soldiers trained to fight the enemy in uniform in open battle find it very hard to fight a subversive undercover campaign. Still, fifty years on, many officers do not easily accept the covert role of modern Special Forces units in their present-day conflict against insurgency and terrorism. In 1940 many of these officers, stripped of the trappings of power in their ministries, were finding it difficult to set up underground resistance cells off the street and were beginning to find how useful reliable non-commissioned officers could be. Men with trades like François who was a mechanic and engineer, could move about anywhere in the country without attracting attention. Already enjoying the respect of his superiors before the war, François found himself entrusted with various jobs which took him away from Brussels. His common sense, natural reserve and great determination gave him the perfect characteristics for clandestine work. His sister had the same characteristics in abundance.

Hortense guessed he was up to more than working for the Red Cross. He was often absent for days at a time and it was well known that there were large numbers of British servicemen at large, more than 2000 in fact, after the defeat of May 1940 in Belgium and France, and that efforts were being made to help them evade capture. In addition a few of the two million French and 52,000 British servicemen taken prisoner in May 1940 began to escape the Stalags in Germany. They too were milling round in Belgium and needed to be fed on to the burgeoning escape lines. Two of these were the Pat O'Leary line run by Captain Ian Garrow, a British infantry officer, and Albert Guerrisse who was a Belgian naval doctor; and the Comet line which was started by a Belgian girl, Andrée de Jongh. The evaders, escapers or shot-down aircrew were located by local people brave enough to give them shelter, and collected by those like François who played an active part in the Resistance. Then they were put on the lines through Brussels *en route* for the south. Hortense dared not ask François too much but her interest was obvious to him and to their parents, and François could see that she badly wanted to help, even though she was only fourteen.

'Will you take some of these and leave them about for people to read?' he asked one day, handing her a small bundle of *La Libre Belgique*, the most famous and popular paper from the illegal presses.

'Of course, Brae!' Hortense said, overjoyed to be of use and pleased she could do something against the Germans.

'Just be careful,' François warned her. 'If you're seen, you'll be in real trouble. The Germans'll send you to prison.'

'I shan't be caught,' she laughed but she saw her brother was deadly serious.

François knew his younger sister had plenty of enthusiasm and hated the Nazis, but there was much to learn about secret work. At that time he too was a beginner. They had to be cautious.

Following the example of the Great War, clandestine newspapers and broadsheets were produced in Belgium within weeks of the invasion of May 1940. *La Libre Belgique*, with a Catholic bias, had the widest readership but others from every shade of society represented the Belgians' instant rejection of the Germans. *De Warrheid* and *Vrij Volk* were Flemish and *De Vrijschutter* was produced for Democratic Christians. In all, more than 650 different titles were produced during the Occupation, all united by a common purpose to publish news censored by the authorised newspapers: *La Nation Belge* for French speakers, the Flemish *Het Laatste Nieuws* and *Le Soir* had all shrunk in size to no more than six to eight pages. Hortense's father often brought back illegal papers from the shoe factory and she continued to distribute them from time to time while the family stayed in Brussels.

François's instinct was to discourage Hortense from doing anything active but he realised she was quite old enough to take matters into her own hands. There was a strong possibility that she would do something stupid if he did nothing to help her.

One evening the family were chatting in the apartment and François found a moment to speak quietly to her. His thin face utterly serious, he told her, 'If you want to help, there is something you could do.'

'Oh yes, Brae, please. What is it?' she replied, trying to keep her excitement under control. She knew François was watching her very closely and wanted him to trust her completely. She wanted him to know she could do whatever he asked. She would take every precaution. No one would catch her.

'Will you take this letter to someone for me, on the way to school tomorrow?'

There was never any doubt. She got to the rendezvous early to check who else was about and saw her contact arrive. He sat on a park bench under the trees in the Place du Petit Sablon opposite the Comte d'Oultremont's house, exactly as François had described. The excitement was intense; a feeling of achievement overwhelmed her in the mere fact of his being there at all. She watched him under the trees for several minutes, but as she started towards him the thrill inside her abated.

'Whatever you do, behave normally. Don't walk too fast or make sudden movements,' François had insisted. 'That way you won't draw attention to yourself. And for God's sake keep your eyes open.'

43

Without being aware of it she concentrated on what had to be done and forgot her earlier wild thoughts of the thousand and one things that might happen. She walked casually across the grass to the man and, as though she had been passing messages to strangers in the park all her life, handed him the letter. Not with a flourish, but quietly without fuss. It never crossed her mind to question what was inside it. Just as casually the man thanked her politely and walked away.

She wanted to do more. But as time passed François seemed to be able to visit the family less often. They got on well and she spoke to him when she could, when she thought he was not preoccupied with other problems, when she was sure her parents or her sister Julia could not overhear and when she could no longer contain her impatience to ask.

François watched her and checked her constantly. He gave her as little to do as would keep her quiet, just the occasional message to carry, and coached her as best he could for their enemies were formidable.

Under General von Falkenhausen, the Military Governor, the Wehrmacht had authority to carry out all the police work and for some months, perhaps into 1941, the excesses of the SS were concealed behind the stolid work of his troops in occupation. Their principal concern was not sabotage, as may be thought, but setting the Belgian economy back on its feet to support the Nazi war effort. The most frequent crimes were commercial, such as black market trading or selling goods to the Germans at inflated prices. However there were powerful police agencies ranged against people like François who were involved in escape lines. Two groups of the Geheimefeldpolizei (GFP), Nos. 530 and 740, were primarily responsible for destroying resistance in the Brussels and Brabant areas, which included Louvain. Easily recognised in grey uniforms with green collar patches and metal breastplates, the GFP units tightened their grip during the first year.

They worked closely with two infamous units of Heinrich Himmler's SS, the Sicherheitsdienst (SD) and the Gestapo. Both were part of the central controlling office of the SS in Berlin, the Reichssicherheitshauptamt (RHSA) or Reich Security Division. The SD in Department Six was responsible for 'security' in occupied countries and the Gestapo in Department Four was responsible for general 'state security'. As their objects were similar there was often intense rivalry between the two. Their internal chains of command were complex and while they did not always share information, they shared a common purpose in ruthlessly searching out and destroying anti-Nazi groups. By the time they reached Belgium they had already accumulated seven years experience in Germany since Hitler came to power in 1933, and their particular enemy was inevitably the left wing. Ably assisted by the GFP, which carried out the routine police work and midnight raids on suspects' houses, these SS security forces were the chief enemy of the Resistance. With no experience at all Hortense Daman had made a bold choice to fight them.

The house at 130 Pleinstraat was repaired and Hortense and the family moved back to Louvain in October 1940. Stephanie Daman started her corner shop and flower business again and soon found that the grocery business suffered badly from the constraints of rationing. The girls she had employed before the war could not get in to work, and the Germans had requisitioned most of the petrol, though her deliveries could be made by bicycle. Stephanie Daman settled down to the special problems of running a food store when food was in such short supply and made an effort to do the best for her customers. Naturally Hortense helped.

By December 1940 rationing was very tight and never really improved throughout the Occupation. Hortense watched her mother checking customers' ration books, and noticed her adding small extras here and there.

Officially a person's daily ration was 225 grammes (½ lb) of bread, 33 grammes of sugar (the same as three lumps), 50 grammes of meat of which 25 per cent could be bone (the equivalent of two small sausages), and 500 grammes (just over 1 lb) of potatoes. There were a few other items on the list, such as a small amount of jam, and a butter ration, in theory 4.2 grammes a day but which in practice was never available in the shops. Cheese did not appear until December 1942 when the authorities generously permitted 5 grammes. The national average consumption was 1400 calories a day per person throughout the war, compared with twice that in England at the same time. Today people can tuck away this amount at breakfast.

Food was always in demand in the Resistance where people on the run had no ration cards. François asked Hortense if she wanted to help supplement the rations her mother handed out over the counter. Again there was no doubt in her mind. After school in the afternoons she set off on her bicycle to the farms in the country round Louvain to scrounge what she could. She went from farm to farm asking if she could go into the fields and pick up the grains of corn dropped during the harvest. Working up and down the stubble, she filled the pannier on the front of her bicycle and came home. It was slow, arduous work. Gathering up pieces of beetroot and kohlrabi in the winter was easier because the pieces were bigger and filled the pannier faster, but it could be bitterly cold in a sharp wind on the bare fields.

The farmers knew the Damans and came to trust the young teenage girl. Sometimes they could be persuaded to sell flour, which Hortense would buy with money given her by François. But they had to be careful. This was black market activity. Indeed the military government strictly banned the sale or purchase of any foodstuff, or its transportation, without documents of authorisation. The German penchant for organisation was applied in full measure to the food chain, from the farmer, who had to account for his harvest in detail, stating the area of his fields, the likely yield of crop and size of his family; to the grocer, like Hortense's mother, who had to have papers to buy anything at all at market; and to the consumer, whose purchases were controlled by the rationing system. Hortense's innocent bike trips to the countryside to scrounge a few grains off the stubble fields made her a black marketeer as far as the Germans were concerned and she risked a year in prison if she were caught.

So strict were the German controls that even the basic foods which Hortense gleaned to feed young men on the run had a price on the black market. In 1941 the official price of bread was 2.5 Belgian francs per kilogramme (it had been 1.8 in 1939) but 37 francs on the black market. Potatoes were sold by Hortense's mother at 83 centimes a kilogramme but cost 10 francs illegally, and new potatoes were unobtainable in the marketplace. The Germans ordered the farmers to inform the authorities when their harvest was due, arranged trucks to be at the fields and the entire Belgian crop was transported into the Third Reich. More exotic food was always available through the real wide-boys, the black marketeers called Smokelaars, who could get anything, for a price. Chocolate cost 2 francs in the shops in German official theory, but in surreptitious Belgian practice could only be obtained for 400 francs, and at a time when the average working wage was 1200 francs a month.

Hortense could fit two 25 kilogramme bags of flour on her bicycle, one at the front and one slung over the rack above the back wheel and tied down. It was warm work pedalling with a full load but when the price of corn was ten times the official rate (145 francs per 100 kg) it was very important that she got home safely. The farmers tried to warn her of German patrols in the area and several times she saw the grey uniforms of soldiers, usually in groups of seven, moving across the open fields in the distance. Hortense treated these forays into the countryside as a game. The Germans were on bicycles too, but she prided herself on being much faster on hers and knowing all the back ways through sunken lanes and valleys. Later she would find she needed all that skill.

The dramatic success of the German army in May 1940 compared to the stagnant trench warfare of the previous generation had been demoralising to the occupied people, who had little confidence that the new Wehrmacht could be beaten at all. They watched preparations to invade England with dread, fully aware that no other power in Europe was in a position to help them Their chances of release from the German yoke disappeared the moment England succumbed: so, late that summer, it was with more than passing interest that the people of Belgium listened nightly at 7.30 to the BBC broadcasts, an activity punishable by imprisonment. Goering's Luftwaffe was thrown against London in the Battle of Britain, and its defeat, coolly and accurately annotated day by day by BBC announcers, gave hope to all who listened, huddled round their sets, while the Germans patrolled the streets outside. The Damans did not have a radio in their house because Jacques thought the high profile of the shop in the community might attract searches. They went to Hortense's grandparents' house. The news boosted the morale that one day a greater victory, this time on land, would restore their freedom.

There was little else to be cheerful about as winter gave way to spring in 1941. The British successes against the Italians in North Africa had brought the capture of Tobruk; but Rommel and the Afrika Korps arrived in February forcing the British into retreat. In Europe the Wehrmacht had extended Hitler's control with the capture of Yugoslavia, Greece, and then Crete in May. Throughout the occupied territories the Nazi security forces, the SD and Gestapo, followed behind the Wehrmacht to begin their campaigns of terror, with pogroms against Jews and gypsies to ensure racial cleanliness, and arrests of any political opposition.

These police activities made helping evading service-men increasingly dangerous work and yet in the winter of 1940-1 there were still numbers of British soldiers left behind from the summer evacuation. François had built up a net of contacts in the countryside east of Brussels and Louvain, who would get in touch with him if they had any information about evaders. Gradually over the months he had identified twenty British soldiers and he decided to move them into Louvain.

· When an Allied soldier or airman knocked on a door and threw himself on the mercy of a stranger living under the Nazi occupation he placed that person, and the whole family, at risk. Notices were pasted up in public places which made it clear that those harbouring the enemy would be sent to a concentration camp. Breendonk, the king's old GHQ, was turned into a prison with a particularly brutal reputation. The prisoners were cruelly treated, not allowed to speak, often tortured and worked twelve hours daily to shift earth off the concrete redoubts to a mound at the edge of the surrounding moat. The survivors of Breendonk were sent to Buchenwald and thought themselves lucky by comparison. A terrible fate hung over those brave enough to utter the simple words, 'Come in!'

François found an ideal place for the twenty soldiers, big enough to conceal so many; it was on the top floor of the convent of the Groot Begijnhof and the nuns were just the sort of people dedicated enough to keep the secret. The convent was inside the walls of the town on the same side as the Damans and not far from the Philips factory. However finding food for so many men in one place was a problem.

Hortense accepted François's request for help without hesitation. Stephanie Daman had picked up her old connections in business with most of the religious orders in Louvain, so it was reasonable for Hortense to make deliveries to the convent. The Germans never appreciated that the frequency of the attractive young teenager's visits increased when she was supplying so much extra food for the twenty hungry men. Concealed under the steep grey-slated roofs of the old convent, the men led a claustrophobic and boring life. They had little to look forward to except mealtimes. They were banned from talking or moving about too much for fear the noise would be heard in the cobbled street below. True to the principle of 'need to know', most of the nuns were ignorant that twenty members of the opposite sex were hiding in their convent. Even the lavatory had its security rules; the men had to be reminded time after time to put the seat down after use.

Laden down with flour, Hortense bicycled the short distance along the old walls of Louvain, past Parkpoort and into the town through the gates of Naamsepoort to the red-brick buildings of the convent which stood along the banks of the river Dyle. Sometimes her mother gave her vegetables, celery and leeks, but it was always hard work over the cobbles with such weights. For several weeks she was a regular visitor to the convent but never at any time when unloading her panniers did she talk to the nuns about the real reason for such an increase in supplies. Then suddenly François told her to stop going.

'What's happened?' Hortense asked, worried that the Germans had discovered them.

'They've been moved,' he told her off-handedly, as though he was talking about packages, not people who could be arrested, and whose helpers could be tortured and disappear into camps.

'Where to?'

'I hope they'll reach England,' was all the explanation François would give. There was no need for Hortense to know the details, and, besides, he was not a man who talked of his own achievements. The Channel coast was not yet the endless line of concrete bunkers which was later to form Hitler's Fortress Europe to prevent Allied invasion; but from the first months of the Occupation the Germans made every effort to stop escapes to England. The area was swarming with troops. Movement was strictly controlled along the coast and documents were necessary to approach within ten kilometres of the sea. Yet François had managed to conduct the soldiers to the coast where they had been put on a small boat to cross the few miles home to England.

For Hortense the months passed quickly. She was busy with schoolwork and helping in the shop. Gradually she did more and more for François, passing messages or taking food to addresses he gave her. The Resistance always needed more food. Her mother saw she was reliable and by the time she was fifteen years old she was getting up at five several days a week to go to the Old Market in Louvain, buying for the shop. There were no special privileges for age in the cut-throat business of market trading, and wartime restrictions made life in the market harder still. The regular Belgian buyers took advantage of the young girl, a novice in their hard-nosed world, and to begin with palmed her off with poor quality vegetables. They reckoned without her obstinacy and natural cunning. She hated the idea of letting her mother down by coming home with bad produce and went direct to the German official who controlled the market and issued the 'bonds'. Admirably concealing her hatred she buttered up the Germans, flattering them with her good looks and chat, and speaking in German which she was picking up quite well.

'Wait there,' the official ordered, waving her rudely to one side as he dealt with several other buyers jostling for their paperwork to be stamped. For several moments Hortense thought she had been forgotten.

'Here! Will these do?' The German shouted at her and pointed to two large crates of leeks which he had set aside, just what her mother wanted, in perfect condition.

'*Vielen Dank, mein Herr,*' Hortense said, genuinely delighted. She had beaten the older buyers, and her mother would be content. The German smiled at her obvious pleasure. Soon, Kleine Hortensia, as the Germans called her, was able to buy the best quality of the day.

Then she finished at school. The German officials in the education department of the military government had identified talented Flemish boys and girls at the schools in Louvain. Seeing Flanders as part of the Greater German Reich they wanted children brought up to support Hitler's view of the world. They tried to encourage Flemish parents with a generous offer of further education in Brussels for their children, fully paid for, with travel organised by the authorities. Hortense Daman was one of those selected but her mother was deeply suspicious of the real motives behind the offer. Stephanie had no intention of letting her daughter be seduced by the propaganda of National Socialism, though she admitted to herself that it had little chance of success with Hortense. She declined the offer by simply telling the truth. Her problem was running the corner shop at home. She had to travel on the train to Brussels to the flower market, while her daughter went to the Louvain Old Market. Hortense made the grocery deliveries round the town and took food to the Philips factory canteen for the workers' lunches. She also helped in the shop at busy times, for example when there were flowers to lay on clients' graves in the cemetery.

Reluctantly the Germans conceded her point, little imagining that the young schoolgirl was using most of these excuses to help the Resistance. Her deliveries of groceries now included several addresses which François had given her, where she simply knocked on the door and left food she knew would never be paid for. The extra mouths inside without benefit of ration books had to be fed somehow on their long journey to freedom.

Under persistent questioning by Hortense, François had long ago admitted he was organising the distribution of the clandestine newspapers, of which she had previously passed a small bundle for him. Finally he agreed to let her in on it. Providing lunches for the Philips workers was a perfect opportunity. François brought copies of *La Libre Belgique* in quantity to the corner shop and Hortense smuggled them into the canteen where she left them lying about for the men to find at lunch. The drastic consequences of this act of resistance were highlighted at the end of February 1942.

'*Morgen, Herr Kapitän,*' she called to the captain of the guard as she passed through the gatehouse into the huge factory.

'Heil Hitler!' the elderly captain replied.

The captain was overweight and arrogant, with a duelling scar on his face typical among older German officers, but Hortense took care to appear cheerful. She had quickly learnt that a smile worked wonders.

'*Morgen Karl, morgen Paul,*' she said to the two German soldiers as she passed inside the building.

They waved her through. They were so used to seeing her taking in the lunches that the chances of her being searched were small indeed.

Inside, she waited till there was no one about, swiftly pulled the illegal papers from under her coat and left them where suspicion would never attach to her, in the men's locker room.

She took special care that time. She had been badly shaken by the news François had brought earlier in the day.

'Commandant Lambert has been arrested,' he had told her, sitting in the kitchen while she prepared the lunches. Their mother was in the shop serving a customer and they spoke softly. 'With a lot of others.'

Commandant Lambert, an officer in the Belgian army, had been organising the distribution too.

'What happened?' she asked, stopping her work and staring at her brother. She noticed his thin face was drawn and he looked tired.

'Too much talking. Too many doing things they didn't need to,' François replied. 'February the 24th was a black day.'

He looked at his sister and realised the news was a tremendous shock to her confidence. There had been arrests before, but none so far had hit so close to home. She knew François had been working with Lambert and the others since the beginning. Copying her brother and always taking his advice, Hortense had developed a certain cunning and was determined never to be caught, but she knew that the more important the job, the more dangerous the work became. Like Lambert had been, François was now permanently on the run. He never stayed in the same place more than a few nights, sometimes only one night. The leaders were especially exposed to danger.

In a small voice she asked, 'The SS have them?'

'Yes.' François had no doubt what pressures would be brought on the captured men. 'We've warned everyone but this'll slow us down badly for a while.'

It was a success for the German security forces. The SS had not taken long to settle in and had spread their net wide, making free use of Belgian sympathisers, collaborators with the Nazis, and their own crude methods of interrogation. These were powerful weapons against the Resistance. Each time there were arrests the Resistance had to find out what had happened and why, re-group and start again.

The officers and men arrested with Commandant Lambert suffered the full consequences of resistance to the Nazis. Cruelly interrogated, Lambert was finally executed on 31 October that year.

The shock took some time to wear off. Hortense had no doubt that she must continue her work for François, but she took more care. Evading the Germans was no longer a game. She was growing up fast.

In Brussels von Falkenhausen's officers at the Kommandantur in the Hôtel de Ville had run out of patience. Edith Cavell's immutable stone gaze, silent encouragement to resist, was no longer admired. There were too many flowers. The authorities surrounded the statue with several dense rolls of barbed wire and declared that anyone seen leaving anything at the memorial would be sent to St Gilles prison. But the flowers, just a few, just enough, kept appearing.

# 4

# The Point of No Return

*'Le Peuple sait que le sang des Patriotes n'est pas versé en vain, qu'il est fécond et que la Liberté en sortira.'* From *Le Partisan*, clandestine copy No. 92, October 1942.

'I need your help,' François told his sister one day in the summer of 1942. 'I've been asked to get in touch with a man here in Louvain and so far everything we've tried has failed.'

'Why?' Hortense asked, pleased François wanted her to do something.

'He's under close house arrest and we can't get near him,' her brother replied bluntly. He paused to see the effect of his words on his young sister who seemed quite unmoved, and then explained, 'He's called Professor de Vleeschauwer. His brother escaped to England after the invasion and is part of the government-in-exile. He's Minister of the Belgian Colonies which is a very important position. Since the Germans occupied us, our country's finances depend on the colonies. The Germans know this and that's why they've locked up the Professor in his own house. His brother's sent us a message to get in touch with him.'

In May 1940 the Belgian government had escaped first to France and on 18 June Prime Minister Pierlot had ordered de Vleeschauwer to leave Bordeaux, where they had been pushed by the German advances, and travel to London to be the Administrator of the Belgian Congo, Ruanda and Urundi. He was joined by the Minister for Finance, Camille Gutt. With the king a prisoner of war in Belgium by his own choice, the Prime Minister and Paul-Henri Spaak were uncertain what to do and eventually moved to Spain where they were interned at once. The Spanish refused to release them. Finally with British help, Pierlot and Spaak slipped out of their prison but they did not reach England until October 1940.

'What's the problem?' Hortense was filled with the importance of the mission and wanted to know all the details.

'He's guarded all the time by soldiers on the gate and patrols in the grounds. We also think his servants are supplied, or at any rate vetted, by the Kommandantur. There's no way the lads can reach him on a secret approach to the house without raising the alarm. But you might be able to.'

François told Hortense that the house was No. 239 Tiense Steenweg, set back in its own grounds and surrounded by a high wall. The way in was through the gate on the main road. They discussed the options and decided the simplest plan offered the best chance. The house was not more than ten minutes away on her bicycle and Hortense would deliver groceries. As always authority from the Germans would be required.

Hortense biked into the centre of town to the Kommandantur, which had been the Palais de Justice. She used her best German which had become quite fluent, and all her charm to flatter the German officials. She had learned all the German ranks and deliberately upped them by a notch or two. When she was admitted to see the duty officer she smiled and explained sweetly that someone had come round to the corner shop and asked them to make deliveries to the professor's house.

'Rather silly of me, but I can't remember his name or anything much about him,' she smiled at him and adjusted her dress.

The duty officer could see nothing but an attractive and pleasant young girl who wanted to deliver groceries. Her explanations made sense to him: the mother ran a grocery shop and had always had authority to buy at the market; the professor obviously needed groceries, and besides they were Flemish.

Hortense and her mother prepared the first delivery and she biked down Pleinstraat and on to the Tiense Steenweg. As she approached the house she could see two soldiers with rifles standing at the big double gates and beyond them a little guard hut inside by the wall.

'What's all this then?' the Gefreiter demanded, lifting the red and white chequered cloth over the front pannier. When he saw the vegetables and a small basket of eggs, he became less aggressive and said, 'The grounds of this house are controlled. Maybe it's better if we take this to the kitchens ourselves. You can stay here by the gate. We don't want to get into trouble, do we?'

Hortense smiled inwardly, genuinely amused. Rationing was difficult and the sight of a few eggs and the tiniest amount of butter would turn people's heads. Clearly the soldiers intended that a proportion of the delivery would never reach the kitchens.

'Please, I'm only doing my job,' she wheedled them in a small voice, 'I really ought to go up myself. If I don't, my mother might . . .' she finished lamely, looking pathetic.

The soldiers seemed disappointed. The Gefreiter inspected her authority from the Kommandantur and conceded, 'All right then. But we'll have to come with you.'

'I can manage,' Hortense replied, trying to control her alarm. No one at the house had ordered any groceries and no one knew she was coming. There was no way of warning the professor. She and François had looked at the problem from every angle but could see no way round it. This part of the plan had been left to her own initiative and she had not bargained on two German soldiers hanging around while she explained things to the professor. What if the soldiers overheard? She ignored the idea and concentrated on what the unpleasant corporal was saying.

'No. It's our duty,' the Gefreiter declared self-righteously, his attitude hardening again. He glared at her from under his steel helmet. The opportunity to help himself was denied and he was going to make damn certain the delivery reached its destination.

Leaving a soldier on guard at the gate, the Gefreiter ordered another to accompany him and Hortense followed them up the drive pushing her bike. She watched their broad backs under the field grey uniforms. They looked so solid. She wondered who would open the door, whether the professor would be there, what she would say?

She watched them bang on the door and when the housemaid opened it, Hortense boldly asked to speak to the professor. The woman looked at her suspiciously, and then at the soldiers who were standing close by the bike and the pannier full of vegetables. Hortense saw at once that the woman was Belgian and disliked the soldiers, but there was nothing in her surly manner to suggest she was going to be helpful. Almost shouting, Hortense launched into a story about the delivery of groceries, off the top of her head, all the time repeating how important it was to speak to the professor himself so she could bring the sort of vegetables he liked, in the hope he was somewhere close and would hear. Just as she was beginning to run out of variations on this theme she heard a man's voice inside the house.

'What's the matter?' Professor de Vleeschauwer asked, clutching a book to his chest and peering curiously round the door at the strangely assorted group.

Hortense saw this was her opportunity. Her only opportunity.

'May I speak privately, sir?' she asked him directly, her expression as much as to say that soldiers and housemaids had no idea about the complicated world of groceries nor about a customer's preferences. Professor de Vleeschauwer was a neat man who wore steel-rimmed spectacles, a mathematician and scientist, but he was not unkind. He motioned for Hortense to come in.

This was the hardest part. She was not out of the wood yet. She stepped briskly into the house, moving with the professor as far as she dared, away from the housemaid who was standing inside the front door and the soldiers who were peering round the door. All three were watching her. She observed the professor carefully for a moment, trying to decide how he would react. She had no idea of his real political sympathies, nor did she really understand why he was under house arrest. All she knew was that in the next few moments she had to make him understand she was a link to his brother in England. She began to explain about the deliveries again, speaking in a quieter tone than before, so the others could not hear. The professor began to look puzzled as to why he should be subjected to such a detailed discussion about vegetables, and then, to her horror, he grew bored. She had to act. She glanced at the door and saw the housemaid turn to say something to the soldiers outside.

'I've a message from your brother John,' she whispered suddenly.

The statement coming so abruptly after an explanation of his groceries took the professor completely by surprise, especially from so unlikely a source as this young girl. Fortunately he was not facing his housemaid and only Hortense had the satisfaction of seeing his astonishment. She did not have to wait long to see what would happen next.

He recovered quickly, and very deliberately said to her, 'Well, I look forward to seeing you again, and thank you. Stuck in the house with little to do, I would like to take more interest in what I eat. We'll discuss this further next time you visit.'

He turned to the housemaid and said, 'Marie, take these excellent vegetables to the kitchen.'

The soldiers escorted Hortense back to the gate on Tiense Steenweg. They were irritated by her sudden cheerfulness. Hortense relished the thought that she had made contact between the Belgian government-in-exile, far away in England, and the prisoner inside the house on the Tiense Steenweg, in her home town, right under the noses of the German guards.

François's obvious delight at her success was a further boost to her morale and confidence, but the task had only just begun. Every time she visited the professor's house she carried in with her a part of a radio set hidden beneath the groceries. The plan all along had been to set up the professor in contact with England by radio. As Hortense bicycled in with wires, resistors, valves and switches, Professor de Vleeschauwer assembled the radio. Every time she visited she had to pass inspection by the sentries on duty at the gate, and every time they escorted her to the house. Sometimes she had to give them an apple or even an egg to prevent them looking right through the pannier. Every time she risked her freedom for those small radio parts. She was never certain if anyone else in the house in Tiense Steenweg supported the Allies and was careful to speak only to the professor. Once he knew why she was making the deliveries, he made it as easy as he could for her to see him. The rest of his family and the staff assumed that his excessive interest in groceries was due to the boredom of being confined to the house, and was an extension of the vegetable garden he had started on the terrace.

Hortense generally met him in this garden, where he had laid out neat seed-beds with meticulous scientific care. With the air of a mad professor, he refused to allow the two German soldiers near his precious vegetable garden, apparently convinced they would trample all over the beds, and ordered them to wait at the end of the terrace. This gave him the chance to speak to Hortense.

Finally after several weeks of deliveries, standing in his garden between immaculately dressed rows of baby carrots, she gave him the last little piece of radio. Three days after that he whispered to her, 'I've assembled the radio. It's ready.'

'Good,' replied Hortense, pointing vaguely at the lines of bright green carrots to satisfy the curiosity of the two Germans watching them from the edge of the terrace garden. 'Because there will be a broadcast tonight, from your brother, from London.'

Before she could explain the codes which would be used, she stepped back in astonishment as Professor de Vleeschauwer suddenly leaped in the air and began to dance about all over the neat rows of little carrots, laughing and shouting with happiness.

Thoroughly alarmed Hortense looked round at the Germans. She need not have worried. Still standing stolidly side by side at the end of the terrace, they watched this performance with total indifference, quite convinced the professor had gone mad. Ordinary infantry soldiers in the Wehrmacht, under orders by the military governor von Falkenhausen to guard the professor, they were not surprised to find their suspicions about educated people, especially Belgians, at last confirmed. They watched as the professor cavorted over his precious vegetable garden, where they themselves had been banned for fear of treading off the neat paths. They watched as he calmed himself chatting to the delivery girl – more talk about groceries they supposed – and then they escorted her down the drive to the road.

# The Point of No Return

Hortense's job with Professor de Vleeschauwer was finished. London had made contact with the professor as they wanted, through the organisation of Belgian army officers working underground in Brussels and through François. The job was well done and Hortense had every reason to feel proud of her success. François was pleased that his sister had shown such intelligent initiative. The first contact had been crucial and the risks considerable, passing the sentries every day with the radio parts. There is no doubt it had been a considerable achievement for a sixteen-year-old.

But why were they asked to do all this? Was it simply so that the Minister for the Belgian Colonies could cheer up his brother under house arrest in occupied Belgium? The radio which Hortense supplied in parts was a receiver with no possibility of transmitting signals back to England, so what other explanation could there have been? Perhaps the professor was supposed to have collated information about the Occupation, but under house arrest he could not collate very much and dependent as he was on the link through Hortense he could not add much to the information already filtering back to England from other sources in Belgium, on escape lines or through couriers into neutral countries like Spain and Switzerland.

So was it worth it? Was it worth risking the freedom of a young girl, and the inevitable indictment of her family? She risked arrest on every journey. Interrogations would have followed. The Gestapo would have been extremely interested to find out the names and addresses of everyone behind the operation, an operation which obviously stemmed from London. She was perhaps lucky the German soldiers were bored with their job, and were anyway infantrymen, not policemen who are naturally more suspicious and might have searched her pannier more carefully. Certainly the operation worked and its success was due to Hortense's preparedness to take all these risks. But just to keep the minister and his brother happy? It seems a cavalier treatment of the men and women who risked their lives daily by their commitment to resistance.

Hortense did not see François every day as he was on the move. But he was always in the background and she learned from him all the time. She knew the Gestapo were by now very keen to catch him. His work with the escape lines from 1940 onwards was known to too many people. Many of those arrested had, in spite of themselves, let slip a name here or there. The SD and the Gestapo did not work well together but their crude methods had quickly produced a list of persons suspected of being in the Resistance. An image of François Daman was beginning to emerge through various sources of information and under different names and aliases. So far the Gestapo seemed not to know his real identity or his family's real address but the net was growing tighter. A man with his contacts would be a fine catch for the German anti-terrorist intelligence cells.

François frequently reminded Hortense what would happen if she was arrested and she was determined not to be caught. She took a considerable pride in her professional efficiency, and François realised she had a natural skill as an agent

'Do you want to become a soldier?' François asked suddenly one evening shortly after the night they had re-buried the pilot in the cemetery.

Hortense looked up immediately across the kitchen table. Over the last couple of years she had learned to be economic with what she said. But this was different. This was something she never expected to hear from her brother.

'How? What d'you mean?' she asked, with difficulty matching her voice to François's low tone, and glancing in the direction of the shop where she could hear her mother serving a customer. She suddenly found it difficult to control her excitement. Before the war, for years as a little girl, she had envied François his glamorous life in the army. He had been, and in a certain way still was, serving his country, which had always been a very important issue to Hortense. She resented the Nazi swastikas hanging from all the requisitioned Belgian public buildings, the notices stuck on walls banning the freedoms of normal life and the streets filled with German troops, and she had done her best to help François in his resistance work. She envied the young men their opportunity to fight and it had never occurred to her that a more formal possibility existed for girls.

'What can I do?'

François watched her carefully, taking in the pretty face framed by long blonde hair, seeing the vivacious energy in her, but really concentrating on the serious expression in her wide-set blue eyes. He saw her glance at the shop. For all her young enthusiasm she had become cautious too.

'Do you want to join the Partisans?' he asked. 'The Belgian army of Partisans. They've started recruiting in Louvain and they need people like you.'

Even now he was uncertain whether he was right to make the offer. The decision had not been easy, but reluctantly he thought she must be given the choice or she would take some other course, sooner or later risking all in some personal action against the Nazis and jeopardising the family, and his own contacts.

'I know what you feel about the country, wanting to join up,' he said quietly and earnestly. 'Now's your chance. This isn't the same as the regular Belgian army, but the Partisans are officially recognised and supported by the government-in-exile in London. One day, when the English armies come again and the Germans are beaten, you'll be able to wear your uniform. Some of the lads round here have joined and they need more volunteers.'

'Girls too?'

'Certainly.' Although a career soldier, François had quickly accepted that the Resistance could not operate without the women volunteers. He just hoped he was doing the right thing recruiting a girl of only sixteen, his own sister.

Hortense listened, hardly daring to speak. Her thoughts were a turmoil of excitement but the appalling sight of the British pilot's cruelly tortured body in the dark morgue had quite convinced her. If strangers were prepared to leave their homes far away and give their lives in such agonies how could she refuse to join the battle too? This was her country. There was no option. The soldiers and airmen from abroad, her own people like François and all the others in the Resistance gave her no option. She had seen something of the dangers and knew of men like Commandant Lambert who had been executed. Yet there was no shadow of reluctance in her decision to join the Partisans. She did it willingly, knowing it was more than her duty. It was her right.

'Of course, Brae. Of course I'll join. What do I have to do?'

François looked over to the shop door in the corner of the kitchen, almost hidden in darkness under the steep stairs. It was late and though there were no customers their mother was still busy. They could hear her moving stock about on the shelves.

'It isn't like an ordinary army, as you know,' he went on. 'There aren't uniforms, of course. Or camps. No place for those in secret work, but the Partisans are well organised. They've divided everyone into cells, and the idea is that a person in one cell has no connection with a person in another. No one knows what the others have done, or are going to do.'

Hortense frowned. 'I can see that's fine for security, but how do they all know what to do?'

'You'll be a courier, so let me tell you something about the organisation,' he said. So far he had taken care to employ her in the minimum number of jobs, just enough to keep her busy and out of trouble. He could not deny she had done well, and he was proud of his sister. However once she joined the Partisans she would be really committed. A courier's life was generally very busy, dangerous and often short. Most were girls and their job meant they were constantly on the move and always with incriminating evidence on them. With collaborators and denunciation a real threat, being good was not good enough. Couriers needed luck to survive. François had decided his sister could be given the chance.

'The lowest level in the hierarchy is filled by people whose sole interest is in fighting the Germans. These men are organised in cells and are the backbone of the Partisans. They're the activists. They aren't concerned with reasons, they're just committed to attacking the enemy. When they're not in action they go about their daily lives pretending they're God-fearing citizens like every other man and woman in this town. Some are on the run but they're always in danger of denunciation.'

He paused. He thought for a moment of explaining the tremendous psychological pressure some of these men lived under. Sometimes not even their wives knew they were involved. He decided Hortense was too young. Pressure like this was alien to her and she had no experience of her own pain and grief. She was still filled with the callous optimism of youth.

'Although the cells are supposed to be separate it's frankly impossible to insist on this. In a small town people know each other from schooldays, or working together, like in the factories along the canal. Then as Partisans they see each other during an attack and soon get to know one or two more people in the group, or maybe in another group. When the Gestapo arrests someone we have real problems limiting the damage.' François looked his sister straight in the eye. 'You should be in no doubt how you will be treated by those bastards if they catch you. Just remember that poor lad we re-buried in the cemetery.'

'That's all right, Brae,' she replied with unnerving candour. 'I'll do my best not to say anything.'

She wanted to know everything, but tried to keep her questions short. Normally a man of few words her brother had become especially cautious and alert. Now he was looking round again, listening to noises in the shop and outside in the street. He turned back and continued.

'The cells are controlled by a central organisation in Brussels and are part of a network across the country. There are similarities to the regular army. The cells are called battalions which are grouped by areas into corps. Actually Louvain is Corps No. 34.'

Hortense interrupted, 'So are there a lot of people in the Partisans?' She thought of all the soldiers in the battalion billeted in the Philips factory before the invasion.

François smiled. 'The BAP calls them battalions to give the impression that there are masses of men fighting the Germans. It's propaganda really, but the network of command and control is very important. Even though we work in secret there has to be a structure so we can send orders to all the battalion cells, to coordinate them for an attack, for example, and then receive reports back again. The reports might be about attacks or contain information collected daily about German units which can be turned into useful intelligence for the Allies. This system of communication depends on couriers taking messages, letters and parcels from one level of command to the next. That'll be your job.'

'The same sort of thing I've been doing for you?'

'Yes, but you'll have much more to do. You'll be busy every day for the Partisans, plus there'll be more of the jobs you've been doing for me. The English are now sending more planes to bomb Germany and there'll be more airmen shot down. We have to help them get back to England to fight again. Then, in addition to orders and reports, you'll have to take messages about guns and ammunition needed for a particular attack. Not all the Partisans are armed all the time and before an attack the leaders have to coordinate bringing the guns which are hidden in one place to the Partisans who'll gather in another place. Then we have to get them all back into hiding afterwards. Our system of command and control is what the Gestapo wants to destroy. They want the commanders, but the next best thing is to identify the couriers, the links between so many contacts and addresses, hoping they'll give away the leaders. Be in no doubt, little Hortenseke, those bastards won't hesitate to beat you up to get what they want.'

François could not help thinking how strange it was to be discussing guns, explosives, torture and death with his teenage sister. They should have been talking about his chances of being picked for the Louvain Athletic Club relay at the next sports meeting, or what Hortense was going to do now she had finished her schooling. The Occupation had changed their lives so much. He felt sure Hortense understood the dangers, at least in theory, so he went on describing the partisan structure.

'The corps reports to a sector which is controlled by the National Commando in Brussels.'

He did not complete his picture of the structure by adding that the National Commando was in turn controlled by Moscow. The Partisans were the active wing of the Communist-controlled Front of Independence, a Labour Party group formed in March 1941. Before that, in Louvain, a mix of socialists and the extreme left had combined in 1940 to form the Revolutionary Anti-Fascist Front, or RAFF, as an action group of the Labour Party. At first the Front of Independence had refused to recognise the RAFF. Because of this, and because they could see no future in the narrow confines of the RAFF, two men, Edward Seymens and François Nijsen, left the RAFF in the autumn of 1941 and started the Belgian Army of Partisans in the Louvain area. The third founding member who joined them at this time was Hortense's cousin Pierre Hermans, and the fourth, suggested by Hermans, was Louis van Brussel. All these men were dedicated to fighting the Occupation with armed action.

The fledgling Louvain Partisans had struggled for nearly a year. Then two factors boosted membership enormously. First the Germans took a decision which struck at the heart of Belgian families. From the start of the Occupation the Reich had offered Arbeitsfreiwillige, or voluntary work, in Germany with colourful stories of good pay and conditions. Reality was quite different and the truth filtered back home. Pay was not sent back to Belgium as promised and deductions at source for food and accommodation were made at punitive rates. In May 1942 already 300,370 Belgians were working in Germany, but Fritz Sauckel, Reichscommissar for labour, was not satisfied. In August he obtained authority to increase this by 150,000 and that month alone 25,000 were sent. On 6 October he made the selection compulsory and by 1943 over half a million men were working in Germany whether they liked it or not. Young men immediately went on the run, rather than be called up. The clandestine life was not easy without support and many were precipitated into the Partisans, which offered food, a structure and a little money from time to time. They were not all as dedicated as Hortense, perhaps, but faced with the choice between deportation into Germany and joining the Partisans at home, a lot stayed at home.

Secondly the Front of Independence, essentially a political organ, gave its approval to the Partisans. After the Nazis invaded Russia in the summer of 1941 Moscow had decided that the Communists in occupied France and Belgium must carry out active resistance and from 1942 onwards encouraged the maximum of attacks. It followed that many socialists who hated the Germans but had done nothing so far, now felt they could join the Partisans with the support of the Front.

Soviet support was not given merely in pursuit of the ideological struggle. In the autumn of 1942 Russia needed all the help she could get as she was under tremendous pressure from the Wehrmacht on the banks of the Volga, at Stalingrad and in Sebastopol. Moscow wanted Partisans everywhere to put pressure on the Germans. There was perhaps another reason. For two years Moscow had been receiving intelligence reports from a spy circuit in Belgium but it had been brilliantly uncovered by the Gestapo, which called the group the Rote Kapelle (Red Orchestra). After arresting several leading members including the leader Leopold Trepper, who subsequently escaped, and several German socialists in Berlin, they ran a radio game with Moscow sending false information to the Russian Director of Intelligence throughout the winter of 1942–3. During this period they continued to pursue and arrest members of the Soviet circuit, until by the spring of 1943 the Gestapo was confident that it had virtually eliminated effective Communist agents in France, Holland and Belgium. Suspecting that its Rote Kapelle source of intelligence had been destroyed it is not surprising that Moscow encouraged the Front of Independence to support the Partisans who could send them the information on German forces they needed so much.

François also avoided an explanation of his own motives, and those of his masters in the Belgian Legion, like General van Overstraten. The army officers of the pre-war Belgian army and the government-in-exile were particularly interested in the Partisans. The BAP quickly became a considerable force all over Belgium, second only in size to the Belgian Legion, but their political base was clearly quite different. Under the Occupation they were fighting the same enemy; but what orders would Moscow send to the Partisans once the Germans were defeated and the democratic government returned from London? General Overstraten thought François Daman could provide some of these answers if he joined the Partisans and kept the Belgian Legion informed about their organisation, activities and future intentions. In the meantime it also made sense to encourage cooperation between resistance groups, so François combined his work for the escape lines and the Belgian Legion with his job as Intelligence and Liaison Officer for the Partisans.

François Daman was in no dilemma joining the Partisans. He was never a Communist, but he was always a man of action and could not have stood by and not be involved in the Resistance in his local area. His cousin Pierre Hermans had arranged for him to join the Partisans knowing that his existing wide range of contacts in the Resistance would be extremely useful to them. François never confused his priorities by discussing matters that had nothing to do with the Partisans. He saw no reason to describe this background to Hortense. To the vast majority the simple aim was to remove the Germans, and the Partisans were committed to using force. Politics belonged in the debating halls and François was a career soldier who believed there was no place for politicians on the field of battle.

'The risks are enormous,' he told Hortense. 'But I think you can do the job.' François felt sure she would do well.

'Just tell me what I have to do, Brae,' she said.

'As a courier you'll take orders from the Corps Commandant and work mainly here in Louvain, but be prepared to go anywhere. Your cover working in the shop is perfect. Remember, keeping all the command links alive is vital, from National Commando level to sector, corps and to the battalion. Your Corps Commandant will depend on you completely.'

'Who is the Corps Commandant here?'

'Louis van Brussel.'

When she started work as a courier for Louis van Brussel her life became very busy, as François had predicted. Every day she had to take orders from van

Brussel to the Partisan battalion leaders in the town, and bring reports back to van Brussel. She quickly learned all the places to visit and who to see, bicycling round the town, along the canal and beside the railway tracks of the huge depot and marshalling yards. Her cover delivering groceries for her mother was ideal. She was often stopped by German patrols but they seemed satisfied by her authority for the vegetables she carried.

François and Louis saw how quickly she learned her new trade and seemed to thrive on the work. She showed initiative and resourcefulness, using her appearance and age to the best advantage. François continued to give her advice but increasingly encouraged her to make up her own mind about the things she had to do. He recognised that it was wrong for a commander to insist his courier went to a meeting even if she thought the rendezvous was compromised.

'But Brae, what if the message is important?' Hortense said. She often wondered what was in the reports and orders she carried but she never asked questions.

'Nothing's more important than being able to walk away free to carry on the fight,' François replied, and added bluntly, 'and keeping the message from being captured with you.'

Several times Hortense had decided not to go into a particular house or make a certain rendezvous with another courier, and came back to tell van Brussel or François that she felt unhappy about it. On one occasion when there was nothing amiss the other courier got very cross that Hortense had failed to make the meet. François backed her. He saw no point taking risks for a routine report and would rather she used her feminine instincts to protect herself than blindly followed orders. It did not pay to take chances.

But she was young. The same impulses which made her stay away from a rendezvous made her take risks which men like François would never dream of. They realised that sooner or later she would run into trouble. It happened to them all. The fortunate ones survived, their self-confidence battered, their judgment tempered, and their chances of ultimate survival increased from the experience.

In November Louis van Brussel had such an experience when the Gestapo raided the house in De Ridderstraat in Louvain where he and his wife Simone were staying. Acting on source reports from Belgian collaborators, the SS had posted members of the Belgian SS and the GFP at the front and the back of the terraced row. As soon as the hammering began on the door, the two woke, leaped out of bed and realised they were in bad trouble. Their options were few. They could give themselves up, which invited certain death after torture; fight it out, which probably amounted to the same thing when all he had was a pistol; or make a run for it. Louis decided on the last and led his wife into the attic, out of the skylight on to the roof, and they ran the length of the roofs of the long terraced street to escape. The Germans were just too slow to realise what their prey had done.

Stephanie heard the story from François and it brought home to her what risks Hortense was running. It tore her heart to think what the Germans would do to her if she was caught.

Shortly after van Brussel's narrow escape he introduced another Partisan newly arrived in Louvain, Godefried Dreesen, known as Gaston. He arrived from Maastricht late one night looking dreadfully thin. Sallow and ill at ease, he stood in the kitchen where Hortense and François were sitting with their parents and Julia. Stephanie looked at him, at the dark circles under his eyes and the hunted expression on his face. Then she looked at her son. François himself was very thin now. It saddened her to think that these young men were chased and hounded in their own country, driven from their homes and families. Firmly and gently she told Gaston to sit down. Then in silence she fetched him some food, a wonderful thick soup and bread which he wolfed down like a man starved for months. Hortense had moved from the table and watched in the background without a word. François had taken his mother to one side in the corner by the door to the shop and spoken to her in a low voice for some minutes. Gaston had looked at them, at Louis, at the girls and then concentrated on his soup. Hortense noticed he ate as though someone might suddenly take it away from him. Stephanie came back to the table.

'You can stay here tonight,' she told Gaston. 'Then tomorrow François will find somewhere else for you. This is a small house and I have a large family, but it upsets me to think you have nowhere else to go. François need hardly have asked. So tonight anyway you're welcome here.'

Gaston was at the end of his tether and too grateful to find the right words to thank Madame Daman. He had been arrested but escaped from the Gestapo interrogation centre in Maastricht the day before, so he knew precisely what risks they were taking. Harbouring a wanted man meant Hortense's mother and father Jacques would be arrested. Quite simply, giving him shelter for one night risked the destruction of the family group. It did not matter that they were already involved with the Resistance, Gaston knew very well what his presence meant.

Hortense had seen a number of François's friends fed and looked after by her mother. For many of them it was their only decent meal in days. But that was the first occasion her mother had agreed to take in someone for the night.

After that night in November Gaston slept with the Storckels across the street, but he spent all day with the Damans and worked with Louis in the Louvain Corps of Partisans. Every evening he slipped over Pleinstraat under the noses of the guards at the Philips factory to eat with the Damans. There were such a lot of comings and goings at the Damans' with the grocery and flower business, that the guards never noticed. None the less the presence of the Germans so close was a constant reminder of the blow that would fall if they made mistakes. Or if they were denounced.

Hortense had wondered why Gaston continued to stay in Pleinstraat until she learned from François that Louis van Brussel wanted him to take over command of the corps quite soon, as he was a Partisan of good experience. Gaston himself had reservations because he was not familiar with the area. Knowledge of the ground is vital for all those engaged in a secret life, whatever their style: freedom fighter, subversive, revolutionary, terrorist, criminal, resistance fighter or partisan. He knew Maastricht, his home town, but little about Louvain when he came. However he learned fast and was valuable to the group, offering advice on tactics and plans which was always useful during the endless discussions that took place in the Daman kitchen after supper and late into the night.

François, Louis and Gaston tried to keep Hortense out of the armed operations, which the Partisans called actions. Hortense carried the orders for these to the cells or battalions, and was involved in setting up the administration for them.

One day early in 1943 the Partisans were preparing to attack a Post Office in Kessel-Loo on the outskirts of Louvain. Post Offices were regularly attacked as a source of money and ration cards. Mostly the Post Office staff made only token resistance and 'allowed' the robberies to take place. On this occasion Gaston decided to use a sub-machine-gun which was cached in Pleinstraat. The weapon was hidden in Josephine Roost's little house on the corner of Kerkhofdreef. Josephine was fiercely loyal to the Damans and hated Germans. She would do anything to help. Already materials were hidden under the ground in the back room of her small cottage. There was a trap-door concealed beneath a carpet under her bed and she lived and slept over several hundred pounds of high explosive, blithely content as long as Germans would be killed as a result.

During the morning, another of Hortense's cousins, Pierre van Goitsenhoeven, had picked up the sub-machine-gun. He was the same age as François and had joined the Partisans about the same time. As a very close friend, almost a brother, he had gone into the Damans' house where Hortense found him when she came home on her bicycle. The gun was loosely wrapped in a brown paper parcel on the kitchen table.

'What's the news?' she asked him. While she spoke she automatically peered through the little window to check the gate guard at the factory. The officer there often wandered over to buy a few things from her mother's shop to break the boredom of his job.

'I'm on the action today, and I've got to take this into town,' he said, and lifted the brown paper slightly so Hortense could just see the dull steel of the sub-machine-gun muzzle.

'What's the problem?' Hortense asked. Attacks on Post Offices had to be carried out during the day, in working hours, and she knew it was important to stick to the timings set down by the Corps Commandant's orders.

'I noticed quite a lot of Germans about earlier, on the main road.'

'Where?'

'Near the Tiensepoort,' Pierre indicated the other end of Pleinstraat. He had decided it was wiser to wait a little while for the Germans to move on.

Hortense agreed there had been more than the usual number of Germans about when she had passed the old walled gate to the town near the bottom of Pleinstraat,

77

but she had seen nothing to suggest that any special effort was being made to check everyone.

'They seemed pretty aimless when I went past just now,' she told him. She was well aware that Pierre had been compulsorily called up for work in Germany by the order of Fritz Sauckel in October 1942, and had refused to go. She doubted the Germans had any idea of exactly who was supposed to go from Louvain as there had been a highly successful attack on the Arbeitsamt, or Labour Control offices, very soon after Sauckel's order. Her cousin Pierre Hermans, codename Georges, and the courier Simone, van Brussel's wife, were among the nine people involved. They had worked through the night and shortly before dawn every record, every filing cabinet had been systematically emptied, carried into the street and dumped in the river Dyle. Over 800 kilogrammes of paper containing lists of names eligible for deportation were turned to pulp. The compulsory programme, which had replaced volunteer labour, was put back months.

Hortense knew it was harder for the men to avoid searches, especially when they were on the run and using a false identity. She had a perfect right to move round the town at that time of the day and decided on the spur of the moment to take the parcel herself.

'I'll take it,' she said abruptly, and picked up the parcel before her cousin had time to think. 'Where's it got to go to?'

Pierre told her where to go and she tucked the heavy brown paper parcel on the back pannier of the bike, climbed on and pedalled down Pleinstraat, bouncing over the rough cobbles. She felt she was really contributing something to the attack.

As she turned at the bottom of Pleinstraat and crossed the wide open space of the Tiensepoort into the old town, she saw her mother under the trees by the old walls on the other side. Stephanie Daman had her hands full of the flowers she was taking to the shop for the cemetery.

Hortense told her very little of what she did for the
Partisans or for François, but she knew Stephanie realised
what was involved. She was grateful for her parents' tacit
support and proud to be working in the Resistance. She
felt very strongly that she was fighting for her family as
much as for Belgium itself.

As she crossed the Boulevard she looked carefully
about for any sign of Germans. She could see no patrols or
long-nosed black Citroën saloon cars which the Gestapo
used. She bicycled along the side of the pavement towards
her mother, thinking she was doing rather well, and quite
as good as Pierre or François, even if they were a bit older
than her.

'I won't be long, Mama,' she called as she passed. She
wondered why her mother was staring at her and why she
did not reply.

'Hortense! Stop!' Stephanie Daman burst out at last,
her lips pursed together, and trying not to let her voice
carry too far.

Hortense braked at once, shocked by the controlled
violence of her mother's outburst.

'What's the matter?' she said in some alarm, balancing
the bike with one foot tiptoe on a cobblestone. Her
mother hurried over, looking about to see if anyone had
noticed. Two people on the other side of the Tiensestraat
were watching out of idle curiosity. She walked swiftly
into the street and stood between them and Hortense on
the bike.

'What on earth do you think you're doing?' Stephanie
asked her sixteen-year-old daughter. Her eyes fixed
accusingly on Hortense a second and then without actually pointing she looked fiercely at the brown paper
parcel on the back of the bike. 'Look!'

Hortense twisted round to see the brown paper had torn
as the bike bumped over the cobbles and the unmistakable
butt of the sub-machine-gun was sticking out for anyone
to see. The sight made her feel sick.

Without speaking, her mother tidied the paper over the weapon as best she could, using some more paper which had been wrapped round her armful of flowers.

'Go back at once,' she commanded. Her voice allowed no argument. She watched her pretty young daughter turn and pedal back towards Pleinstraat, her heart beating with fear and the aftermath of her shock. Ever since François and then Hortense had become involved in this secret war against the Nazis she had dreaded the day of their arrest. If she had not seen Hortense her daughter would almost certainly have been seized. By enormous good fortune she had been there. She found herself sweating and felt faint, like waking from a terrible and realistic dream to find everything was still all right. But for how long?

François was cross, but Gaston for some reason was furious. He blamed the incident on Pierre because he was the older, but he left Hortense in no doubt what she had risked.

'Everyone's in danger when someone is arrested,' he shouted at her. 'Your friends, the Partisans, your family, everyone. They'll beat you and torture you without mercy. This is not like being caught cheating at school,' he finished, with emphasis which cut deep.

The words did not need saying. She knew what damage had been done. She had let her brother down not behaving as he would have done. But she did not believe she had done the wrong thing in taking the weapon in the first place. Even Gaston admitted that for the Gestapo there was probably no difference between the sub-machine-gun and the illegal radio parts for Professor de Vleeschauwer. She still thought a girl had a better chance of getting past German checkpoints than any of the boys, but she was deeply embarrassed at having made such a mess of it.

Hortense was right to think she had a better chance of wheedling her way past German checkpoints with her striking blonde good looks. François was delighted she could fool the Germans but more worried that she would turn the heads of the young men in the Partisans. He did not want them flirting with his sister and trying to impress her. He made it clear to them that amorous hanky-panky was out of the question. If anyone messed her about, they could reckon with him. Romance and personal security did not mix well in his view and he could see nothing but trouble and danger if Hortense became involved with any of them.

But if he could warn off the lads with practical male commonsense, there was not much he could do to control his sister's feelings. She saw much less of Jan Sprengers now, for there was virtually no public social life in Belgium during the Occupation. Most towns, even Brussels, closed their shutters on life after six o'clock in the evening. People visited each other at home, and went to their favourite café. Young people met each other in clubs. In fact many of the Partisans in Louvain were members of the Louvain Athletic Club. The Germans applied Aryan ideology in an attempt to woo the Flemish in support of the Third Reich and encouraged the young men of Louvain to train and take part in competitions. François was an accomplished athlete, Louis van Brussel was an excellent 1500 metres runner, Josef Homblet played football at national level, Jan Sprengers's speciality was the 200 metres hurdles and his good friend Eugene Haesaerts ran the relay. After they went into hiding, one by one, their time at the LAC was over, but till then the Germans had no idea these young men were using the opportunity to keep fit for a purpose quite opposed to the pursuit of the Aryan ideal.

Hortense saw Jan at athletics meetings, but more often they met in the club above the Lyric café by St Peter's church in the centre of town. She did not have the time to go there often but it was popular with a lot of her school friends. They played ping-pong and the talk inevitably revolved around the war. Some of the boys boasted of their anti-German feelings, showing off their bravado to the girls even though the café downstairs had become a popular meeting-place for German soldiers who came to drink beer off-duty. Increasingly Hortense found she had little in common with the friends of her own age. Helping François and her work in the Partisans had given her a different and more sober outlook on life and she saw through the big-talk for what it was. There was another reason why she saw less of Jan Sprengers. By the beginning of 1943 he was also in the Partisans. They were well aware of the dangers of seeing each other and the need for security at all times. But Hortense tried to see him when she could. She was still not quite sure how much he liked her, but she was fond of him and enjoyed his company; even in the war he was amusing and the centre of conversation. When she went to the Old Market for her mother she sometimes went to see him in his tailor's shop. The other, rarer, occasions when they saw each other briefly were when Hortense, as courier, brought orders for a new Partisan attack. For Hortense and Jan, who had seen a lot of each other before the war, it was hard to follow the Partisan rule to be separate. It was harder still when Hortense knew that he was going to be involved in an attack.

Inevitably their relationship came under pressure. A few days before Pentecost, on Thursday, 10 June, Hortense was ordered by Gaston, who had now taken over as Corps Commandant, to deliver the final orders to Jan's battalion for a big attack on a collaborator.

The Partisans, like all the Resistance movements, were always threatened by Belgians who collaborated with the Germans. They were called traitors by the Resistance which could not condone fellow-countrymen giving information to the GFP, the SS or the Gestapo. They must have known this would result in the destruction of lives and families. From the perspective of the Resistance all the worst human characteristics were responsible, and there is no doubt that information was passed, sometimes anonymously, for the basest reasons of jealousy, hate, personal revenge and, of course, money: the 'thirty pieces of silver'.

Nothing has changed. These reasons still account for many of the source reports available to modern police forces fighting insurgency and revolution in every country of the world. These are the streaks of evil in every society, no matter what its politics.

In the war some Belgians supported the German National Socialist view that all resistance was terrorism, and pointed to the disruption of society by attacks on Post Offices, banks, the railways, telegraph lines and members of the public. Others, not necessarily Nazi supporters, insisted that attacks on German soldiers always ended in retaliation. Resistance, they said, always ended with Belgian suffering. There is some truth in this. Keitel's hostage order of 1941 was used to full effect by the Germans who were never reluctant to take harsh reprisals for serious attacks on their own armed forces. A number of prisoners in Breendonk were shot in reprisals for incidents they had nothing to do with months after they had been in the prison. But they generally took little action if Belgians attacked Belgians, even the Belgian SS or Black Police.

Whatever the reasons, there is no doubt that collaborators were a real danger to the Resistance. The founders of the Louvain Partisans, Seymens and Nijsen, had been denounced by collaborators, arrested in September 1942 and sent to Breendonk where they were tortured to give information about the Underground. They withstood the most unpleasant treatment until three months later, on 12 December, the SS tired of them, tied them to posts behind a bank near the moat and shot them. With the black shadow of Breendonk prison ever present, the Partisans were ruthless.

The messages which Hortense carried round on 10 June gave the order to attack a collaborator that night at home, in the Rue Promenade near the Fish Market in Louvain. The word went out to the Partisans in Jan's battalion, to his closest friend Eugene Haesaerts, and to Georges Omloop among others. They attacked during the early hours of Friday and by the afternoon Hortense knew there had been a disaster.

François was called in to an emergency meeting in the Daman kitchen. Faces were grim as they went over what they knew.

The attack had started badly when a home-made grenade thrown at the window of the house had bounced back and exploded in the street. The noise of this and the shooting had been heard by a German patrol which by sheer bad luck had been close by. General von Falkenhausen was constantly criticised by Heinrich Himmler for the bad job his infantry made of police work keeping internal security in Belgium, but he could reply that at least they were trained to fight. This attack was quickly disrupted, taken by surprise in the fierce fire-fight and the Partisans withdrew in disorder, pursued by the German soldiers. One Partisan was killed and one was captured seriously wounded.

'The problem is that we don't know yet who was killed and who was wounded,' Gaston explained.

'Who's involved?'

'Omloop and Haesaerts.'

Hortense relaxed. She had not seen Jan since the attack and was terrified he had been hurt. There was no comfort in what she heard next.

François stared at Gaston a moment. 'Listen, it makes a huge amount of difference which one's alive. Omloop's been away a lot. He fought in the Spanish Civil War. He doesn't know much here. But Haesaerts does. He's the Company Commandant of that group. He knows all the names.'

'Whichever one's alive, he's not talked yet,' Gaston said. 'The Gestapo are all over the place, watching people they know are friends of those two. But they've made no arrests yet.'

Hortense knew that Omloop did not know Jan Sprengers but Haesaerts was one of his closest friends. They often trained together at the athletic club.

'They're obviously waiting to see if anyone panics, and gives themselves away,' her brother said. 'We must find out which one they have.'

'We'll have to find out what we can from the gendarmerie,' Gaston said, after they had been over the story again. He glanced at Hortense who understood she would be asked to visit Marcel Van den Borght and Walter Philips, both policemen in the Belgian gendarmerie. She made regular trips with groceries to the gendarmerie where Marcel used to find some excuse to bring Hortense into the privacy of his office so he could give her his notes about the SS and Gestapo. He was a brave man in an invaluable position.

Everyone at the table knew there was no time to lose. The one who was still alive would be tortured by the Gestapo, who wanted to act immediately to catch the 'terrorists' responsible before they could go to ground. The victim would be given no mercy at all.

In the next two days Hortense was busier than ever. Sick with worry about Jan, she went to the gendarmerie to see Marcel and then bicycled round the town bringing messages back to Gaston. She dared not see Jan. François had banned visits to any of the Partisans involved in the abortive attack and Hortense could see why. The Gestapo were out in force and there was no means of knowing whether they had broken Haesaerts and were already watching Partisans he knew – such as Jan. By Saturday there was more information and François and Gaston had another meeting in the little kitchen behind the shop. Hortense stood in the background again, determined not to miss a word.

'Have we heard from the police?' François wanted to know.

'Yes,' Gaston replied quietly. 'Apparently the Gestapo are keeping the facts very much to themselves. He had to be very discreet and it took time. He went to the mortuary himself.' Gaston paused.

'And?' François asked impatiently.

Hortense could hardly speak with the tension, waiting to hear.

'Omloop was killed during the attack.'

Hortense's heart sank.

'They captured Eugene Haesaerts and took him at once to the Kommandantur where they've had him since.' Gaston could not help pausing again. What he had found out might be the fate of all of them. 'They've been torturing him ever since, using electric shock treatment, straight into the wound in his stomach.'

'Poor bastard,' François hissed, his face tight and empty of expression.

There was a moment of silence in the kitchen, punctuated by the soft ticking of the clock on the dresser. Hortense became aware of it and it seemed to measure the remorseless destruction of Haesaerts's life. Somewhere in her home town, in a harshly lit cellar, men were systematically torturing a wounded man, to death if necessary, to give information so others could be seized.

'Has he broken yet?' François realised that no man could suffer like that and be expected to stay silent for ever. Already it was thirty-six hours.

'Not yet.'

'You realise what will happen if he talks?' François looked up at Gaston who nodded. He glanced at Hortense, wondering whether she should be listening, and what she was thinking.

'All the men closest to him are being watched,' Gaston said. 'It'd be mad to try and get near them. The Gestapo

86

are waiting to see anything unusual and they'll grab anyone they think might be involved.'

Hortense could not stay quiet any longer. Normally she was conscious of her age, and her rank as courier in the Partisans, and listened to her brother and the Corps Commandant. She considered it a privilege to be able to know what was happening. This time she could not remain silent. 'You've got to warn them,' she burst out. 'We have to get them out before the Gestapo pick them up.'

François looked up. He was quite well aware of what Jan Sprengers meant to her and the danger he was in. But there was no place for sentimentality in this brand of war.

'The Gestapo are waiting for us. They might already have broken poor 'Gene Haesaerts. I don't know,' he said heavily, deliberately choosing his words to make his young sister understand the extreme danger they were all in. 'But they'll be hoping to flush out more of us, the ones they expect to go and warn the people they're already watching. That way they cast the net wider, they catch more. The attack last Friday was a disaster for that battalion, but it'll be a catastrophe for the whole corps if we give ourselves away.'

'So what're you going to do?' Hortense asked, beginning to feel angry and horribly frustrated at the same time.

'There's nothing we can do,' said Gaston bluntly.

'Nothing we should do,' François amended accurately.

'You're just going to sit here?' Her voice rose with the energy boiling up inside her.

'Listen, Hortense,' François began, seeing his sister working herself up for a furious argument.

'Just wait till you hear they've been picked up too?' she shouted at him, moving towards the back door which gave on to the small garden at the back.

'You damn well stay here,' François snapped at her and began to get up. Suddenly he could see what she was going to do. She kept her bicycle against the end wall of the house by the garden. But she was too quick for him. She dodged round a chair and was out of the door before he was on his feet. Outside she grabbed her bike and shoved it into Pleinstraat. Nothing mattered to her now. She had decided there was no alternative. Maybe the boys could not warn Jan, but she could. They would never suspect a girl going there. She caught a glimpse of François running out of the shop as she leaped on to the bike and started to pedal furiously down the street.

'Stop! Hortense, for Christ's sake!'

She closed her ears to him. It was the first time she had disobeyed him, but she never hesitated. Just before the bend in Pleinstraat, she looked back. He and Gaston were standing by the shop window staring after her.

She pedalled into the centre as fast as she could. They could come for him at any time. Poor Haesaerts could not last much longer. However she still took some care approaching the shop in Parijsstraat. There were quite a number of people in the streets, being the Saturday before Pentecost, but no tell-tale signs of the Gestapo in their smart suits and hats. She circled round and came back to Parijsstraat, stopped and left her bicycle with several others in a stand near the Sprengers' tall gabled tailor's shop. She turned back to the shop and wondered whether she should ring the bell on the private door which was side by side with the shop entrance. She decided she was safer pretending to be a customer and pushed into the shop.

That was when she realised the danger and why she had seen no Gestapo on the street. Two men dressed in dark grey suits and wearing soft felt hats were talking to Jan Sprengers's mother. Hortense stood for a moment in the background, deferentially as any sixteen-year-old while her elders talked. She saw Jan's mother was frightened. The woman knew nothing of Jan's involvement with the Partisans but she knew the Gestapo when she saw them. They spoke fluent Flemish so they were certainly Belgian SS, hard-looking and their language was rude and arrogant.

'Is Jan home?' she asked sweetly, smiling at Jan's mother who looked relieved to speak to someone else.

'Yes, he is.'

'Oh, good. My father ordered a suit some time ago and Jan said it would be ready today. Mind if I go up to see?' She spoke all in a rush of words, making it up as she went. The two plain-clothes SS were visibly irritated by the intrusion.

'Oh, really? Well, I suppose so,' said Mrs Sprengers, gesturing vaguely upwards where the tailor's cutting-room was on the first floor.

Hortense was round the counter and starting up the back stairs before anyone could say more. She went as softly as she could, three steps at a time, her ear cocked to hear what happened below. Thankfully she heard a deep growl as one of the two men started speaking to Mrs Sprengers again. Jan was not in the cutting-room. Feeling rather desperate, she opened several doors at random until she found him in his own room, on the second floor. 'Hortense!' Jan jumped off his bed in surprise, a look of real pleasure spreading in a wide grin across his face. 'What're you doing here?' He put out his hands in a happy welcoming gesture and caught her arms. Gradually his smile faded as he saw the expression in her blue eyes. The time for happiness was completely over. Events, the war, the Occupation, the disaster before dawn not two days ago had overtaken them. He knew at once what it was. Hortense spoke first, feeling her throat dry, 'Quick. There's no time! You've got to go, now!' In a few seconds she told him what she had heard François and Gaston talking about. His face crumpled as he heard what the Gestapo were doing to his friend Eugene Haesaerts.

Hortense allowed him no time for self-reproach or questions and shoved his coat at him.

'We've got to go at once,' she urged him, trying to get him to concentrate on the danger. 'Listen, Jan. They'll search the house soon enough. Have you got anything here to do with the Partisans?'

He shrugged and shook his head slowly. He found action impossible when all he could think of was the collapse of his life, his future thrown into total uncertainty as a fugitive, maybe for years, if he escaped now, and maybe never to see Hortense again. He watched her checking through a chest of drawers and then opening his clothes cupboard.

Hortense saw her photograph pinned inside the cupboard door. Her heart jumped at the sight. In a rush of tenderness she forgot her businesslike search to savour the implications of the find. She had had no idea he had ever bothered enough about her to have her picture in his room. Certainly he had never asked her for it, but just as certainly he had got hold of it somehow because he wanted it there.

She took it off the cupboard door and slowly she turned and looked at him. A small smile appeared for a moment on his face, and he shrugged, a little embarrassed, like any young man whose love is discovered.

This precious moment was born to a short life. Hortense heard a commotion downstairs, and in panic she realised the other implication of her photograph. If it had been found during a search by the SS, she would have been associated with Jan and the Partisans. Suddenly she saw the truth of François's warnings.

'Come on,' she whispered urgently, shoving Jan out of the room and down the front stairs. 'There are two SS in the shop downstairs.'

'What?' Jan Sprengers gasped at her as she bullied him down the steep stairs, urging him to be as quiet as possible.

'Yes, yes. I only hope your mother can keep them talking. We'll use the front door.'

# The Point of No Return

In the shop Mrs Sprengers knew from the vague distant noises she could hear upstairs that something was wrong, and it reflected in her face. The two men were well experienced in the fear they caused and quickly noticed her look. Abruptly they told her who they really were and demanded to know who else was in the house.

Hortense and Jan heard the raised voices as they reached the narrow hall on the ground floor and ran for the front door. Jan seemed to take for ever to open it.

'Hurry, for God's sake,' she shouted at him.

Suddenly the door to the room behind the shop burst open as the Gestapo forced their way past Mrs Sprengers and their shouts became louder. A dark shadow of one of the suited SS fell along the passage reaching out towards the two young people who could hear Jan's mother ineffectually demanding to know what was going on.

Hortense and Jan fell through the front door into the street and turned to the bike stand.

'Take my bike,' Hortense ordered him, without any hesitation. He stopped and looked at her, pleadingly.

'Take it and go!' she screamed at him, and began looking for another from the stand. Jan Sprengers pedalled off as fast as he could and it was the last she saw of him. For a fraction of a moment she saw him go, then seized another bike without any qualms at the theft, shoved it past the derelict site beside the shop and down Drinkwaterstraat, pushing at the pedals for all she was worth. She was thankful Drinkwater was so short. She turned the corner just as the shouting filled the street behind her, bouncing off the tall houses as the two Gestapo agents ran out of the shop to give chase.

Eugene Haesaerts finally broke a day later. The Gestapo made a number of arrests, but Jan Sprengers had got away. His mother's shop was raided the following day at dawn but Jan was by then hiding in a house in Heverlee on the outskirts of Louvain. Whatever his private thoughts, François knew the case could not be left as it was and made arrangements to see that Jan could not be reached by the SS. After a week Jan moved to another safe house in Harboortstraat and then spent the rest of the war in a small village called Dion-le-Val, working as a farmhand.

His close friend Haesaerts was not so lucky. The Germans finally gave him medical attention, classified him a terrorist and sent him to Breendonk. His wound mended gradually and he suffered the appalling regime there for eight miserable months. Then he and twenty others were marched out on 10 February 1944 and shot in reprisal for another attack by the Partisans, executed against the same posts where Seymens, Nijsen and many others had died. The February attack which caused that reprisal also had far-reaching consequences for the Daman family.

All that was in the future. For now, her bid to save Jan had been incredibly foolhardy, or brave. François was cross but again Gaston was furious. They acknowledged her success and could not fault her determination and it seemed the Gestapo had not been able to identify her as she escaped with Jan. Her parents soon heard the whole story and were badly worried. None of them had any doubt Hortense had become a talented and resourceful operator, but at what risk? At what cost to the others? For all her experience in this dangerous game, she was still a young girl in her mid-teens. So far, she had got away with it.

# 5

# The Rabbit Tasted Fine

*'Ik bid voor u, ik strid voor u, ik leg eieren voor u.'* 'I pray for you, I fight for you, I lay eggs for you.' Neerlandes saying from Emile Lousse, *La société d'ancien régime*, Louvain, 1943.

On 1 July 1943 in Middleton St George near Newcastle in England, the pilots of 419 Squadron had the afternoon off to play softball. Sergeant Doug Arseneau played for the wireless operators against Bob Bell, the captain of his Halifax bomber, and the other pilots, while his good friend Bob 'Willy' Williston played with the bomb aimers against the navigators, including their own 'Nav' Sergeant Simpson. White clouds raced across the blue sky and the wind was cool but the Canadians were by now used to British weather and anything was a pleasant change from the incessant bombing missions over enemy territory. Dressed in shorts and a variety of coloured sports shirts, the crews exhausted themselves in good-natured rivalry and felt a hundred per cent refreshed to get away from the war.

The Canadian bomber squadron had been working hard in the last months fully committed to the Battle of the Ruhr. Doug Arseneau and the crew of Halifax JD 159 had bombed all the important German cities, taking the war into the heartland of Hitler's Third Reich to break the German spirit and destroy their war industry. Doug and Willy Williston had done what the crews called 'ops' over Hamburg, Essen, Duisburg, Dortmund, Bochum, Krefeld, Stuttgart, Nuremberg, Frankfurt, Dusseldorf, Cologne and the capital Berlin. The majority of ops were over the industrial Ruhr valley, which they called 'Happy Valley' in spite of the intense anti-aircraft flak and searchlights which arced up through the night to slash great holes in the vulnerable bellies of the slow bombers.

It was a strange and frightening war in the bombers. They sat for hours on end in inky darkness in a confined space, pasting the unseen enemy thousands of feet below with high explosive. The lucky ones who survived the flak and enemy fighters returned home over the friendly English countryside to touch down in the half light of dawn, frozen and stiff when they dropped out of the aircraft on to the tarmac, but glad to be back and breathing the cold morning mist off the North Yorkshire moors. As aircrew, they were allowed an egg for breakfast after ops and a few hours off duty when they could forget everything in the bar or pub. These were luxuries denied to the Resistance in Occupied Europe but the pressures mounted with each operation.

The bald statistics were that the losses of early 1942, 1 per cent of planes per op, had risen by July 1943 to an average 4.7 per cent. To the likes of Williston and Arseneau that meant their squadron lost an average of one plane on each sortie.

Doug Arseneau's crew had twenty-eight sorties to their credit since his first bombing raid on Kiel on 13 October 1942. One op had been a mind-numbing nine and a half hours to Pilsen in Czechoslovakia. But they had been well trained at Croft near Darlington, on the four-engined Halifax and, though they were all young men not many years older than Hortense Daman, they considered themselves professionals. The crew became very close to each other, each man depending on the others for his survival. After every six weeks of operations they would be given one week's leave which they enjoyed to the maximum until the money ran out. Then they would go back to Middleton. On 2 July, after the extra day off from war and the softball matches they knew there would be ops the next day.

In Belgium during those two days nothing had changed. The GFP had hardly slowed the pace of the extra patrolling they carried out after the Partisan débâcle on 11 June, and the Partisans had then dynamited the Louvain-Liège railway line at Korbeek-Lo on 14 June. The strategy chosen by the National Commando was to show the Germans that nothing would stop their march to freedom and defeat of the Nazis. The cost in Partisans' lives and in the deaths of those like Haesaerts who were shot in German reprisals cannot easily be counted but was enormous.

Modern 'freedom fighters' or 'terrorists', depending on the perspective, try to show the same power of action against their enemy. Security force successes worry the IRA tremendously, since they are so often due to 'source reports' or 'betrayals' (again terms depend on perspectives), but they always try to strike back quickly to show they are still in the game.

This effort to keep up the pressure on the Nazis and their collaborators took its toll on the Partisans. Some found they could not live the clandestine life and had to go into hiding till the end of the war. Hortense spent a good deal of her time slipping money and ration cards through letter-boxes to their families, who still had to be taken care of. Their wretched wives usually had no idea what had happened to their husbands and the children grew up without fathers.

Every arrest set the Partisans back and it was a constant battle to tighten their security and prevent the GFP penetrating their plans with sources and denunciations. Gaston worked out of the Damans' house though he continued to sleep across Pleinstraat with the Storckels, and he kept Hortense busy. In the mornings she bicycled out with orders, and in the afternoons she went out again to receive reports. All this was in addition to her early morning marketing, working for her mother and her errands for François, who was more than ever involved with escaping and evading aircrews. With more planes being shot down there was more work rescuing crews from the Germans, and hiding them until the right moment came to put them on the long escape route to the south and the Spanish border.

Busier than ever, Hortense had no social life at all. She had still not got used to the idea that she would not see Jan Sprengers for a long time, though she comforted herself that at least she had managed to help him escape. She got considerable satisfaction from the thought that she had managed where the men had failed. It had surprised her that Gaston had been more angry than François. Maybe her brother understood her feelings better and Gaston was conscious of not being so familiar with Louvain, but he had left her in no doubt that personal feelings had no place in clandestine warfare. He had not shouted at her but his words smarted and hurt.

'What you did confirmed the Gestapo's suspicions about Jan and you risked them arresting his parents,' he said, his face expressionless but looking at his eyes she knew how angry he was. 'Worse, if you'd been caught, they'd have turned on your own parents. You heard what happened to Jan's friend Haesaerts. For God's sake, Hortense, to them we're just animals to be hunted down, just terrorists to be eliminated. They don't care how brutal they have to be. We're all damned lucky they didn't recognise you.'

At midday on 3 July, thirteen crews of 419 Squadron attended a briefing for operations that night. For Williston, Arseneau and the others in Halifax JD 159 the break was over. They were back at war. No one wanted to mention the unlucky number of planes on the operation. The big four-engined Halifaxes took off that night to bomb Cologne, passing over Belgium as they had so many times before. The squadron log states 'Twelve successfully bombed the target and returned. One aircraft is missing', a bald understatement of the dramatic events of that night during which 24,000 lb of high explosives and a massive 47,520 lb of incendiaries shattered the uneasy calm of the blacked-out city 3000 feet below, while the bombers lumbered through the wild pattern of swinging searchlights, and the ack-ack fire curved up the pillars of light towards them.

The log continues with information on the missing plane, JD 159, 'up at 22.30 hrs', leaves a blank for its return time, 'down at hrs', and then: 'This aircraft took off to attack Cologne. Nothing further was heard from the aircraft after take-off and its failure to return is presumed to be due to enemy action.'

They never made Cologne. About two hours after take-off they had slipped some twenty or thirty miles off course and were flying over Belgium. The Halifax was suddenly raked with 0.30 calibre shells and the rear turret put out of action immediately.

'Get ready to bail out,' Bob Bell called over the intercom.

Doug Arseneau drew back the curtain over his window to see the enemy fighter attacking and recalls how frightening it was to feel the enemy shells slamming into his plane. Two Luftwaffe FW 190s were attacking the lone bomber. For a brief moment Doug wished his Flight Commander had been in the plane with them. He had decided that the mid-upper machine-gun turret impeded airflow and speed and had removed them from his Halifaxes. With the rear turret out and no mid-turret, JD 159 was helpless. Against two enemy fighters perhaps there was never any chance. And they were still loaded with bombs.

'Bail out,' Bell shouted a few seconds later. 'And make it fast!'

Doug Arseneau moved into the body of the stricken Halifax and grabbed his parachute. Very carefully he put it on and tried to remember the exact drill he should follow to exit the plane and pull the rip-cord. He was staring at the all-too-small 5 by 3 foot hole in the bottom of the plane. A blast of heat made him look up and he saw a raging fire down the end of the fuselage. He jumped.

In the sudden rush of cold air, his mind refused to react and for several seconds, each one an eternity, he tumbled in free-fall unable to find the rip-cord handle. Then with a bone-shaking jerk the parachute burst open above him. As he floated down he felt his feet becoming frozen. He reached down as he swung in the harness and lifting a foot up he felt his stockings. His flying boots, which he had never bothered to lace up fully in the plane, had been ripped off when the parachute opened. With them he lost his escape and evasion kit and the money which MI9 taught them always to keep hidden in their boots.

The Halifax had been flying high and it was some time before he hit the ground. He landed safely and made his way over to a wood to hide, furious about his boots. Then, amazingly, considering his change of fortunes and his situation in occupied territory, he wrapped himself in the warm folds of his silk parachute and went to sleep.

By mid-morning on 3 July François Daman knew that a Halifax had been shot down north of Louvain and that several of the crew had bailed out. A farmer near Boortmeerbeek, by Mechelen, had heard the noise of the bomber during the night and the sound of the attacking German fighters. In the morning he was making the rounds of his fields and noticed Doug's trail of soft footprints into the wood. He found him but, speaking nothing but Flemish, and Doug being Canadian who spoke no French, they could not communicate. Doug was fortunate. Many of the Belgian farmers were sympathetic to the Resistance, the same men from whom Hortense collected extra corn at harvest time, and this man's report reached François and the Partisans the same morning. Time was short. Everyone knew the Germans wanted to capture the airmen first. Later that morning Louis van Brussel ordered a young Partisan and an eighteen-year-old girl, a courier like Hortense, to fetch the downed airman. They bicycled out to the wood and found Doug Arseneau still hiding in scrub.

The bicycle was an essential part of the Resistance. Everything was done on bicycles, delivering messages, carrying illegal documents and radio parts, collecting downed airmen and escaping from the German patrols after an action. With petrol rationing, it was a common sight to see two sharing a bike, one sitting on the back pannier or even on the handlebars. Of course, like everything else, bicycles had to have licences and a number plate, and this simple regulation caught out several SOE agents, after they had come all the way from England with months of specialist training as saboteurs.

The two rescuers had brought civilian clothes for the flyer, and the farmer had warned them to bring a pair of shoes. They buried his parachute and uniform and set out towards Louvain. The girl sat on the handlebars of one bike, her friend pedalling, and Doug struggled on behind, very out of practice on a bicycle and never getting closer to them than about a hundred yards. The ride took nearly three hours and was tiring, but Arseneau's mind was on other things. It was a Sunday afternoon and everyone was out enjoying a stroll, including German soldiers who all seemed to turn and look at him as if they knew who he was. He expected to be stopped and arrested any moment, but the long ride ended without incident in Parkstraat, just inside the walls of Louvain and not far from the Philips factory.

Meanwhile Williston was picked up and taken to Madame Bos's house in Regastraat, two streets from

Parkstraat and closer to the Damans' house. Here François questioned Williston. He was fairly certain that the Canadian was telling the truth but he had no dog-tags, the identity discs worn by all servicemen. He noticed that Williston's chest was badly bruised, which appeared to fit his story of parachuting from the Halifax, but it never paid to be too credulous. François reported his identity and story to London and waited to hear that all was well. François Daman had never had any arrests while he was running his part in the collection of airman and feeding them on to various escape lines. This was a record he kept up throughout the war and it pays a remarkable tribute to the care and attention to detail which he devoted to every aspect of his dangerous job.

In this case however François was not on his own in organising the Canadians' future escape. Louis van Brussel, the first Corps Commandant of the Louvain Partisans, had been involved in the pick up. Senior to François, he generally took his advice on escape and evasion work, since he knew François had been feeding men on to the lines since the early days in 1940. Williston complained that he was not at ease in Madame Bos's house so François and Louis decided to move both airmen to another safe house. The move would have to be made in darkness for added security, which at that time of year meant after curfew. François briefed Arseneau and explained that he should do exactly what he was told. He would be picked up by a young girl with blonde hair and there would be another group behind him. All the men with him would be armed, and if they were challenged by a German patrol they would fight their way out.

That evening it poured with rain, which was uncomfortable but increased their chances of not being stopped. Soldiers and policemen do not function so well when wet. After dark Hortense left her parents' house in Pleinstraat with her brother and cousin Pierre van Goitsenhoeven. They slipped across the Boulevard using the shadows of the trees, and keeping close to the walls of houses made their way first to Parkstraat. François knocked softly on a door, was let in silently and after a moment reappeared with a very tall man, Doug Arseneau.

'Stay with this girl,' he ordered Arseneau brusquely, in a thick English accent. 'Do what she says.'

With Pierre and François in the lead, several metres ahead, Hortense hurried along with Arseneau hunched up against the rain. They reached Madame Bos's small house in Regastraat, picked up Williston who was ordered to stick to Pierre, and soon the two groups were walking swiftly down the blacked-out streets. Darkness favoured the Resistance on nights like that but the enemy could hide too, and François, Hortense and Pierre grew weary staring into the darkest corners to see if they were being watched or were running into an ambush set by the Belgian SS, Black Police or an infantry patrol.

Williston never knew his fellow crew member was behind him as they walked the deserted streets. Nor did either of them know how close they had to go to several places which were best avoided by day, let alone after curfew. After Dekenstraat they turned out of Maria Theresiastraat, down Bogaardenstraat rather than pass the Little Prison of Louvain further down. In Bogaardenstraat they ran quickly past the junction with Leopold I straat where the Gestapo had a private building which they used for their more unpleasant interviews. They followed Stationstraat for a couple of hundred yards and with the dark bulk of St Peter's church looming over the end of the road they turned down Vaartstraat between the SS headquarters, visible a hundred yards away on the corner of Vital Decosterstraat on one side and the Kommandantur on the other.

All went well until they skirted the end of the Kommandantur. Not much more than fifty yards distant under yellow lights, Hortense could see the sentries outside the huge neo-classical building. Above them hung the Nazi flag, its frightening red, white and black pattern muted in the darkness.

As Hortense and Doug passed this point she saw the sentries look over towards them, peering into the black night. They were suspicious and had obviously heard something through the dull beat of the rain. Swiftly she grabbed the astonished Canadian and pulled him into the shadows of a doorway and held him close as if they were lovers. She sensed his embarrassment but there was no time for explanations. Holding him tightly she manoeuvred him around with his back to the Kommandantur so she could see past him to the sentries. Ahead, she knew François would be hidden in another doorway, his hand closed over his pistol in case the sentries came across. After a moment the sentries relaxed again. Night duty guarding key, or important places, is always boring for a soldier. The ears and eyes play tricks after an hour or two and something more than complacency settles in. Whatever the German sentries thought they had heard, they preferred to stay chatting at their post rather than get drenched running around the streets of Louvain chasing shadows.

Hortense saw them turn away and without hesitation or instructions from her brother she pulled Arseneau out of the doorway and they continued on more briskly over the cobbles down the full length of Vaartstraat. François slipped along behind the two groups. He had learned to have complete confidence in his little sister. He had known she would be a good partner for one of the airmen, not just because as a girl she could pretend they were lovers, but because she had a knack of finding a way out of difficulties. On reflection this was odd, as he never remembered Hortense having the reputation of a slippery character at school. On the contrary she had always had a name for holding the strongest views and sticking to them. Resistance, he thought, was evidently her mission, and the tricks she had learnt instinctively were her weapons.

Louis van Brussel and François had made arrangements to hide the two men with Joan and Philemon de Witt. This excellent young couple lived in a tiny terraced house on the opposite side of Louvain to the Damans. Hortense knew them and had taken five people to the house two years before, in 1941. The five, a family with three small children, were Jews and were hidden by the de Witts until they could be moved away. They were among the lucky ones. Eventually they made good their escape from Hitler's 'Final Solution of the Jewish Question' and reached Israel after the war. In gratitude they dedicated a tree to Philemon and Joan and it stands in a long avenue of trees, all dedicated to those who risked their lives to help the Jews persecuted in the Third Reich.

Joan's mother lived next door and ran a small alehouse. Much to the old lady's disgust, German soldiers guarding installations along the canal came to her for beer and she dared not refuse them. For Joan and Philemon the Germans posed a greater nuisance. From the start they had distributed illegal newspapers, but once they began to hide men in their house the chances of being caught increased enormously.

Pierre reached the de Witts' house first, left Williston with Joan and slipped away by another route. Hortense and François kept Arseneau back for a while until they were certain there was no one in the narrow street. Then, at a pre-arranged signal from the house, they moved in and the second airman was taken in. It had taken a long time to come right across the town from Pleinstraat, and it was well past midnight. Hortense and François did not delay and made their way home along streets shiny with the rain.

Inside the house Doug Arseneau met Bob Williston. They were delighted to see each other, but Willy had depressing news. He had been told by the Partisans that Bob Bell, their pilot, had been killed. So had Anderson, the co-pilot on his first mission, and Bill Taylor, the flight engineer. The other three, Simpson the navigator, 'Digger' Graham, mid-upper gunner, and George Aitken, rear gunner, had been captured immediately. Arseneau and Williston had been the only ones to get away from the stricken Halifax.

They did not know that they were the subject of careful examination. François was always careful who he took on to the escape lines. Williston could not produce his identity discs and Arseneau could not remember whether the crew had been seven or eight men. Both François and Louis van Brussel decided that the two men would have to wait until their bona fides had been established before moving them on to the lines south to Spain.

The Gestapo had had too much success in 1943 penetrating the early escape lines for François or Louis to risk moving potential stooges on to the routes and allow the Germans to make further arrests. Andrée de Jongh, the prime mover of the Comet line, had been arrested in January; more than a hundred of her helpers had been picked up in Brussels in February; and another of the line's key men, Baron Jean Greindl, code name 'Nemo', whom Hortense had met in one of her contacts for François shortly after the family's return to Louvain, was seized a week later. The Pat O'Leary line suffered as well. Ian Garrow had returned to England but the radio operator was arrested in January and two traitors, Harold Cole, an Englishman, and Roger le Neveu, who was French, betrayed large numbers to the SS. Le Neveu met Guerrisse in a café in March and handed him over to the SD who were waiting for him. Badly battered, both escape lines miraculously regrouped and continued work, but more slowly and more carefully.

The Canadians found hiding up in the tiny house very

frustrating. Both Arseneau and Williston were very tall men, and on one occasion when Joan de Witt suddenly called, 'Germans! Quick, hide!' Williston, who was six foot four, knocked himself out on a door lintel as he and Arseneau made another dash for the attic where they lived. Fortunately the Germans did not come to the house.

Joan de Witt was cautious. She realised that bravado and mistakes cost all. One day Louis van Brussel had thrown some Partisan documents into her stove without telling her. She discovered them later, only slightly burned and realised what would have happened to her and Philemon had the Germans raided the house. She burned the whole lot but kept one sheet to show van Brussel. 'Never do that again,' she told him severely. 'Or it'll be the last thing I'll do for you.' She was petite, but her anger was frightening and van Brussel apologised profusely, deeply embarrassed.

The Damans' responsibility for the two Canadian airmen did not end with their delivery to the de Witts. François was reporting on them back to London, via the Légion Belge and its radio operator. Hortense brought food for the extra mouths and some money to the de Witts, while their mother, the Louvain Partisan supplies officer, had to fix them up with suitable civilian clothes. Both men were so tall that none of the standard suits fitted them. Belgians, it seemed, were shorter than Canadians. What they had available was only just adequate to bring them out of the fields into the safe house. They would need something more convincing to move down the escape lines through Belgium, France and into Spain.

The Germans had tightened up the security enormously since the first months after their victory in the West. Hundreds of soldiers, and increasingly airmen, had been moved in almost open style down various lines, like the twenty soldiers Hortense had supplied food for in the convent in Louvain. By 1943 the SD, Gestapo, Geheime Feldpolizei and the Abwehr were all very much better organised to catch those helping escapers. They had found the most efficient way of doing this, by informers, and by infiltrating men and women into the lines masquerading as links in the chain to freedom. These treacherous connections, taking advantage of the trust so necessary between helpers, would occasionally deliver the unsuspecting airmen into the hands of the Germans. Often the loss of 'packages', as escaping airmen were known, was hard to explain and traitors were slowly identified. Not every airman was betrayed, or that would have raised the suspicions of genuine Resistance workers.

Hortense's mother volunteered to find suits for the two men. She obtained some material cheaply on the black market. Stephanie was pleased with the buy but Hortense thought the good price related more to the garish pattern than to a discount for quantity. However the Partisans had little choice, for money was scarce, and the two airmen had none. The tailor, Marcel Goemans, ran a shop called 'de Witte Duif' (the White Pigeon), and he was not impressed either. When Goemans saw the colours of the cloth he was surprised. When Stephanie told him the size and measurements for the suits his surprise turned to fright. He knew very well that few Belgian were so tall. However Stephanie put some pressure on him: Marcel was her eldest daughter Bertha's husband's cousin and though the family connection was tenuous it counted. He made the suits, saying, 'For God's sake don't tell me who they're for.'

Hortense bicycled round several times a week with groceries in the front pannier and the two young men looked forward to her visits. Her code name on this occasion was 'Henri', which with the Canadians' bad French pronunciation became "Ory'. Arseneau and Williston always waited for her visits and became despondent on days she was unable to find the time. It was hard being cooped up in the tiny rooms, being careful not to make too much noise and having to climb through the attic into the house next door to use the lavatory.

Hortense enjoyed her visits as well, for she had little social life. Jan Sprenger's departure into hiding had brought home to her the foolishness of becoming involved with one of the Partisans. Furthermore François's warning to all the young men that there was to be no messing about with his little sister had been taken seriously. The war had turned François into a hard man, ruthless and aged beyond his thirty years. So, once or twice Hortense would stay on with the de Witts and their temporary and dangerous house guests. They made agreeable company. Joan de Witt had, and still has, an excellent voice and there were sing-songs after supper. Doug Arseneau and his friend Whitney, the navigator who did not come with them on that fateful trip to Cologne, used to sing in the Golden Fleece in Darlington, where their renderings of risqué ballads went down well with the local Yorkshire girls. Although Joan de Witt spoke no English at the time, they sang songs to each other and the Canadians introduced them to one especial favourite, the lilting Hawaiian love song which Joan still sings beautifully to this day:

> To you sweetheart, Alloa, Alloa,
> From the bottom of my heart.
> Keep a smile on your lips,
> Brush the tears from your eyes,
> Once more, Alloa, I say goodbye.

Willy wrote out the words and gave them to Hortense who hid them with some photographs in Josephine de Roost's house in the secret compartment under the floor.

Hortense did not get a chance to say goodbye to Willy and Doug. Louis van Brussel arranged for them to be removed one Sunday after four weeks at the de Witts', without reference to François. Hortense never knew what happened to them. François only found out after much careful questioning, aware that somewhere there lay a minefield of treachery.

On leaving the little house Doug Arseneau had walked with Philemon, and Willy with Joan some way behind. They were taken to the house where Monsieur Ely's mother lived. Ely was Chief of the Department of Works at the Hôtel de Ville in Louvain and a friend of the de Witts. He hated the Germans and his office gave him an excellent chance to know what was going on and to help the Resistance. They stayed there another four weeks and were visited several times by a woman from Brussels who spoke excellent English. The woman, a Belgian, was an agent of the Gestapo. She did not do it for the money but because it made her feel important. Neither the two airmen nor Madame Ely suspected anything, but they were on the brink of the trap, the victims of an elaborate game played by the Germans to infiltrate the escape lines and at the same time capture airmen loaded on to them. The cards were always in the favour of the German authorities.

An elderly white-haired woman led them into Brussels on a tram in daylight. The two Canadians were told to keep several paces behind her and make no contact with her. Nervously they sat wedged between civilians and groups of German soldiers. One of them tried to begin a conversation with Doug Arseneau who turned away with a half-smile, scared to death he would be found out. The soldier shrugged and said no more, presumably used to the indifference of conquered races.

Once they were in Brussels the old woman continued the journey and left them in a vacant building with another member of the network. They stayed one night there before being handed over to a man who was known as the 'Captain'. He took them to a large house which had belonged to the Swiss Embassy before the war, where they found ten other airmen, an older Belgian civilian and a priest. All these men thought they were waiting to be taken along the escape line into Spain. One day Willy Williston and Doug Arseneau were taken by a short fat jolly man called 'Marcel' into the centre of Brussels. He got them to sit in a photo booth for the passport-size photographs they would need for new identity papers to travel south. Then he treated them to ice-creams, which neither really enjoyed for they were in the middle of a large group of German soldiers. The Canadians were tired of hanging about in one dingy house after another, always having to be quiet and not being allowed outside. They were delighted when this same 'Marcel' came to pick them up a few days later with the news that they were off to the south with an American airman, John Anderson, and the elderly Belgian. The Canadians were thrilled to be on the way as they drove towards the French border.

The feeling of euphoria did not last. After half an hour they were flagged down by a German soldier. When the fat jolly Marcel stopped, the car was suddenly surrounded by Germans pointing rifles and machine-pistols at them. The trap was sprung. They were all dragged out of the car except Marcel, who passed some papers over to the officer in charge and drove on. The two Canadian airmen were gaoled in St Gilles, Brussels' main prison on a hill in the southern quarter of the city, and after more weeks of waiting were finally sent by train to a prisoner of war camp in Germany, where they remained until liberated by the Russians in April 1945.

At no time were these airmen subjected to a particularly severe interrogation. An officer in the Abwehr questioned them both in St Gilles. Every evening for a week he came to the cell and said, 'If you don't tell me where you got the civilian clothes you will be shot.'

The threat was idle. Anyway, since the arrests had been prearranged with the jolly fat man, Marcel, and probably several other collaborators, the officer probably thought he knew all the answers. The German had succeeded in infiltrating the escape line with these collaborators to create what was called a 'loop'. Using Belgians posing as members of the Resistance, the Germans had introduced themselves as a link in the line itself. So genuine members of the lines like the Damans, Louis van Brussel and the de Witts unwittingly fed men into the treacherous 'loop' where the enemy were able to pick and choose which men should be arrested. The aim of the 'loop' was twofold: to foil efforts to bring Allied servicemen back into the war, and to extend intelligence on the Resistance. Some men, but sadly not the two Canadians, were allowed to go down the line to freedom, to justify the link and maintain the 'loop'.

The interrogation of the airmen was not pursued for two reasons. They were held in the prison of St Gilles, which was run by the Wehrmacht as part of General von Falkenhausen's military command, rather than by the Gestapo; and secondly they claimed status as prisoners of war under the Geneva Convention.

Civilians like Hortense, François and all the others in the Resistence could fall back on no such protection. The Germans were ruthless in their interrogations. The very least that could be expected was a prison sentence in Belgium – in St Gilles perhaps. The norm was incarceration in Breendonk for the men, and then deportation into the concentration camp system in the Reich.

However the Germans made a distinction between the different Resistance groups. Ideologically they accepted that the establishment would set up resistance in the form of escape lines and that army officers would form an association like the Belgian Legion. They also expected opposition from the Communists, but as good National

Socialists they hated it all the more. Even if activists like Hortense and most of the others at grass roots level had no interest in nor knew of the Partisans' connection with Moscow, the SS knew. So the BAP, the sworn enemy, was dubbed a terrorist group to which no mercy would be shown. This does not mean the Germans were soft on the men and women they caught helping evaders. Too many who sheltered wanted men were arrested and killed, like Viktor Robrechts, the owner of a garage in Louvain. Five airmen on one occasion and a single man on another had stayed for a short time in his house. One was caught further down the line, in France, and talked. Both Viktor and his wife Elise Vanderveeren were arrested. He was beheaded in a concentration camp at Siegburg in Germany.

It may be thought that the concentration camps were an anarchic environment produced by hysterical minds let loose without restriction. This is quite apart from the truth. As early as September 1941 General Keitel, Hitler's Chief of General Staff in Berlin, had promulgated an order that the SS should seize anyone they considered dangerous and that these prisoners should be made to vanish into a system called 'Nacht und Nebel', or Night and Fog. No questions were to be answered about the whereabouts of prisoners, and no confirmation or denial was to be issued about their fate. Associates and relatives of 'dangerous persons' were also to be arrested. The whole design of this extraordinarily anti-democratic order was to terrify people with uncertainty. From it developed the concentration camps, a system of misery which was nothing less than deliberate.

François lost many friends into Nacht und Nebel. When he found out that Arseneau and Williston had been moved along a route he would not have chosen, and learned that they had been arrested, though not who had betrayed them, he kept his findings to himself. Hortense did not need to know. Under interrogation her knowledge could compromise genuine members of the lines.

François was determined not to allow men in his area to be moved without his agreement in the future. There was always a great mixing of the various Resistance groups throughout the war, so that the finer distinctions of command and liaison were grey, to say the least, but he had been working on the escape lines since the early days and had more experience than most. So when the fate of two more Canadians had to be decided François insisted on complete control while they were in Louvain.

Art Bowlby and Elmer Dungey of Squadron 408 were shot down in their Halifax over Belgium the same night as Arseneau and Williston. They were more fortunate. Bowlby came down in Werchter and Dungey not far away. Both were brought to Louvain, Dungey dressed as a priest in a black cassock and dog-collar. They were handed over to François a day later and questioned in the house of Madame de Gyssels, again in Parkstraat. He sat at the kitchen table and called the airmen in one by one. Their faces lit by a dim electric bulb above the table, the two men stared at each other, François, a civilian representing his country's secret resistance to the Nazi occupation, the other, still in his flying jacket, representing the combined Allied war effort. One had learned his trade by trial and error, throwing off his formal military background to pick up the grey life and style of a clandestine. The other had enlisted thousands of miles away in Canada and been specifically trained to fly and to bomb Germany.

As before, François questions were vital to establish that these men were not German *agents provocateurs,* posing as evaders to infiltrate the lines. He frequently had one or two others in the room listening, and more particularly watching the faces of the men he questioned. On this occasion Hortense stood in the shadows outside the circle of light. She stared at the faces of the young airmen trying to assess their honesty, without realising she was instinctively measuring their commitment against her own.

'What did you think?' François asked her, after the second interview.

'They seemed all right to me, Brae,' she replied, thinking she had seen nothing in their faces but tiredness and a real concern to convince her brother they were genuine. 'But the one called Bowlby's very young.'

'Only eighteen,' François agreed. 'He'll have his nine-teenth birthday in a few days' time. He's not much older than you.' He reflected that at least this boy had been trained to do his job. It irked him that the Resistance had to learn on the street, by their own mistakes.

The German guards in the Philips factory at the end of Pleinstraat did not know that several groups of enemy airmen were being moved about and housed for weeks in the narrow terraced streets so near them. It gave Hortense a sense of considerable pride that she was helping the airmen right under the noses of the German soldiers. It was somehow the next best thing to actually fighting them.

Every day Hortense bicycled over the Boulevard and through the walls to Madame de Gyssels with extra food in her pannier for the two men, and the days turned into weeks while François waited for a reply to the message he had transmitted to London. She looked forward to seeing them, as she had with Doug and Willy. Her visits brightened up their hours of boredom in the cramped house and they enjoyed seeing the pretty blonde sixteen-year-old. They used to talk about how amazingly cheerful she always was despite the tremendous risks of helping them and of living under the German occupation. They knew something about the way the escape lines operated and how to behave as evaders, having attended training lectures given by MI9 officers, the branch of Military Intelligence responsible for assisting escape and evasion in the war. Men like Captain Airey Neave, who escaped from Colditz and had come down the Pat O'Leary line in 1942, were their instructors, and Bowlby and Dungey knew what to expect. The two Canadians were impressed by the way the Belgians managed their clandestine and dangerous life without any training at all.

Like Arseneau and Williston, they called Hortense "Ory'. Equally they never forgot the girl who brought them food and whiled away a few hours in a period filled with fear and an overwhelming sense of oppression and helplessness. The frustration got too much for them. Madame de Gyssels came round to the Damans' corner shop in a hurry one day in August.

'The two men are talking about leaving on their own,' she told Stephanie Daman when they had a quiet moment together in the shop.

Hortense glanced up from the tray of food she was preparing to take to the workers in the Philips factory.

Stephanie Daman looked serious and replied in a steady voice, 'Go back quickly and tell them anything you like, but stop them going.'

Madame de Gyssels nodded. She trusted the Daman family implicitly.

'I'll get word to François,' Stephanie said.

François, who usually came without ever saying he would, or when he would, was told immediately. He went out, crossed the Boulevard into Parkstraat, through Parkpoort to Madame de Gyssels house. He was not a man to waste words.

'It's out of the question to go on your own,' he said emphatically.

François, at thirty, was about the same age as Dungey but more than ten years older than Bowlby. He had always been slim but three years in the Underground had made his face thin as a hatchet and his eyes hard and unsympathetic.

114

'You'll wait till I say you can go,' he snapped leaving them in no doubt how he felt in spite of his poor English.

'When will that be?' Bowlby asked. At nineteen it is hard to stay quietly in an old woman's house with nothing to do but wait. They had no idea when they would be moved by the Resistance, or whether the Gestapo would suddenly burst in and find them first.

'Maybe next week.'

'Well, that's not good enough,' Dungey replied, his frustration clear.

'Yes, we're going to get our things together and make our own way,' added Bowlby, fingering the escape kit issued to him by MI9.

'You will stay here,' shouted François in a furious temper. 'If you walk out of here, you have us to worry about. I'll not have you blundering about putting us all at risk. I'll make sure we find you before the Gestapo does, or we're all in trouble. D'you understand what I'm saying?'

The bleak expression on François's face left them in no doubt that there might be little to choose between the Partisans and the Gestapo.

'OK, OK,' Bowlby said with some embarrassment, but the intense boredom of the past weeks made him add none the less, 'But when?'

'Maybe next week,' said François. 'You'll leave when I say.'

It was all they got out of him. There was too much at stake to say more.

François realised how annoying it must be for the young men, fit and keen to be active, to lie low while the war passed them by, but he had no intention of telling them the arrangements for their escape. They had no business to know who or why or when. Just to be there and do what they were told.

After six weeks waiting the report was cleared, a space was found for them on the line and François was told to make them ready to go. On 10 September he made arrangements with Anne Brusselmans who gave him 750 francs for each of the airmen for incidental travel expenses. She made a note of these figures on a receipt. Other names on the same receipt were Darling (825 francs), Judy (825 francs), Di Minno (1350 francs), Aquino (1575 francs), Street (1125 francs), Sarnow (675 francs) and Minnich (675 francs). There is no explanation of the different costs of these evaders but the list indicates both the numbers involved on the escape lines and the funds needed to keep them open. These were a fraction of the sums which had to be paid for the travel fares, the food while they stayed in safe houses, payments to the mountain guides and other expenses including bribery.

Anne Brusselmans worked throughout the Occupation helping more than 200 airmen escape to England and was awarded the MBE after the war.

Hortense was disappointed to see Elmer and Art go. One evening she had bicycled round with a rabbit in her pannier, which Madame de Gyssels made into a stew for them. Fresh meat was scarce and rabbits particularly special as they were not on the list of rationed foodstuffs. Next day François moved them out of Louvain to Brussels, to the start of a long journey to Spain. They were lucky, avoided capture and arrived back in England later in September.

MI9, which had trained them in what to expect, now wanted to know what had actually happened. The two were thoroughly debriefed, each on his own, by MI9 staff in London. Both Art Bowlby and Elmer Dungey told them about the girl and her brother in Louvain and both were asked what sort of things they ate while they were in Madame de Gyssels's house.

'What, for example, did she give you the evening before you left that house?'

Both Canadians innocently said they had enjoyed a rather fine rabbit stew and thought no more about it as the staff officer studiously wrote down the answer in his notebook.

Weeks after they left Louvain, and as they were being posted back to their squadron in the north of England, François received a report from one of the escape line helpers. His job was to listen to special messages sent out by the BBC on the radio waves over occupied Europe. François went home to Louvain and told Hortense.

'We've heard the 'rabbit tasted fine',' he said, smiling, as they sat at the kitchen table. Hortense grinned broadly with pleasure.

She knew nothing of MI9, but she knew the convention was for the English to transmit a signal about the airmen's last meal in a safe house if they reached safety. It was good to know the risks had been worth it in the end.

Hortense helped some three dozen airmen working for François, many of them paid for by Anne Brusselmans, among them an Englishman called Fred Heathfield, a pilot of 51 Squadron flying Halifaxes. He left Snaith airfield in Yorkshire late on 21 June 1943 to bomb Krefeld in Germany. His plane was hit over the target and he struggled to return to England with two engines on fire and losing height all the time. The Channel was just too far for them. He ordered the crew to bale out over Belgium at 5000 feet but had to stay at the controls while they jumped or the stricken bomber would have cartwheeled and made parachuting impossible. By the time they had all gone there was no altitude to jump himself and he sat it out all the way down to a crash landing in a field.

Luckily unhurt, he was picked up and taken to Louvain by people associated with another Resistance movement, the Witte Brigade, and hidden in a safe house belonging to Jean Crab near Parkpoort.

The case illustrates the mix of resistance groups which on the face of it operated separately but in practice worked together from time to time.

In this instance, Hortense made several visits to the tiny terraced house with food and on one occasion she came to collect several revolvers which the Partisans needed for an attack. Heathfield remembers her as a pretty young girl whose calm surprised him as she slipped the weapons under some books in the front pannier of her bicycle. She covered them up with a white cloth drawn tight over the basket before cycling off down the cobbled street, seemingly without a care in the world.

Heathfield's experience further underlines the danger of collaborators on the escape lines and compares the fate of airmen and local helpers who were caught. He was moved into Brussels and from there to Paris. A Belgian calling himself Captain Prosper de Zitter was involved in some of these arrangements and Heathfield thought everything was going well until the bogus captain betrayed him to the Gestapo. Another Belgian, Matthias Boghe, who lived in Louvain, was also implicated and arrested. Heathfield spent the rest of the war in a prisoner of war camp in Germany run more or less according to the rules of the Geneva Convention. Boghe was tortured by the SS and taken to Breendonk where he was tortured some more and then executed. De Zitter survived the war in the pay of the SS but was caught after the liberation, tried and executed as a traitor. His passing was mourned by few and was certainly cleaner than the deaths of the men and women he betrayed into the hands of the Gestapo.

Allied aircrews were not the only ones to be helped by the Underground. There were displaced persons, men and women on the run for one reason or another; and languages of all kinds could be heard in the big railway stations as people of all races crossed Nazi Europe. After the German invasion of Russia in 1941 a considerable number of Russian prisoners of war were brought into Germany and the occupied countries as slave labour. They built camps in Norway, mended railway lines in

# The Rabbit Tasted Fine

Denmark and worked in the coal mines in Belgium. One such group of Russians was identified near Louvain in the summer of 1943, and word reached Gaston.

Pierre van Goitsenhoeven, Hortense, and Guillaume Vanderstappen who was known as 'Jommeke', were sent on bicycles to fetch the four from the countryside farm where they were hiding.

The ride out was the easy part. The weather was fine, the air warm and they enjoyed the forty minute trip to the farm, chatting and racing each other on the downhill stretches. After that nothing seemed to go right. When they reached the small farmhouse they discovered the four Russians could not speak a single word of any other language than Russian. Even 'Ja' or 'Nein' in German produced puzzled frowns and incomprehension. Worse still, none of them had the slightest idea how to ride a bicycle.

'There's nothing for it,' Hortense said, shrugging her shoulders. 'We'll have to carry them on the handle bars.'

'You're joking?' Pierre said at once, glancing at Jommeke who grinned and moved away from the four Russians.

'What else can we do?' Hortense asked them, hands on her hips and smiling encouragingly at the confused-looking Russians. She found herself unable to stop staring at their hair which stood straight up on their heads stiff with black soot. The fact was the Russians smelt. It was as plain to the nose as the eyes that they had not washed for months.

'Leave them here?' Jommeke suggested, still grinning. 'Anyway there're four of them and only three bikes.'

'We'll have to go in relays.'

'All right,' Pierre said, resigned to the idea. 'We'll take it in turns to go back and pick up the fourth one at the end of each leg.'

They agreed but it was easier said than done. First the Russians did not understand what was required. After

119

much gesticulating and mime they grasped the rudiments of the scheme but then they found it nearly impossible to balance on the bikes. Every yard of the way they wobbled about and wriggled for fear they would fall off, and all the time Hortense, Pierre and Jommeke did their best not to have too much contact with their charges as the smell was truly awful.

The journey took three hours of weaving about the tracks, falling off, swearing, laughing at the others falling off, at the Russians and at Jommeke's comments on the smell. The Russians remained cheerful and helpful but they never got the hang of the bicycle.

The usual safe houses were full of evading airmen at the time so Hortense had been told to bring the Russians to the house in Pleinstraat. This was a breach of a rule which François had instigated with the full support of Stephanie and Jacques. There was so much other clandestine activity at the house, with François, Gaston, Louis and of course Hortense moving in and out all day, that it would have been quite wrong normally to have used the place to hide airmen or any other evaders. On this occasion there was no alternative. Also, no one else wanted the Russians. Stephanie Daman was not enthusiastic either. When she saw the condition of the four, she refused outright to have them in the house and a prolonged argument took place in the kitchen with Gaston, Hortense and the others while the Russians sat equably in the garden apparently content to see what would happen next.

Finally Stephanie agreed to have them in for one night only, provided they had baths immediately and cleaned up. This solution was put to them by Gaston and Hortense with more mime which produced satisfied smiles and vigorous nodding from the Russians. There was no bathroom with running water in the little house. Stephanie filled the bath tub in the kitchen with hot water. Then she hustled Hortense and Julia upstairs while the men made sure the Russians had a really good scrub. This operation took some while for the visitors were not in practice, but when it was over Stephanie came back and decided the next step was a haircut all round. Even washed, their hair rose like a forest of black needles straight off their scalp and would have attracted attention in the street. Once again, the intention was more easily expressed than carried out. Stephanie sat each one on a chair in the kitchen and soon found there were no scissors in the house sharp or strong enough to cut their hair.

'Let me get the secateurs,' Jacques Daman said eventually, smiling broadly as he went out to the garden shed.

'I think you're right,' she admitted. 'Nothing else works.'

The Russians were rather pleased with themselves when they were shown their new appearance in the mirror and even more impressed when they were taken upstairs after supper to Julia's room where they were going to spend the night. After escaping from a slave labour detail working in the coal mines in Northern Belgium they had been sleeping rough in the hedges and fields for nine months. Baths, sheets and pillows were a novelty.

Stephanie was a great deal less impressed the following morning when she discovered that one of the Russians was a bit of an artist and had covered the newly papered walls of Julia's room with freehand drawings of nude women. 'That paper's unobtainable now!' Stephanie shouted furiously at the Russians who looked confused and hurt.

'Rather well drawn, I thought,' Jacques whispered to Hortense and then ducked out of the back door for a drink in the bar opposite till things quieted down. Hortense agreed, without daring to say so, but it made no difference. The Russians had to go.

That day the four Russians, now at least clean, were moved. One who was called Georg went to Madame

Berges's house. He stayed there quite happily for the remainder of the war hidden in the cellar and making models out of small pieces of metal. Two went to Henri Coulear's house and the fourth left the Louvain area altogether. One of those hidden by Coulear joined the Partisans and fought well until he was killed in action.

Stephanie was emphatic. She would have no more Russians to stay in Pleinstraat. Life returned to normal.

# 6

# Action!

'Human action is a seed of circumstances.' Friedrich von Schiller (1759–1805).

Those listening to the BBC in 1943 could hear more optimistic news as the year went on. On the eastern front General Paulus had surrendered his entire army to the Russians at Stalingrad on 31 January with a loss of 92,000 German troops. Only 6,000 ever returned to Germany. The Russians continued their pressure after Stalingrad with successes at Kursk and in the Caucasus. In North Africa the American and British armies met in Tunisia and on 13 May Colonel-General Jürgen von Arnim surrendered over 170,000 German and Italian troops at Tunis. In the air British bombers were committed to the Battle of the Ruhr to bludgeon German industry. Everywhere the Allies were closing in; but life in the centre of Hitler's empire continued as before.

The organisations in England tried to encourage the Underground in Europe to fight the Germans, but the Resistance was always short of supplies. There were never enough weapons or explosives. The Partisans in Belgium felt they were badly supplied. Very little in the way of parachute drops was made to the BAP and we must assume the government-in-exile was reluctant to give too much to an organisation which they believed would be a direct threat to the return of democracy after the liberation. Possibly the British government, through MI6 and SOE, took a similar view.

The alternatives were thoroughly explored. Partisans always tried to steal the weapons off the Germans they attacked. The GFP carried rifles and the Gestapo revolvers or the MP40 sub-machine-gun. The Partisans had a policy of only attacking Germans in uniform. Hortense and her fellow Partisans hated what the Germans were doing to Belgium, but they felt very strongly that it was wrong to attack the enemy 'off-duty'.

The principle highlights an important difference between the actions of the Partisans who were called 'terrorists' by the Germans during the war, and the actions of 'terrorists' nowadays. For example, what was the principle at work behind the two IRA men who killed off-duty Sergeant-Major Meakin in August 1988, as he drove through Ostend in his own car in civilian clothes on his way home to his family in England? Or what possible explanation (other than a delight in sheer criminal murder) is there for blowing up the Pan Am Jumbo 747 on flight 103 which fell on Lockerbie in Scotland filled with people going home to New York for Christmas at the end of that year?

The German soldiers were often in large groups and it was not so easy to take their weapons, so the Partisans were sometimes forced to barter or buy them. Pierre Hermans, Hortense's cousin, bought six Sten guns once at the exorbitant price of 6,000 Belgian francs each, the equivalent of five months wages.

An alternative to seizing weapons when the soldiers were carrying them was to break into an armoury. A plan to rob the armoury in the Central Prison in Louvain, just across the Boulevard from the Damans in Pleinstraat, was carried out in 1943. An informant working in the prison told François, Pierre and Louis van Brussel that the prison guards kept their pistols in the armoury, which could be easily reached without anyone knowing until it was too late. They questioned the man carefully and estimated the whole affair could be carried out silently in a matter of twenty minutes.

In the event the attack did not go according to plan, like so many military skirmishes which appear at first sight to be the essence of simplicity. Two Partisans were detailed to go inside. After scaling the eighteen foot walls, and reaching the armoury deep inside the prison without being detected, they were faced with an unwelcome shock. The informant had failed to mention that the Germans had locked the pistols inside a cabinet secured with iron bars. Cool determination was clearly an essential ingredient in the Underground. While the normal routine of the prison went on around them, the two Partisans spent the next two hours silently forcing their way into the cabinet.

Outside, the lookouts, among them Pierre and François, waited patiently in the darkness of doorways in the streets around the back of the prison. As time passed, they knew something had gone wrong but, before the time of two-way radios, had no way of knowing exactly what. They expected the Germans to raise the alarm if the two were captured. But nothing happened. So they waited. Two hours is a long time to wait in the dark, plenty of time for the imagination to conjure up visions of disaster, such as the Geheimefeldpolizei stealthily moving into ambush positions in the streets, waiting for the Partisans to step out of their protecting shadows.

Finally the thieves appeared over the wall and dropped to the cobbles beneath. Pierre Hermans saw them momentarily silhouetted on the top of the wall and prepared to move from his spot to help. At precisely the same moment, by sheer bad luck, two Germans on a routine patrol came round the corner of the wall in front of him. They spotted the movement at the foot of the wall, drew their pistols and seized the two men, whom they took for escaping prisoners.

Pierre paused only a moment. He checked up and down the darkened street. The two Germans were alone, one a policeman and the other a member of the GFP. Pierre stepped swiftly and quietly over the street towards the little group by the prison wall. Neither German noticed. They were thrilled by the good luck of their capture, but their success was short-lived.

'Partisans!' Pierre hissed savagely, suddenly jabbing his pistol hard into the back of the policeman who had grabbed the man with the bag full of stolen pistols.

The man gasped in surprise and pain, and immediately burst out, 'OK, OK. For God's sake don't shoot. You can all go!'

His friend in the GFP was less intelligent and began to scream for help, 'Don't shoot! Don't shoot!'

Terrified out of his wits by Pierre's sudden appearance out of the dark, he threw away his pistol screaming hysterically. Pierre turned to silence him for good when the man collapsed in terror, crying like a child. Disgusted, Pierre found he could not kill him in cold blood.

But the alarm had been given. The Partisans made their escape as fast as they could, leaving a rising volume of shouts behind them. They scattered to various bolt holes and safe houses, Pierre to Pleinstraat slipping through the darkness under the trees in the Boulevard, over the garden wall and through the kitchen door into the house. Hortense met them in the kitchen and they spent the rest of the night with the Damans. In the prison, where the guard was doubled and troops turned out to search the streets, they discovered sixteen pistols had been stolen.

It might seem a lot of effort and danger to obtain only a few pistols, but nothing was easy for the Resistance, especially by 1943 when the German counter-resistance was largely controlled by the SS. Perhaps the easiest way to obtain weapons and explosives was the most traditional: looting the battlefield.

126

# Action!

In 1940 large quantities of equipment had been left behind by the Allied armies, but by 1943 this had been picked up either by the Resistance or the Germans. The battlefield in Belgium later in the war was in the air and the bombers which crashed with aircrews also offered the opportunity of unexploded bombs filled with useful high explosives.

In the summer of 1943 Hortense was told by Gaston to go to a small village outside Louvain and pick up a sack of explosives which had been taken from a bomb. She was accompanied by Guillaume Vanderstappen, Jommeke, who had been with her to fetch the Russians. They set out in the afternoon, Hortense on her bicycle and Jommeke hanging behind on his. If they were stopped, even before picking up the sack, he did not want to be associated with Hortense. She had identity in her own name, but he carried a false identity card, as was the custom in the Partisans during operations. And he carried a pistol. Small and wiry, with fair hair and brilliant blue eyes, he was one of the best Partisans in Louvain. He followed faithfully a distance behind as they pushed on through the fields, casting an experienced eye about for trouble.

They reached the village without incident. The sack of explosives was heavier than either of them had expected, more than 40 kilos, and only just fitted over the back shelf on Hortense's bike. They slung it over the frame and tied it on as best they could. There was no time to delay and they set off at once back to Pleinstraat, to the safe house where the explosives were to be hidden. Hortense found the bicycle much harder to pedal with the extra weight and she worked up quite a sweat on the journey back, which went well until they reached the outskirts of the town.

Hortense eased the heavy bike slowly round the corner of a terraced street and saw the German patrol immediately. A group of four soldiers was standing on the pavement ahead of her on the same side of the road. The weight of the sack on her back wheel was hard to control on the cobbles. She concentrated on steering over the rough stones and deliberately paid them no attention as she passed them. Jommeke came round the same corner behind her. He stopped as one of the four soldiers suddenly began to stare at Hortense's bicycle and then at the ground behind her. Jommeke was too far away to see exactly what the German was pointing at but he could guess. A quick glance at the cobbles near his bike where Hortense had turned the corner confirmed it. Hanging over the wheel, the sack had been rubbed through on the way from the village and powdered explosive was falling in a steady stream from a hole to the ground. Trying to be as inconspicuous as possible he moved with his bicycle back to the cover of the corner house as the Germans evidently reached the same conclusion.

'Halt! Halt!' the Gefreiter in charge shouted at the top of his voice, simultaneously pulling his rifle off his shoulder into action. Hortense had not looked back at the patrol, but she was still very much aware of them behind her. All the same, their guttural shouts went straight through her. The shock of hearing their voices made her glance over her shoulder. In a fraction of time, the picture was imprinted on her memory of two soldiers running towards her and the other two taking aim to shoot. Beyond and behind them, she saw Jommeke at the corner with his pistol.

The explosion of shooting was deafening in the tiny terraced street. The crack and thump of shots echoed round her. It was all the encouragement she needed. Desperately, she shoved her feet on the pedals to get away. The next corner was no more than thirty metres but reaching it took what seemed to her an age of time and she hurtled round it at a speed she would not have dared to go normally with such a heavy load.

The firing continued for a moment, the explosions of sound dulled by the houses between her and the patrol. Fortunately the street she had turned into was quite short.

She pedalled furiously to get away round the next corner before the soldiers could reach the turning and have time to aim at her: it would be like target practice in a shooting gallery. By then she was exhausted, out of breath and the muscles in her legs burned with the strain. There was no sound of pursuit and she risked a look back as she turned another corner. The street behind her was clear.

It would take the Germans some time to alert other patrols so she went on to Josephine de Roost's house, where François was waiting to hide the explosives. He dragged the sack into the back where Madame de Roost was holding open the secret trap which covered the old well under the floorboards. She would soon be sleeping over enough explosives to blow her and her small house to kingdom come.

Hortense told François what had happened immediately but it was only later that she discovered how successful Guillaume Vanderstappen's covering action had been. He waited till the two Germans were about to open fire before he shot and wounded one of them. This sudden attack from their rear threw them into complete disorder. Guillaume had fired off a full magazine at them, leaped on his bicycle and made his getaway, leaving the Germans to tend the wounded man, thinking they had been attacked by a large group of terrorists.

Hortense had been lucky. She was rightly pleased with herself. Cycling on the bulky cobbles with 40 kilos (88 lbs) on the back wheel had not been easy, and the drama of the situation, carrying explosives and being shot at for the first time, gave her a sense of achievement. She had survived and come through it quite well.

François saw it differently. The incident showed how easily plans could go wrong. The tiniest detail, the lack of thought needed to strap that sack properly to the bicycle, could have resulted in disaster. This time they had been lucky: but he dared not tell his parents. Hortense's father

Jacques was a mild man. He approved of his family's part in the Resistance, and made his own contribution by distributing illegal newspapers, but he worried about his daughter, of whom he was especially fond. The mistake of not tying up the sack could have been made by any of the Partisans, but François wondered how much the error was due to youthful enthusiasm and a lack of the discipline that comes only with formal training, such as his own in the Artillery. Pre-war army training was never designed for subversive warfare but he appreciated the military grounding.

In spite of their lack of training however, the Louvain Partisans carried out a piece of sabotage as good as any other undertaken by any unit, trained or not, in the war. In addition to all the other ingredients needed in a military operation, an element of luck is necessary to turn mere good management into an outstanding success. In July 1943 everything came together.

François Daman was given information from his contacts in the Légion Belge that two important German troop trains were due through Louvain at the end of the month and they should be attacked. There was enough time for a good reconnaissance, so a few selected Partisans, Pierre Hermans or 'Georges' as he was known, among them, spent several nights observing rail traffic leaving Louvain on the routes to Brussels through the districts of Old Heverlee and Erps-Kwerps. In the dark shadows of the bushes Pierre watched the trains rattle along the straight section of line which passed alongside the big woods to the south of the town and picked what he thought would be the place for the ambush. He is a meticulous man and took great care to measure distances and calculate the speeds of the trains.

After some weeks François received word that the attack was on for the night of 30 July. He sorted out the plan and Hortense bicycled round town with messages which gathered the men at the shop late that evening.

# Action!

'How's it to be done?' Pierre wanted to know. He did not think the mix of explosives they had accumulated from various places, including the sackful Hortense had brought in recently, would be suitable. The problem of achieving good detonation of the loose explosives might seriously affect the velocity and reduce the cutting power necessary to derail a train travelling at speed.

François said nothing but unwrapped a package on the kitchen table. Hortense and the other young men crowded closer to watch fascinated as François laid out charges, primers, detonators, detonating cord (Cordtex), and initiating devices.

'Extraordinary,' Pierre breathed, genuinely amazed. He had never before seen such a fine display of explosives equipment. Indeed he never again saw such supplies for the rest of the war. 'Why can't we get this sort of thing more often?'

François ignored the question. He thought Pierre knew that the best drops were made to the underground Belgian army, which was the new name for the Légion Belge since the arrival of Adelin Marissal with an SOE mission code-named 'Stanley' from the government-in-exile in London. Pierre certainly knew that the Partisans' socialist background did not especially endear them to the government-in-exile. There were those who strongly disapproved of the Partisans' policy of continually attacking the Occupation forces. They argued that these attacks brought an unacceptable toll of reprisals on the already suffering population. Some critics of the Partisans went further and claimed the policy was deliberately chosen by the Communists under directions from Moscow, in order to disrupt the country in preparation for the end of the war. The Communists, it was said, wanted to destroy the infrastructure, by actions like blowing up lines of communication, and damage morale by actually encouraging vicious reprisals against the population for those attacks.

131

Whether there was any truth in these allegations against the high command of the Belgian Army of Partisans, the Partisan policy clearly suited the Belgian army's strategy that evening in July 1943. They had provided all the equipment, and the young Partisans were only too willing to use it to kill Germans.

François showed Pierre how to set up the charges. He picked up a round, flat object the size of a small vanity compact with a large spring attached to the bottom.

'This is what the English call a 'Fog Signal' initiator,' he explained. 'This spring fits over the railway line and the detonator slides in the tube on one side of the round part.'

Hortense was absorbed in his demonstration and it never occurred to her that there might be an appalling explosion in the house which could destroy them all. She did not appreciate the aspects of safety involved. However her brother knew what he was doing. He made a good instructor and Pierre, with his meticulous eye for detail, a fast-learning pupil.

'I'll fix up the charges for you now,' he told Pierre. 'There'll be plenty to do without worrying about this when you come to lay them. We'll fix this explosive line, Cordtex, to the detonator in the Fog Signal,' he explained, picking up a coil of what looked to Hortense very like a length of washing line. 'Then the velocity of the explosion travelling down the Cordtex needs boosting at the end so we'll fit a primer where it goes into the charge itself.'

Hortense watched him pick up a cork-like object with a hole in the middle, push a length of Cordtex through the hole and quickly tie a knot in the end. He pulled the primer tight on the end of the Cordtex knot and fitted it into a hole in the top centre of the standard charge. Then he pulled the black cloth bag back round the charge and tied a piece of string round it to hold the Cordtex firm.

'All you need to do now is tie this to the place you've picked to cut the rail at the side, and attach the initiator further up the track. Make sure you use both sets of gear, just in case one fails.' François narrowed his eyes. 'But remember this warning, Georges,' he said. 'You're the boss and you must hang on to the Fog Signal initiator till everything else is done. That way, you have the detonators and therefore complete control over the attack. You'll know no one else can set the charges off by mistake or too early. Only attach them at the end, when you're sure everything else is ready. All you have to do is push the Cordtex into the clip on the end of the detonator.'

François mimed the action and looked up at the keen young faces around him.

'Is that enough?' Hortense could not help asking. The two small packages on the kitchen table, no bigger than a medium loaf, hardly seemed sufficient to destroy an entire train.

'Certainly,' François stated.

Pierre, or Georges as he was that night, had a few questions. Then he packed the pieces of equipment in satchels and set off with the three others in the team. They walked pushing their bicycles behind the houses in Pleinstraat keeping out of sight of the Philips gate guards and round the cemetery on the far side. Then they mounted their bicycles to ride through Heverlee woods to the railway line beyond Old Heverlee. The other team left shortly afterwards to go to Erps-Kwerps.

Pierre said afterwards that the operation went smoothly though he had difficulty laying the Cordtex. It was too springy and would not lie down. By this time in the war he had been in numerous fire-fights with the Germans, but he had no experience of sabotage on this scale. An SOE agent or SAS soldier in his place, with all the benefits of training or actual operational experience, would have automatically brought a supply of masking tape to stick the errant detonating cord to the underside of the line. However Pierre Hermans was a determined young man.

He placed the charges, tied down the Cordtex and fitted the Fog Signal initiator carefully over the line at the exact place he had selected on his reconnaissance. He had chosen a spot just up the line from a small bridge over a cutting through the embankment. Then he checked the placing of the charges once more, sent his other men back to a rendezvous in the shadow of trees away from the line, and finally connected the detonators to the Cordtex.

Old Heverlee is more than six miles from Pleinstraat, but at half past three in the morning the still night air carried the sound of the explosion clearly to Hortense who lay in bed unable to sleep. The dull crump she heard gave no indication of the utter devastation at the scene. The train had been travelling at more than 100 kilometres an hour on the straight when the front wheels struck the Fog Signal initiator. The charges went off in a searing blast which cut the line and blew the engine off the track as it rocketed over the little bridge, exactly as Pierre had calculated. Toppling sideways it crashed upside down in the cutting. The carriages plunged after it, twisting and cartwheeling off the embankment into a mass of torn metal in which there was no room for life.

Photographs captured after the war showed that the destruction had succeeded beyond all expectations. The statistics give a clue to the disaster: one general, two colonels, eighty-five assorted officers were among a total of 285 dead soldiers. It would have been well-nigh impossible to have killed more.

A quarter of an hour later another explosion rocked the countryside as the line near the village of Erps-Kwerps was shattered. The other team were responsible for the deaths of over sixty soldiers and the destruction blocked the lines out of Louvain for eight days.

Trained soldiers from the best units in any army would have been more than satisfied with these results. The incident shows that good intelligence and a reasonable supply of equipment in the hands of men with courage and an eye for detail can achieve remarkably effective results.

The attack raises points which are still relevant. The principles applied by Pierre are still the prime concern of both freedom fighters and the security forces who combat them. First, the number of men actually carrying out the attacks was very small; only four in each case. This figure might have been reduced if necessary. Very few people are required to cause havoc with bombings and ambushes, even on a long campaign if it is well planned. The scale of terrorist attacks is no yardstick of the size of the group responsible, or the support for it among the general public. Secondly, setting up a well-sited ambush does not need previous military training. It requires intelligence and imagination. Pierre's choice was perfect: on an embankment near a cutting, on a straight section of line where the train would be travelling at its maximum speed. The casualties were enormous.

By contrast, the IRA attack on a bus full of British soldiers (in civilian clothes returning from leave) at Ballygawly in Northern Ireland in August 1988 was incompetent. They used a 200-pound radio-controlled bomb hidden in a drainage culvert. In spite of this sophistication, the ambush site was badly chosen on a fast stretch of road, the bus shot past escaping much of the blast and twenty-nine soldiers survived.

Thirdly, obtaining and using good intelligence does not depend on modern communications. Long before the age of satellite communications, radios with 'burst' facility and two-way radios with 'scrambled' voice, the Partisans succeeded rather well with just the telephone, the bicycle and good reconnaissance. Lastly the equipment Pierre used was as good or better than that used by freedom fighters now. At a detonating speed of 25,000 feet per second, his plastic explosive in the train attack was slower than Czechoslovak Semtex but it produced a far higher 'brisance', or shattering effect, than any of the fertiliser mixes, for example the Ammonium Nitrate Fuel Oil (ANFO), so popular with the IRA in their car bombs. Then, his Sten gun may look old-fashioned and have a slower cyclic rate of fire than many of the sub-machine-guns in use nowadays but it is quite as effective. Many would say its simplicity puts it ahead in ease of use and in cleaning. His pistol was an automatic 9mm made by Fabrique National at Herstal in Belgium, still the preferred hand gun of the modern SAS and used at Gibraltar in March 1988 when three IRA terrorists were shot there. Pierre, François and Hortense operated decades ago but their techniques and equipment are still valid. One may suppose that Pierre could still teach the IRA a thing or two; but I very much doubt he would be inclined to.

One of the most useful tools available to the Resistance was the grenade. Very often the Partisans made their own, using explosives hidden in Josephine de Roost's house. Home-made grenades, like the ones that Jan Sprengers's battalion tried to use against the collaborator in that ill-fated attack, were thoroughly unreliable. Real grenades, like real plastic explosive, were extremely valuable. They were jealously guarded and stored, cautiously moved and used prudently.

Hortense therefore rightly considered it an honour to be asked by Gaston to move no less than twenty-five Mills Grenades, type No. 36 Mark I, from one safe house in Louvain to another, in preparation for an attack. It was decided that the best way was to conceal the grenades in the front pannier of her bicycle under a layer of eggs, and pull a red and white chequered cloth over the top of the basket, rather like the cloth she had used picking up the revolvers from Matthias Borghe's house. When Hortense set out to cross the town the weight of the grenades loaded down the front of the bike. She was used to filling the pannier with vegetables from the market, but grenades weigh more than turnips. With all the weight at the front she found she was fighting to keep her balance over some of the older cobbled streets. She chose a route through the quieter streets round the outskirts of the centre, near some of the university buildings which still showed shell damage from 1940. She crossed the main road to Brussels, and seeing some German soldiers ahead, turned into Wandeling Straat. Suddenly Germans appeared at the top end of the short street. She slowed intending to turn round as casually as she could with the heavy pannier-full of 'groceries' and escape the way she had come. To her horror she saw the road behind blocked by the Germans she had passed. It was a 'razzia'.

The German patrols carried out these razzias frequently, mainly to catch black market trade, young men avoiding the labour draft or those with illegal papers. Normally Hortense had permits for her vegetables. This time she was carrying twenty-five items for which there was no excuse. With blunt efficiency the Germans advanced along the street from both ends, rounding up everyone, shoving them into the centre, pushing one or two reluctant young boys with their rifles.

'Men on the left. Women on the right side!'

Hortense could not help thinking of the story of the Great War when the Germans had done exactly the same thing and then shot all the men and boys. Perhaps someone had denounced her. Perhaps someone had told the Germans she would be crossing the town with arms and they had sprung a trap for her.

Watching the soldiers carefully, she eased towards the side of the road with all the other women, still pedalling slowly, and keeping near the kerb so she could put one foot down to steady herself. She dared not get off her bike for fear the heavy pannier-load of grenades would swing round and topple over as she tried to hold the handlebars from the side. Briefly her imagination swelled with a vision of what would happen when the Germans saw two dozen unbroken steel-grey 'eggs' bouncing off the stones in a cascade of broken shells and splashing yellow egg yokes.

'You! Get over there,' a German soldier shouted at her, waving his rifle to where a crowd of frightened women and children were waiting to see what would happen to them.

'Where's your officer?' Hortense replied, her fear of what they would do to her if they found the grenades momentarily banished in the immediacy of deciding what to do.

'Never you mind about that,' the soldier advised her rudely. 'Just get over there with the other women.'

Hortense looked past him for the officer she desperately hoped would be close by. Annoyed at her disobedience, the German soldier reached out to grab the handlebars and shove her towards the wall. She pulled back to avoid the man's hand and nearly lost her balance.

'Herr Hauptmann,' she shouted at the Wehrmacht lieutenant, deliberately upping his rank to captain. Her voice and the rank made the soldier hesitate. The officer was some yards away but he heard Hortense shout and looked up.

'Herr Hauptmann, can I speak to you for a moment?' Her German was not perfect but sufficient to make herself understood.

The soldier scowled at the young Belgian girl but held back his rifle at the ready across his chest, watching his superior walk over. It irritated him that the stupid girl had got the lieutenant's rank wrong.

'What's the matter?' the young officer demanded when he reached them.

Hortense gave the soldier no chance to answer first and immediately launched into a long story of worry and upset, about fetching supplies from the market for her mother's shop, being late and what would happen to her when she got home.

'Why're you late?' the officer snapped, unmoved by this tale.

Hortense hesitated a moment, let her eyes drop and put on an expression of awful guilt and embarrassment.

'Come on,' the German snapped, but Hortense heard a slight whisper of interest behind the hard tones. Encouraged, she plunged on.

'I was talking to someone,' she admitted in a soft voice.

'Who?' the officer demanded, as though he was conducting an interrogation. He noticed the girl was attractive.

'A friend, Herr Hauptmann,' she said, continuing to flatter him with a higher rank.

'A boyfriend?' the officer suggested.

She nodded and he relaxed a little, evidently pleased he had guessed right. Hortense hardly realised how well her story had diverted him from the main object of his street blockade. Her mind seemed to function on two planes. One side of her was terrified by the idea that she was standing astride her bicycle loaded down with grenades and talking to two German soldiers who might any second reach out, discover her treachery and drag her off to be shot. Physically she could hardly stand the tension, the surge of adrenalin each time the German officer spoke, as if he knew all along that she was carrying grenades and was simply playing with her for a while to amuse himself. Her stomach knotted painfully and she had no feeling in her legs. The other side of her mind was conducting this banal but vitally important conversation.

'Well now, what have you got here,' demanded the officer, pointing at the pannier. His tone had mellowed but he was obviously motivated by his duty to search.

Hortense stared for what seemed an age at the inoffensive red and white chequered cloth which covered her own arrest, torture and death under a thin layer of chicken's eggs.

'Just eggs, Herr Hauptmann,' she said in a small girl's voice, looking up at him, her eyes wide with young innocence. Her mind was doing a convincing job of keeping up the dangerous charade. Taking enormous care not to lose her precarious balance, she let go the handlebars with one hand and lifted one corner of the cloth so he could see the brown eggs underneath.

She noticed his eyes widen. Eggs were rare indeed in the occupation in Belgium, even for German officers. In July 1943 an egg cost 1.61 Belgian francs in official theory, but in practice was rarely seen except on the black market where it cost more than 8.80 francs. In February 1940 before the invasion an egg had cost 49 centimes.

'Where's your authority for these?' the lieutenant asked, without taking his eyes off the eggs.

Hortense struggled to hold herself upright with the bike and pulled out the official papers she had been given by the officials at the market that morning. She handed them to the officer.

He examined them carefully, just in case they were false and the eggs could be seized. Hortense reached forward and made as if to check the eggs were safe in the pannier. Sure enough the officer kept glancing at her hand running over the smooth round shapes. As he handed the papers back to her, she said, 'Would you like a couple?'

'Ja, bitte,' the officer replied rather quickly. Pressing home her advantage, Hortense reached under the cloth where he could not see, pulled out two big brown eggs and gave them to him. He looked at them a moment, cradling them in his hands, then dismissed the girl abruptly.

'All right. On your way! Hurry up!' He waved her away, conscious he had weakened his position by accepting the eggs, and turned back to deal with the others in the street.

# Action!

Without waiting for a second and ignoring the German soldier who had stopped her and looked as if he might hold her back for an egg himself, Hortense started pedalling at once. The end of the street suddenly seemed a mile away. As the tension drained away her strength seemed to vanish with it. Her bicycle felt as though it weighed a ton, her legs became sluggish and weak and every cobble threatened to throw her off. She hardly rounded the corner. Struggling, she passed a few bystanders watching the German search from a safe distance, and with a final effort pushed the loaded bike to the nearest wall. She leaned against the rough bricks, unable to dismount with the nearly-fatal weight of the grenades pulling at the front and quite without the strength to try. Completely exhausted, she stayed like that for some minutes, while her legs shook uncontrollably and spasms of relief racked her body.

When she reached the safe house eventually they had to hold her bike for her while she got off. They all knew that any of the young men would certainly have been seized had they been in her place. She had only escaped because she had so cunningly played on her sex and youth. Her mission had succeeded, but Hortense could think of little else but that it had been her closest brush with the Germans yet. Like plunging under a freezing shower, the experience cooled and tempered her youthful enthusiasm. It also increased her capacity for 'streetwise' cunning and boosted her confidence.

The incident worried François and Gaston, however. They had noticed a considerable rise in German activity against the Partisans, especially after the successful train attacks. The SS had mounted a series of sudden searches, venting their fury in brutal arrests and interrogations.

Later in 1943 Hortense was given a promotion and became a courier between the Corps in Louvain and the National Commando in Brussels. She still worked for Gaston, bicycling with messages around the town as before, but now she moved further afield into the capital, working again for Louis van Brussel who was by now in the Partisans' National Commando.

Sometimes Gaston accompanied her and on one such trip to Brussels he said he wanted her to pay particular attention because the man they were going to meet was very important.

In a perfect world, perhaps with the benefit of the formal training he had never had, Godefried Dreesen would not have mentioned anything about the man they would meet. In theory Godefried himself was known only by his code-name Gaston, and Hortense only by hers, 'Lisette'. It was not necessary for Hortense to know even the code-name of the contact.

But Hortense met Camile van Acker, Sector Commandant for all Belgian Flanders. The meeting was brief but made a profound impression on the sixteen-year-old girl. Van Acker took special pains to thank Hortense for her work as a courier and praised her efforts as a Partisan. He did what all general officers in command should do, reached down to give his encouragement, and not many have his gift of being able to convey a real personal interest in only a few words. Hortense came away feeling she had met someone very special and was more than ever determined that there was nothing she would not do to support the cause against Germany.

Going home on the train she remembered how exhausted van Acker had looked. He lived in such difficult circumstances, on the run all the time, and was pale and thin, with great black circles round his intelligent eyes. On reflection she was all the more amazed that he had troubled to speak to her at all. She could not forget the tiredness in his face and mentioned to her mother that she had met someone with Gaston who seemed badly in need of a good rest and a square meal.

Stephanie Daman realised there was little she could do to provide a rest, but she could do something about his nourishment. She knew enough about the life of key men in the Resistance; always under pressure, they never knew where they would be the next night or where their meals would come from; they were at the top of the Gestapo's wanted list, often with a reward on their heads, and told their plans to the barest few to avoid the breaches of security which led to arrests. She spoke to Gaston briefly one evening about the man he had taken her daughter to meet in Brussels. Without giving his name, Gaston confirmed that their contact was working too hard and that the Gestapo had several times nearly succeeded in catching him, but like many other fine Resistance men and women he had rejected all the seductive avenues of escape.

When Gaston went to meet Camile van Acker again he carried with him a tin inside which were two cooked rabbits prepared by Hortense's mother. The meeting went as planned, on a street corner in Brussels. Camile van Acker was delighted and touched at the gift.

'I'll keep this till later,' he told Gaston, a smile of genuine warmth lighting his thin face. 'I'm on the way home now, but I've one more visit to make first. It'll be difficult to concentrate when all the time I'll be thinking of sitting down to enjoy these excellent rabbits.'

He made Gaston promise to thank Madame Daman and her daughter especially for the kind gift and they parted. It was the last time Gaston saw him alive.

When Camile van Acker arrived at his next rendezvous, in a café, he walked into a trap the Gestapo had laid for him. He made his usual circumspect examination of the surrounding streets before approaching the rendezvous, trying to spot the lurking enemy in plain clothes. Seeing nothing, he went inside. He sat down at a table on his own and ordered a *petit blanc*, a small glass of white wine. He had been sitting there for only a few minutes when two men in suits banged in through the door, walked straight up to him and shot him dead at point blank range.

In the aftermath of this 'official' killing, the Gestapo discovered the tin with the two rabbits inside. History does not relate who ate the rabbits, but the Germans offered a reward to find the person who had supplied the 'terrorist Camile van Acker' with illegal produce.

The incident again illustrates the different way the Germans viewed what they saw as understandable national resistance and the activities of the Communist-led Partisans. Hortense Daman, at sixteen, neither knew nor cared what Camile van Acker's politics were. To the Germans he was a Communist dedicated to fighting the occupation of Belgium because it was right wing and National Socialist. More pertinently for Hortense Daman, the incident underlined the danger she ran as a courier for men like Gaston, Louis van Brussel and her brother. Long past were the days in 1940 when she had passed secret messages for François in Brussels, or helped take food to the nuns of the Groot Begijnhof Convent for the British soldiers they were hiding in the attic. Dangerous as these jobs may have been, they did not compare to the summary justice meted out to members of the Belgian Army of Partisans, the organisation which embodied everything the Nazis hated and which brought out the most unpleasant and anti-democratic reaction of the German occupation forces.

Summary justice, as suffered by Camile van Acker, may be appalling to us now, in our comfortable government-supported, consumer-orientated environment, but in the measure of occupied Belgium instant death may well have been preferred to a lingering one at the hands of the SS.

Van Acker's death dispelled any doubts Hortense Daman may have held as to her fate should she be caught. His death and the increasingly successful attacks by the Gestapo, the GFP and the SD against the Resistance, and the Partisans in particular, made various changes necessary in the strategic thinking of the Partisans. Van Acker had clearly been betrayed. Someone had not only known where he was going to be at a certain time, but also identified him sitting in the café to the Gestapo's assassins waiting outside. The collaborators were probably Belgian volunteers in the SS, of whom there were all too many.

So changes of appointment had to be made, new orders issued and plans altered. Reports on all the activities of the Partisans had to be moved, in case the Germans had received information on where they could be found: these included details of Partisan attacks, financial accounts, reports on the German dispositions and morale (which were sent to Moscow but little of which reached the British) and lists of names and addresses of members, often with confidential personnel reports attached. All these were gold dust to the Gestapo and SD searching for information to break the Underground.

As a courier, Hortense Daman was ordered to assist in this reorganisation and to carry a particularly important bundle of files from Waterloo to Louvain. François and Gaston decided that the security aspects of the situation were so delicate that Hortense must first bicycle from Louvain to Waterloo, a distance of nearly forty kilometres, collect the papers and then take the train back. Someone else would fetch the bicycle back to Louvain. Gaston and François finished her briefing by both emphasising how important the job was, and when she went outside to her bike her brother came with her to see her off. They were beside the house, under the trees beyond which they could see the German gate guard on the Philips factory. She recognised Karl on duty. Occasionally he would glance at the people going in through the main cemetery entrance on the other side of the open space between them, or look over their way towards Pleinstraat. Hortense wondered what he would do if he knew that François Daman, a wanted man and Partisan intelligence and liaison officer, was briefing his sister to collect vital papers on the Resistance. The German soldiers with their bland faces seemed quite unaware of the strong currents of subversion running through Pleinstraat and the streets of Louvain beyond.

'It's vital you don't get caught,' François insisted as he watched his young sister check the air in the bicycle tyres.

'Don't worry, Brae,' she replied, smiling at him. 'I'll be all right.' One tyre needed pumping and she connected the pump. 'I've memorised all the contact details.'

François hesitated, looking down at Hortense, so pretty in her patterned dress with its little white collar, with her mass of blonde hair and slim shape, and thinking what the Gestapo might do to her if she was arrested. Not for the first time he regretted she was involved, but like all the other times, he knew there was nothing he could have done to stop her. Without his prompting, she had simply reacted to the situation she found herself in, to the state to which her country had been reduced by the German occupation, the arrests of people who seemed to her good men and women, to the miserable social conditions imposed by rationing and the war, to the damage done to her own family and home in 1940; and she had resisted. She had come out of her corner and fought in the only way she could.

'Well,' he said doubtfully, 'anyway, they'll think it's Christmas if they find those papers. There's everything about the Partisans in this whole sector. If you're picked up with them you'll be in real trouble.'

'It's OK, Brae,' she smiled at him, astride her bicycle and ready to go. 'It'll all be fine.'

'For God's sake be careful,' François urged. He watched her pedal off through the open square in front of the factory, her skirt flapping in the wind round her long legs. He saw the German soldiers at the gate stare for a moment as she passed them, before turning to each other and laughing at some private joke. It made him angry to see them, but he knew Hortense was no longer a little girl. She had chosen a way of life which would allow her no time to grow up if she was captured.

The journey across the low lying fields and through the little red-brick villages along the Dyle river valley to Waterloo took her four hours. She arrived in time for her meeting, checked the area thoroughly and was satisfied there was nothing amiss. The house she had to visit was quiet and there was no one about. She came back at the agreed time, pressed the bell, and when the lady opened the door, Hortense acted as though she had found the wrong house by mistake. She apologised, careful to use the exact phrases she had rehearsed with François and Gaston. The lady acted her part and then asked Hortense if she would mind posting something for her, to save her the walk? She handed Hortense a round parcel, like rolled up magazines, about fourteen inches long and four in diameter. Hortense noticed at once how heavy it was. She guessed it was solid for it certainly weighed several pounds. The lady seemed pleased to see Hortense go when they said goodbye to each other, and almost slammed the door in her haste.

Hortense left her bicycle where she had been told, uncertain whether she would ever see it again, and, tucking the dangerous parcel under her arm, walked to the station.

She bought her ticket to Louvain and noticed at once that there appeared to be an unusual number of people waiting for trains. She supposed that there was some hold up on the line. She hoped it was Allied bomb damage, but German troop and supply transports always took precedence over local traffic. The railway service had become very erratic since the war started and stations always seemed to be full of people waiting for trains. Karl had told her once that on a two weeks leave to his home town in southern Germany he had spent ten days sitting in stations and trains. He was not a bad sort but Hortense reflected that if those delays were due to the bombing by men like the Canadians Elmer Dungey and Art Bowlby she had no complaints. She wondered for a moment what had happened to Doug Arseneau and Willy Williston.

It was already well into the afternoon when her train pulled into the station, emitting huge clouds of stream and smelling strongly of coal and grease. The train was full. The first class carriages, occupied only by German officers, were full, the second class were reserved for and full of German other ranks, and the Belgians got in and out of the third class compartments, trying to find room. Hortense adjusted her hat, climbed aboard and found a corner seat near the communicating door of one carriage, clutching her parcel and trying to avoid having to speak to anyone.

Whistles blew on the platform and the train lurched forward. Hortense settled down, even relaxing a little, and prepared herself for a long journey. Noises at the other end of the carriage snapped her wide awake. The commotion came from beyond the communicating door into the carriage beyond, towards the end of the train, and she stood on tiptoe to see what was going on over the heads of the passengers near her. Geheimefeldpolizei! They were making a search of the train which was common enough, but why, she asked herself desperately, did it have to happen on this of all days? She looked out of the window to see if they were nearing a station where she could escape, but the old steam engine was travelling painfully slowly and the steady wisps of smoke passing the windows gave no indication of a change of tempo as it approached a halt. She was trapped on the train.

She could see the policemen checking everyone as they struggled along the centre aisle which was crammed with people. She looked at the people round her. She trusted no one and certainly did not want anyone to see her taking any particular interest in the search, but every few moments she glanced over as casually as she could to see how thorough the German GFP were being. To her

148

horror she saw them examine not only everyone's identity cards, but they were also checking all the suitcases and bags, shouting for passengers to say which cases on the racks belonged to them and then demanding that they be opened up. One thin-faced policeman seemed responsible for rooting around in the cases and he appeared to be taking his job seriously.

What if they asked her to open her parcel? Hortense felt weak at the thought. She looked again at the people around her, considering whether she could leave the parcel on a rack, or even the floor, and then recover it after the GFP had gone by. Blank faces stared vacantly back at her, eyes tired and cheeks pinched. Everywhere people had closed their faces against the stresses of the occupation. Food was short, social life almost negligible and no one could speak freely for fear of being overheard, reported or arrested by the Gestapo. Hortense decided that she dared not put the parcel down. The GFP would want to know who it belonged to and someone would certainly point to her. They were getting closer, and she noticed a sergeant beginning to look ahead at the people nearer her. She considered throwing the parcel out of the window, and as quickly rejected the idea. That would just as certainly draw attention to both her and the parcel.

There was no alternative. The second class carriages beyond her compartment were full of German soldiers, and making her mind up on the instant she moved quietly towards the communicating door hoping no one would notice. Without a backward glance, she walked into a carriage full of grey uniforms. The atmosphere was thick with tobacco smoke and the men were lounging on their seats talking, laughing, sleeping or playing cards. Their rifles and battle equipment lay strewn about all over the floor blocking the aisle, and their steel helmets filled the overhead racks.

'Hey! What's this? A woman!' a Gefreiter sitting near the door shouted, making Hortense jump.

She tried to ignore him, but his shout had alerted the entire carriage. All the men turned to enjoy this interesting and attractive diversion to the boredom of their long journey. Her progress through the carriage was accompanied by laughs, suggestive jokes and wolf whistles, and was hampered as much by her trying to step safely over the kit-bags without falling off balance with the swaying train, as by the soldiers' mock efforts to assist her.

She had no idea what she was going to do next, except that it would be impossible to stay with the soldiers. She had to go on to the next carriage, and the next, to the end of the train, if necessary, and just trust to her fate. Between carriages she paused to get her breath and to recover from the unusual experience of being the centre of attention of eighty bored soldiers.

Hortense knew very little about men. The invasion had caught her at the age of thirteen, when she was leaving childhood, and her upbringing had been strict, as it was in most Belgian families. Belgium was, and to some extent still is, a very Catholic country. Her social introduction to the opposite sex had been severely limited by the Occupation and had stopped altogether in 1943 when she chose the path of a courier in the Partisans. François had been especially dire with his repeated warnings to the other young men after the incident when she had risked everything to see Jan Sprengers. At the same time there was none of the sexual freedom of today during the war, and for a girl like Hortense ignorance of men and sex was not unusual. But it was a definite gap in her growing up which was to have some strange consequences later.

For the moment her considerable experience in the Resistance gave her, at sixteen, an appearance of self-control and sophistication. Ignorant of sex she may have been, but she knew more about life than most young people of her age; in short, in a rough school she had learned in her own way how to handle herself. She would need all her skills as she moved from the last second class carriage into the first class, reserved for the officers.

By evening François and Gaston were deeply worried. They had expected Hortense back in Louvain about four o'clock, and by five when there was still no sign of her Gaston had sent word to a Partisan ticket collector in the station at Louvain. He was to wait in the station and report anything he saw or heard of her at once.

Stephanie Daman fussed about in the kitchen making soup while François and Gaston sat at the table and talked. Jacques came home from the shoe factory in Brussels and immediately noticed something was wrong. He hardly needed telling that his daughter was missing, though François did not elaborate. His father worried enough about the family's involvement in the Resistance without having to know the extent of the trouble she might be in.

In the early evening a young man had brought Hortense's bicycle back. François questioned him closely, but he had simply picked up the bike as ordered and returned it. He had not seen or spoken to anyone.

They settled down to wait. Jacques went out of the house to the little bar across the street. The kitchen was too small for all of them, filled with so much tension and unspoken fears.

In the first class carriage Hortense looked down the narrow corridor and the long line of sliding doors, each of which led into a compartment full of German officers. She could hear them talking, their voices low, and the occasional rough laugh. This was the last carriage. There was nowhere else to go. Slowly she moved along the corridor, keeping a tight grip on the heavy round parcel. She pretended to look out of the windows, but her whole being concentrated on what might be happening behind her. Unlike the soldiers, the officers did not shout or whistle but none the less she knew they were watching her. Down the train the way she had come through the second class, she could hear the GFP arguing with the soldiers to tidy up their kit in the aisles.

'What d'you think you're doing?'

Hortense turned quickly. A senior German officer was staring at her. Even though he was sitting down Hortense could see he was tall. He had dark hair and was dressed immaculately in the uniform of an Obersturmbannführer of the Geheimefeldpolizei. She could not help staring at the distinctive green background to his collar patches and the letters GFP, strikingly visible on his shoulder straps. His was the very unit responsible for fighting the Resistance and which hated the Partisans above all.

'It's so full at the other end,' she said, adopting a pathetic expression of the little girl lost. 'I felt sick.'

'Wanted some fresh air, eh?' the officer asked, and smiled at his colleagues. 'Then come in here and you can sit with us.' He stood up and with exaggerated charm offered her a seat beside him.

Slightly bemused by the speed of events, Hortense walked into the compartment.

'Here, let me take that parcel,' said the officer gallantly and before Hortense could object he eased it from her tight grasp and lifted it on to the rack above the seats. She watched it go in a daze, fully conscious that it was now the sole key to her continued life and freedom, or arrest, torture and inevitable death.

'My word, that is a heavy thing to carry about. I'm not surprised you felt faint.'

Hortense nodded weakly and sat down.

'What's in it to make it so heavy?' The officer had clearly decided Hortense would make good company. He wanted to talk.

'Magazines,' she replied, off the top of her head.

'Really?'

For a terrible moment she thought he would insist she showed him what sort of magazines, and she nearly vomited. Instead he complimented her on her German and the conversation continued, rather one-sided. Hortense wondered if she should let herself go, and be sick, whether out of fear or as a diversion hardly seemed to matter. She would rather not have said anything at all, least of all discuss herself, but she was given no chance. The German Secret Field Policeman was interested to know where she was going.

'Louvain,' she replied, attempting a smile. She had no option but to tell the truth since when they came to ask for her ticket her destination would be revealed anyway.

'Remarkable,' exclaimed the Obersturmbannführer, and slapped his thigh. 'How extraordinarily lucky.' He looked round at his fellow officers and they smiled back dutifully. Hortense had lost her grip on the conversation but she fixed a half-smile which might serve any purpose. She did not expect the next remark. 'I'm going to Louvain as well,' the officer informed her. 'I'm posted to take over command of the Geheimefeldpolizei there.'

Before Hortense could take in the implications of this statement he continued to explain that there was a considerable amount of terrorism in the area of Louvain and that he had been sent to set up a counter-terrorist cell for a month or two to clear it all up. She should take great care not to get involved, he warned her.

'These Communist swine'll kill anyone,' he told her. 'Just you be careful.'

'I don't think they'll bother me, will they?' Hortense replied, looking as young as she could and wishing she had not brought the hat.

'I doubt it,' the officer replied. 'But I insist on taking you back home this evening. In my staff car.'

Before she could recover from this new shock, she heard sounds down the corridor which told her the search team were in the carriage and closing in. For a brief moment she considered ways of escape, all of them obviously fruitless. The Feldwebel of the GFP whom she had seen earlier appeared at their compartment door.

'Heil Hitler!' he shouted and flicked his arm up in the Nazi salute. All the officers responded in a guttural chorus, and to her own amazement she found herself automatically joining in, her arm raised. For an idiot second she imagined she had given herself away, but it was of course the most natural thing she could have done.

'ID,' snapped the Feldwebel, pointing rudely at Hortense. 'Where're you going?'

She braced herself for the inevitable discovery, for the Feldwebel to rip open the parcel in front of all the officers.

'This girl's with me,' the Obersturmbannführer said, allowing a harsh note of command into his voice.

'Just following orders, Herr Oberst,' the Feldwebel answered with care, and added. 'That your parcel up there?'

Again Hortense's stomach seemed to somersault in fright. Moving down the train and getting involved with the lion in his den had done no more than put off the moment of her exposure. She began to think of excuses.

'Never mind about all that,' the officer replied instead. This time the steel in his voice allowed no disobedience. 'Get out and leave us alone. The girl's with me.'

Hortense never really understood the tiny smile on the Feldwebel's face as he turned away. Had she known what he was thinking, she would not have cared. Her problems were decidedly not over, though a temporary respite had come from the least expected source.

The rest of the journey to Louvain passed in a daze. The Obersturmbannführer continued to talk and give her advice of one sort of another, mainly to do with military matters of no interest to her. Then she saw the familiar platform signs 'Louvain' sliding past the window, and before the train had stopped the German was on his feet and insisting that he drive her home. He straightened his uniform, took her parcel off the rack and led her by the arm off the train. She was not sure whether to be more worried about the parcel, which she could not see under his other arm, or how to get rid of him, or what people would think to see Hortense Daman being escorted by the new commandant of the Louvain section of the GFP.

When they walked through the ticket barrier, she saw a brief look of astonishment on the face of the man Gaston had briefed to watch out for her. The Obersturmbannführer never let go and walked her over to his staff car, a large black Mercedes waiting directly outside the entrance.

'Where can I drop you?' he asked as he held the door for her to get in. The idea of breaking loose and dashing away crossed her mind for a brief, mad moment as she looked round the familiar scene and up the Boulevard towards the area of Pleinstraat.

'Would you take me to Riddersstraat?' she said, naming a street on the opposite side of the town to Pleinstraat.

'Jawohl!'

On the way the officer asked if she liked the idea of meeting him again, over dinner perhaps? Hortense looked as young as she could again and said her mother would not approve. She might well have added Stephanie Daman would have been appalled, but the German seemed to understand. He even grinned wryly when Hortense asked him to drop her at the end of Riddersstraat, because the neighbours would talk if he were to leave her at the door.

'I understand, but don't worry. It'll all change when Belgium becomes part of the Greater German Reich. Your parcel,' he said as she got out. 'Don't forget that.'

After the sleek black car had pulled away she leaned against the wall and breathed slowly and deeply. She felt drained but enormously elated. Against the odds, she had made it.

Pulling herself together, she glanced up the street in case anyone had noticed the strange little scene, and started the long walk back across the centre of town. She avoided the Kommandantur and other places where the officer might have gone, and every time she saw a large black car she started, thinking it might be him again, bringing a fateful reversal of the good luck which had served her so well that day.

The gate guards at the Philips factory watched her walk across the little square between them and the Daman shop just before curfew. She went round the corner of the house and through the shop. Everyone was in the kitchen, alerted by the ticket collector who had run all the way from the station to tell them what he had seen. They had all congregated there, sick with worry, to know what was happening. There was a bedlam of greetings and then she was made to recount the whole story. When she had finished they made her go over all the details again. Her father and mother made no secret of their delight and relief.

The comic aspects of the affair were enjoyed enormously but, as ever, the more serious implications could not be ignored. François lectured her to be extra careful where she went in the near future and said she must cut down her work around town until this particular officer left. It was obvious that Hortense had made an impression on him and he would have no difficulty in recognising her. The Partisans he had been sent to wipe out had contacts in the Belgian gendarmerie, Marcel Van den Borght among others, who would let them know when he was posted out of Louvain.

For Hortense the most satisfying part of the day was handing the parcel of documents to François. She had achieved her mission. Quick thinking under great pressure and a remarkable presence of mind had seen her through. Luck too, that sparkling difference between drab achievement and real success, had not deserted her. Yet.

# 7

# Betrayal

'One of the great problems Liberalism faces is its desperate shortage of adherents who recognise the brutal reality of an illiberal world, and who know that it is not possible to preserve freedom and everything that goes with it unless the defenders are as hard, single-minded and, when it becomes necessary, ruthless as our enemies.'
Bernard Levin in *The Times*.

If Hortense was less active for the next few weeks, the Gestapo and the GFP were certainly not. The Obersturmbannführer she had met on the train, and officers of the Gestapo and the SD were determined to destroy the Partisans. Escape lines occupied much of the Germans' time, and were principally the concern of GFP Group 743-Luft which concentrated on finding out where pilots were secretly fed and housed. While the lines tried to keep their activities secret and wanted no contact with the enemy, the BAP's aim, on the contrary, was to take the fight directly against the German occupiers and their Belgian supporters.

Throughout 1943 the Partisans' activities in the Louvain area increased. Hortense was extremely busy bicycling round the town with orders and reports for Gaston. Every month from July to October the BAP carried out an average of twenty-three actions of one sort or another, sometimes several in one night. Railway installations were attacked, Post Offices robbed for money and ration stamps, and goods, especially petrol, were stolen. Belgians openly sympathising or actively collaborating with the Germans were often the targets: farmers had their crops burned before they could be harvested; informers were attacked and their houses set on fire; and members of the Belgian SS or Black Police were ambushed.

Inevitably with so much activity, the GFP were able to pick up information on the 'terrorists', a little at each incident, which was carefully documented and analysed. The Gestapo had had considerable experience investigating threats to Reich security in Belgium; after three years of chasing escape line networks and breaking other resistance groups like the Rote Kapelle, they pursued the task with a combination of Teutonic professionalism and brutal interrogation. Now, they directed their full efforts towards the Partisans, infuriated by the massive railway sabotage of 30 July and determined to stop the almost daily series of lesser incidents. The Partisans did their best to control their own security but the dossier on them in Vital Decosterstraat grew thicker by the week.

The threat to the Resistance was not so much the scene-of-crime evidence as from information supplied by people. This took many forms, from the eye-witness statements of a surprising number of Belgians to the deliberate denunciations by collaborators. The SS obtained more information from the Partisans themselves in statements and confessions extracted under torture.

Who can say how they would react under torture? Constant beatings were common but the SS was prepared to inflict worse, for example Max Gunter's electric shock treatment of Eugene Haesaerts's stomach wound in the Gestapo's house in Leopold I straat in Louvain; and the sufferings of Seymens and Nijsen in Breendonk where they were hoisted off their feet by a rope which went over a pulley and was tied to their hands behind their backs, and then beaten by Lieutenant Prauss and Major Schmitt. Most of these men and women refused to betray their friends and colleagues in the Underground, but some were unable to stand the pain. The more the arrests, the more statements were obtained and gradually the SS built up a picture of their enemy living in the community around them.

As soon as each Underground group was identified the Gestapo, SD and GFP set to work, and then it was only a matter of time. The Rote Kapelle spy network was set up on 6 March 1939 and broken by Lieutenant Harold Piepe on 27 November 1942. Also in Brussels the Comet escape line, begun after Andrée de Jongh's visit to Spain in August 1941, was badly shaken by the arrests of nearly all its original leaders in January and February 1943. The Pat O'Leary line set up by Ian Garrow soon after the Occupation was severely set back in March 1943 by the arrest of Albert Guerrisse. Baron Jean Greindl, leader of the Nemo line, whom François had helped from the early days, was arrested on 7 February 1943. He died in his cell in prison, ironically the victim of an Allied bombing raid on Brussels. All these organisations had lasted some two years and they were all covert. The Partisans in Louvain were aggressively overt and having become active at the end of 1942 they were entering a dangerous period.

François Daman had been involved with the escape lines from the start and when he joined the Partisans in October 1942, it is likely that he was already known to the GFP by his pseudonyms. By the autumn of the following year the GFP Group 743-Luft had identified his work in the escape lines, and the SS knew he was an intelligence and liaison officer for the Partisans. Worse, they had found out his real name and where his family lived. But by then his wife Elisa had left their house in Frederik Lintstraat and was living in the woods with her son Jacques so that the SS could not arrest her and bring pressure on her husband.

The Gestapo realised François could have provided a mass of information: cheated of his wife and son they decided to watch the area of Pleinstraat. It was not easy for their plain clothes men to mount close surveillance on the community living under the huge Philips factory. The people in the terraced streets of Pleinstraat and Parkstraat were close-knit and knew each other well. They lived side by side, the women washed down their doorsteps and the little piece of pavement outside their houses every day, and not much happened which escaped comment. Strangers were immediately spotted, and the Gestapo in their distinctive suits and heavy trench coats could not lurk too near to the Damans' house without fear of their operation being compromised. In surveillance jargon, there is no doubt that for the SS Pleinstraat was a 'hostile environment'.

In assessing the criteria for the operation to catch François Daman, the SS and GFP would have gone through the same arguments currently used by modern security forces. Always, moving in close to obtain the necessary information risks compromising the surveillance agents and has to be set against the danger of alerting the subject who is being watched. At the time, however, compromise would not necessarily mean the whole operation was blown. Gestapo and SD agents were a common enough sight during the Occupation, and if they were noticed by Partisans they might be taken for another group of German security men employed on another task.

The SS would have considered the approaches to Pleinstraat: from the town side past the Philips factory by Parkpoort and across the Boulevard under the trees; from the cemetery and the railway lines beyond; and from the narrow streets at the end, on the way into town through Tiensepoort. The closer the net of surveillance, the less chance of missing their subject but the greater the risk of compromising the operation.

# Betrayal

The Germans in the war had none of the sophisticated equipment used by modern security forces, such as long range microphones, video cameras linked to laser trigger devices or fitted with infra-red and image-intensifying night vision aids, or covert radios which can be concealed on an individual yet keep him in touch with his base and with all the other agents 'on the ground'. Nor, as a rule, did the Gestapo surveillance agents attempt to disguise themselves as members of the community as British government agents do against the IRA in Northern Ireland with such success. Instead they employed Belgian collaborators, men and women, to infiltrate suspect groups.

So the Germans decided to stand off the immediate area of Pleinstraat, and watch the entrances, from the Boulevard round the walls, from Parkpoort and Tiensepoort. They decided to watch François's parents, a classic option for police everywhere, and hoped to arrest him when he came to visit them. Their problem was that, although they knew François by name, they did not know what he looked like.

Shortly after this operation was mounted, Hortense left the shop in the afternoon with two friends, her cousin Pierre van Goitsenhoeven and Jean Maes, a baker. Both were Partisans and Maes was a battalion commander. Hortense had been busy on courier work earlier in the day, but they were not on Partisan business. To all intents and purposes they were three ordinary citizens riding together on bicycles. As they crossed the Boulevard the Germans pounced. Acting on signals from plain clothes men posted round the area on foot, several black saloon cars which had been waiting in side streets suddenly raced out of Frederik Lintstraat and skidded to a halt in front of them, blocking their escape. Men in the Gestapo and GFP leaped out with MP40 machine-pistols and pulled them off their bikes. They grabbed Hortense and shoved her in a car, wedged tight between two grimlooking GFP in coats and felt hats. With the shock of men shouting, in the flurry of arms, of pistols and machine-guns, and hands hitting her, she only got a brief glimpse of van Goitsenhoeven and Maes being beaten up as they too were pushed into another car behind hers. Without wasting a moment, the Germans drove at speed through the town to the Gestapo offices in the large private house they had commandeered half-way down Stationstraat.

There was hardly time for Hortense to wonder where she had gone wrong, or who had denounced them, before she was searched thoroughly and all her possessions taken from her with her identity card. She was taken straight away to the first floor for interrogation. Two Belgian SS, Lambert Janssens and van Avondt, shoved her into a large airy room and ordered her to sit on a chair. Max Gunter was sitting at a large desk waiting for her.

SS Stafleider Max Gunter, also known as Hamburger Max and van Damme, was a forty-eight-year-old Belgian, born Emiel van Thielen in Antwerp on 2 March 1895. After the 1914–18 war he was accused of collaboration with the Germans and sentenced to death in absentia since he had already fled to Germany where he took German nationality. After the invasion he reappeared in Belgium in September 1940 and assisted the SD by successfully running a series of Belgian collaborators, agents called 'V-Leute', whom he infiltrated into various Resistance groups. By 1943 he was working for the supreme SS officer in Belgium, SS Brigadeführer Richard Jungclaus, a personal appointee of Himmler's. He had considerable power and influence in the SD for which he pursued his particular interest of suppressing Communist groups like the Partisans. He was ruthless and applied torture without compunction, moving throughout the area of von Falkenhausen's military jurisdiction in Northern France and Belgium. He was of medium build with an exceptionally hard face and a prominent, pointed upper lip.

'Hortense Daman?' he asked, checking some papers in front of him.

'Yes,' Hortense replied willingly. Since they had not been arrested during some action for the Partisans she wondered desperately what line of questioning he would take. There was nothing illegal about what they had been doing at the time and she proposed to adopt an attitude of hurt innocence. She was quite unprepared for what followed.

'What were you doing with your brother?'

'Who?' Hortense asked, genuinely puzzled by the question.

'Your brother,' Gunter shouted abruptly. 'The man we arrested with you, the tall bastard.'

All of a sudden she understood. 'He's not my brother,' she said at once, relieved not to have to invent a story that would be all the weaker made up on the spur of the moment.

'He's my cousin.'

'Liar!' a voice screamed in her ear and she staggered under a shocking blow on the side of her head which knocked her to the floor. She had not noticed another SS officer standing behind the door. Thirty-two-year-old SS Sturmbannleiter Robert Verbelen was the SS ideal, tall with a thin face and pinched nose. Like Gunter he was Belgian and had been born at Herent near Louvain. He had escaped military service, did not fight in the Belgian army in May 1940 and was a fanatical supporter of Hitler's 'New Order'. He had no scruples about striking a young girl. All the people in the room were Belgian. The men, all volunteers in the Belgian SS, were fanatical Nazis while the girl they were beating up wanted Belgium for the Belgians.

'We know he's your brother,' Verbelen shouted as Hortense tried to recover her senses and compose herself. Instinctively she realised the interrogation was quickly getting out of control. With her head ringing from the blow, she picked herself up and sat down on the chair again.

'He's not my brother,' she said quietly. 'He's my cousin Pierre van Goitsenhoeven.'

'Liar,' Verbelen shouted again.

To her intense relief Hortense realised she could tell the simple truth. There was nothing to hide. No unprepared alibi was needed, which could be swiftly torn apart by cross-examination of van Goitsenhoeven and Maes. It was plain the Germans had made a mistake, but equally obvious that Gunter and Verbelen needed to be convinced. The Germans were well aware that men and women on the run used false identity cards. In fact Partisans like Pierre and Jean Maes, still living apparently normal lives around the town, used their own names and addresses at all times except when they were on operations. Then they used a different identity to protect their families and friends if they were caught. Only men like François and Louis van Brussel, constantly on the run, used code names and false identities all the time. Since they had not been working for the Partisans, Pierre and Jean should not have been carrying their false identity cards. Gunter's next words shattered the easy picture she had been building up in her mind.

'Van Goitsenhoeven, you say? That name doesn't appear on his identity card. No name like that on the list. He's calling himself something quite different, it seems. If he's not your brother, who is he?'

Pierre had forgotten to change his identity cards and was carrying his false card, actually one stolen from a Post Office filled out with a false name.

Seeing no other course but to tell the truth, Hortense stuck to her story, wondering all the time what Pierre and Jean were saying.

Gunter and Verbelen shouted and bullied Hortense for an hour but she stuck to her story. Eventually Gunter lost patience and ordered her to be taken downstairs.

1 Hortense's parents, Jacques and Stephanie Daman,
February 1946.

2 The corner grocery shop in Louvain which Hortense
helped her mother to run. Seen here from the
cemetery gates.

3 Hortense in 1941.

4 The Louvain Athletic Club which many of the Partisans joined, including Louis van Brussel (standing extreme left), and Jan Sprengers (standing extreme right).

5 Hortense in early 1943.

6  Bob Williston (left) and Douglas Arseneau wearing the
suits that Stephanie Daman had made up for them.

7  'Gaston' (left) and François Daman standing at the
back of the Storckels' house in Pleinstraat in 1943.

8 Hortense in Leopold's amusement park, Louvain, mid-1943. She was on her way to a clandestine rendezvous when she was snapped by a roving photographer. Francois obtained the film from him later.

9 The Gestapo 'private' house on Leopold I straat where Hortense was interrogated and tortured.

10 A group of surviving prisoners in St Margaret, Sweden, after being brought out of Ravensbrück by the Red Cross: Doctor Marie-Claude (centre with prominent white shirt); Hortense (on Marie-Claude's right); Yvonne Desoignes (second on Marie-Claude's left, same row); Stephanie (extreme right of sitting row); Claire Van den Boom who was a founder member of the Ravensbrück Association in Belgium (standing mid-left, in front of door frame, with dark dress and white hair).

11 François and Jacques Damans' reunion in Buchenwald.

12 Celebrations in Pleinstraat after the return of Hortense
and Stephanie from Sweden. (Left to right: Stephanie,
Bertha, Jacques, Hortense, Julia and little Michel Berges).

13 Syd and Hortense on their wedding day, 23 February
1946.

14 Hortense with the Belgian Military Attaché, Captain Hector Stradiot, and Air Chief Marshal Sir Michael Knight, KCB, AFC, BA, D.Litt, on the occasion of being elected an Honorary Member of the Aircrew Association, 26 April 1986.

15 Hortense with her grand-daughter Stephanie Nicole Phillips outside the housing complex which was named in her honour by the Newcastle-under-Lyme Borough Council.

Janssens and van Avondt pushed her roughly out of the room and past Pierre van Goitsenhoeven who had been waiting outside in the hall. A tiny flicker of his eyebrows, imperceptible to the SS, told her he had heard the important parts of her interrogation.

She was taken to a bare office in the basement, furnished only with a table and a few chairs. An elderly German soldier was sitting on one of the chairs working through a large number of identity cards piled up along the table in front of him. He was filling out a report.

He ordered Hortense to sit down on the other side of the room. When Janssens and van Avondt left he talked conversationally for a moment, asking who she was and telling her he had served in the Great War. Then he turned back to work stolidly through his report. Rubbing her head, which ached terribly from Verbelen's beating, Hortense could not help staring at the ID cards as he moved them from a stack on one side of his desk to the centre, where he laboriously recorded all the details inside, and then to a finished pile on the other side. One of those cards was Pierre's false identity. It was the key to their predicament. If it could be made to vanish Pierre could say he had forgotten his identity card at home and stick to the truth; that he was Pierre van Goitsenhoeven and a cousin of Hortense Daman. However if the false identity card were recorded he would face an altogether tougher explanation and there would be sufficient grounds for the SS to continue his interrogation.

It was quiet in the room apart from the scratching of her German guard's pen. Hortense guessed he might not be the same as the younger SS officers who would have hated her speaking without being spoken to first, and unable to take her eyes off the ID cards, she asked him what he was doing.

'All these are the identity cards of the people who've been picked up today. I expect yours is here. They all come to me first. My duty is to record them, make a report and pass a copy upstairs to the officers.'

At once Hortense wondered whether the soldier had already processed the incriminating card, whether she could take it first, and then, a moment after, what she would do with it if she got it. The German seemed fixed on completing his task and was not inclined to further talk. However after more than an hour of slowly and meticulously processing the cards, he suddenly sat back and yawned. Shaking his writing hand, he looked at the Belgian girl, commented that she appeared tired and then asked if she would like some soup. He was tired of sitting at his desk and wanted a break from his paperwork.

She thanked him very much. It was by now late in the evening and Hortense was genuinely hungry. As soon as he left the room, she stood up, listening carefully to his footsteps receding up the passage. She could hear him moving about in another room, but there was no time to waste. She tiptoed across to the table and began sifting through the pile of cards. Belgian identity cards were printed on stiff cardboard which opened out to show a photograph inside and which folded along two lines, like a triptych, one flap inside the other. Folded, the card could be slipped in the pocket of a wallet. Desperately she flicked through the stack on the desk. There were so many. She listened for sounds outside the office in case the German came marching back down the corridor.

To her immense relief, she found Pierre's false ID card on the side which had not been sorted. Quickly she turned to double-check the report which the Great War veteran had been filling out. She ran her finger down the list. The name was not there. If the false name did not appear on the German report, Pierre had a chance. Silently, she crept back to her chair and sat down, clutching the card. Feeling slightly foolish, she could think of nowhere else to hide it for the moment except in her brassière.

The soup was disgusting. Hungry though she was, the

tension of the moment made it hard to swallow the thick gruel. Worse, the only way she could think of getting rid of the card was to eat it. Taking advantage of the German soldier's concentration on his own soup, which he evidently enjoyed, she managed to reach inside her dress, tear off a little piece of cardboard, and bit by bit slip it into the spoonfuls of soup. Some bits she dared to sink under the surface where they became sodden. Dunking made the card easier to swallow but no more palatable.

Having thoroughly eliminated the problem of the false identity card, she could do nothing but wait, wondering what the SS would decide. She knew well enough that if they wanted someone they would have no scruples about arresting other members of the family as hostages. Charges, almost an academic point, could easily be made to 'stick'. The night dragged on and she fell asleep on her chair. Finally at four o'clock in the morning she was woken up. Belgian gendarmes had been called by the SS, and they took her home to Pleinstraat. She had been released.

The SS had found that all three stuck to the same story under interrogation and so they had mounted search operations on the houses of van Goitsenhoeven and Maes. Evidence, in family photographs and letters, had shown that Pierre was indeed Hortense Daman's cousin and the two men were released later the same day. The SS seemed to accept that Pierre had left his ID card at home and that no one had noticed in the mêlée of the arrest.

François questioned his sister closely about the incident, to try to assess what the SS knew about him. She told him everything, and he laughed at the 'cardboard' soup. She had done well considering it was her first interrogation and he reminded her of an incident not many weeks before, in September. She and several young men in the Louvain Partisans had been enjoying the late autumn sun in the garden of a house on the other side of Pleinstraat, opposite the Damans. The boys, led by

Guillaume Vanderstappen, Jommeke, who had helped her escape with the explosives on her bicycle, had teased her about how she would behave if the Germans arrested her. Hortense had a good sense of humour but they chose the wrong day and the wrong subject. She was tired after spending hours cycling in the heat with messages for Gaston. She was not in the mood for fun and games when they grabbed her and started a mock Gestapo interrogation. All in good spirits someone pulled some leeks growing in the vegetable patch and rubbed them in her face.

'You'd have to give in if they attacked you with leeks,' they shouted, laughing.

Hortense completely lost her temper, furious that they could make light of so serious a subject. She grabbed the two holding her, smacked their heads together and lashed out at Jommeke, catching him a real shiner in the eye. The boys all backed off, battered and very shamefaced. Jommeke's embarrassment was made worse by having to explain to Louis van Brussel that he had been thumped by Hortense and had not been risking arrest fighting Nazi sympathisers in the streets. François, who had taught her the rudiments of self-defence, had laughed too, but not much as he was impressed by her reaction and careful not to draw his sister's rage. He was in no doubt about her dedication and determination, but he had wondered then how she would react under interrogation.

In the event, Hortense's swift decisions and action had saved them all from difficult explanations. She was seventeen, still very young, but now she was more experienced than her brother in coping with interrogations. François care for his own security had so far kept him out of the hands of the Gestapo. There was another aspect of the situation about which he said nothing but which must have occupied his mind a great deal. At least he could move from one place to the next if he thought the heat was on. His family, on the other hand, could not. The whole essence of their involvement, principally that of his mother Stephanie as a supplier of food and his sister Hortense as a courier, was their cover as bona fide shopkeepers trying to run a business in the difficult conditions of the time. They could not run away. The incident had made it clear that the SS knew a great deal about François Daman. How much did they know about his mother and sister? The knowledge that the depth and scope of his family's involvement in the Resistance was his own doing must have kept him awake at night.

Photographs of him at this time show he was thin to the point of emaciation, his face sharp as a knife, tight with inner turmoil. His burden was to grow infinitely greater.

There was another problem, more pressing. How did the SS find out about François Daman? Was this intelligence the result of meticulous detective work, dragged reluctantly from the mouths of wretched men and women suffering sticky interrogations, or did it come voluntarily, perhaps even from someone within the Resistance who was a collaborator? François had not forgotten how the two airmen Arseneau and Williston had been betrayed and wondered just how far down the line the Group 743-Luft, the Gestapo and the SD had penetrated. There were other cases, and it was more than possible that the Germans had closed in on the Damans because of information freely given.

It is not hard to see that of the two sorts of collaborators the snake in the grass, rather than the overt bully like Verbelen, was the more dangerous. The damage done by the likes of Gunter, Verbelen, Janssens and van Avondt was more direct, but at least the Resistance could see the danger, whereas the collaborators who were infiltrated into the Partisans and working secretly as 'V-Leute' agents for Gunter were very hard to detect. Both sorts of collaborators were a threat to the Resistance but the 'source', 'mole' or 'grass' was an unseen menace who could cause fatal damage.

It was always difficult to identify a collaborator and as hard to confirm his guilt in the restricting circumstances of the Occupation. François knew of the dangers after the arrest of Commandant Lambert in February 1942 but some Louvain Partisans only realised how much damage collaborators could do after the arrest of Seymens and Nijsen in the autumn. It may surprise us now, with the benefit of hindsight, that the Resistance took so long to grasp that there were those who would betray them to the Germans. They were not simple-minded, but being themselves dedicated and brave they assumed, with good reason, the same commitment in everyone else attached to the cause. Sadly they were too often let down. Traitors sometimes escaped suspicion for months while insidiously passing information to the SS and denouncing their fellow countrymen.

A celebrated case linked to the Belgian escape lines illustrates how long it took to identify the traitor and how difficult it was to do anything about it. It also gives the lie to those blind enough to think that betrayal was (or is) not an English problem. Sergeant Harold Cole was among those of the British Expeditionary Force who were left behind in France, not because he was bravely fighting a rearguard action, but because he was in gaol at the time for stealing the Sergeants' Mess funds. He was a man of charm, used a variety of pseudonyms, and found it easy to spin a web of lies to cover himself from Brussels to Marseilles. Moving around occupied Europe became more difficult after the chaotic early days of 1940, and communications were not easy. Letters and the telephone were always at risk of interception by the Gestapo. Personal contact was the only sure way to discuss suspicions as serious as collaboration. Cole helped set up escape lines in Belgium and Northern France for escaping BEF soldiers and, later, airmen. He also helped link these collections of evading people with lines to Marseilles which were controlled by Ian

Garrow and Albert Guerrisse. It is a measure of the
confusion of reports and suspicions which were so hard
to correlate that no one can say when Cole became an
agent for the Gestapo. He started bringing servicemen
down the lines to Marseilles in February 1941. Guerrisse
smelt a rat in July, but it was not until nine months later
in October that Garrow became convinced Harold Cole
was a traitor.

Having decided Cole was working for the Gestapo,
it is interesting to see what the escape line, which
was controlled by the British, did about him. Garrow,
supported by MI9 in London, and 'approved of' by MI6,
decided Cole had to be killed and that he would take
the consequences on his own head at a court martial if
necessary. He believed the losses of airmen and the arrest
of helpers had to be stopped at once. There was no time to
wait for officers in British Military Intelligence in London
to make up their minds. Untold damage could be done by
a traitor in a matter of a day, let alone the weeks it might
take to get an answer back from London to Marseilles.
There was no law in the occupied countries to which he
could appeal; the writ there was firmly under control of
the Nazis. He therefore decided to take matters into his
own hands, literally, to murder Cole and drop his body in
the port. Unfortunately Garrow was arrested in October
1941 before he could tell Guerrisse of his plan. Guerrisse
acted to cut through the blanket of bad communications,
which Cole had depended on to conceal his treachery,
by bringing François Duprez and Roland Lepers from
Northern France to testify against Cole in Marseilles. The
traitor was revealed at a stormy meeting in an apartment
but his captors were unsure what to do next. During
the prevarication, Cole climbed through the window of
a bathroom where he had been locked up and leaped
across the well of the apartment block to escape. Lack of
determination at the very moment when the traitor was
at their mercy had allowed Cole this slender opportunity

to get away. Harold Cole took it and continued till the end of the war to help the Gestapo, betraying his own country and dozens of French and Belgian men and women, many of whom were executed and never came home from concentration camps after the end of the war.

The reaction of the Partisans was precisely the same as that of Ian Garrow, but there was no hesitation in their retribution. Their problem was finding the evidence to be certain of the collaboration, often begun for no better reasons than jealousy, personal dislike or the hatred stirred up by vicious local vendattas. There was no higher authority to which the Partisans could appeal for judgment. By the end of 1943 the SS in Belgium had even dispensed with the pretence of putting people before the Belgian civil courts. Saboteurs and terrorists had no recourse to the measured benefits of a democratic system of justice. Under the crushing heel of the totalitarian Nazi state, dominated by Himmler's SS, they received summary treatment, brutal interrogations, torture, imprisonment, and transportation to concentration camps. Breendonk in Belgium, Vught in Holland, Ravensbrück in Germany for women, Buchenwald and hundreds of others were filled with victims. To many execution was a release.

The harsh treatment drew a savage reaction against collaborators. An entire family in Louvain was attacked one night and shot. All of them, including the children, had been helping the Germans. The father and mother secretly reported people they had heard expressing anti-German views and encouraged the children, who brought back stories from school about other classmates and their parents. After several people had been arrested as a result the Partisans decided to act. The whole family died except a daughter, who was severly injured with a bad head wound and left for dead. Luckily for her she recovered and survives. Reading this in the comfort of an armchair, the story may sound shocking, in particular the killing of children, but so were Himmler's concentration camps, his Nacht und Nebel, set up to absorb countless thousands of men and women who dared to raise their standards against the swastika in their own country.

The SD often took trouble to protect its valuable sources of information. Haesaerts, Omloop and Sprengers had fallen foul of a rapid German response during an attack on a collaborator. Especially valuable agents were commonly protected by the SS with a twenty-four hour armed guard. Sometimes, if the threat to the BAP was particularly pressing, Partisans were detailed to watch the collaborator and find out when he could be most easily attacked.

Jakobs was a particularly dangerous Belgian collaborator who was often guarded by the SS. He was a Police Commissar of Louvain and a member of the SD whose value to the SS was his intimate knowledge of the area. He had given his full support to the Germans, and the Partisans had been trying to get at him for several months. In the autumn of 1943 he had found out that someone was putting flowers on the grave of Georges Omloop. The SS had buried Omloop in secret in the cemetery in the same area as the British pilot had been found, against the wall furthest from the Damans' shop and Pleinstraat. The superintendent of the cemetery had told Hortense's mother, and she had been putting flowers on the grave on most Sundays. She slipped them quickly out of her basket as she made her rounds of clients' family tombstones.

Jakobs had been seen going into the cemetery and word was passed to Gaston and François. Stephanie confirmed this story when she was selling flowers one Sunday in October. She followed him into the cemetery. He hung around pretending he was interested in a nearby grave from which he had a good view of the place where Omloop was buried. It seemed he wanted to see who came with the flowers, and, as he was a man who knew most of the local people well, he would be able to recognise the visitor who could then be picked up by the SS later. The BAP decided this was the opportunity to kill him.

They did their best to check the evidence of collaboration, cross-checking witnesses' statements, building up a dossier on the suspect's activities and using their own sources within the police, from gendarmes like Marcel Van den Borght and Walter Philips. Recent research has indicated that in the Jakobs case the Partisans had support from a man who represented the nearest thing to a true Belgian court. This was Dr van Oorlé who had been Procureur du Roi, had lived in Louvain, was a member of the Resistance and had been in touch with the Belgian government-in-exile and with the pre-war intelligence community. The charges against Jakobs, which were considerable, were sent to the government-in-exile in London and the message came back authorising whatever action was considered necessary to protect the Resistance.

These tasks were not popular with the Partisans. The young men were prepared to give their lives fighting the Occupation but most found it hard to face the difference between the heat of a fire-fight with German soldiers, the SD or the GFP, and a quasi-judicial killing. Even trained soldiers might have disagreed with such assassinations, but the men and women in the Resistance had no such formal thinking to fall back on.

Georges, another Partisan, was asked if he would do the job and he agreed. He was one of the most experienced Partisans in the Louvain corps. After talking it over with François, he asked Hortense to help him.

The plan was extremely simple. All Saints and All Souls day, 1 November, was coming up when it was traditional for relatives to visit the cemetery and put flowers on their families' graves. Georges would wait near Omloop's grave, shoot Jakobs and jump over the cemetery wall. Hortense would be waiting with their bicycles. They would then make their getaways in separate directions.

The day dawned fine. Georges came to the Damans' house on his bicycle and went through the final arrangements in the kitchen with Hortense. Then they parted and he walked into the cemetery through the entrance, which was in full view of the Philips gate guards, along with others, mostly families, going to pay their respects. In his pocket he clutched his favourite side-arm, the Belgian 9mm semi-automatic. This pistol is very well made, operates reliably and holds a magazine of thirteen rounds which gives a considerable edge over those armed only with six-shot revolvers.

They had plenty of time. Georges wanted to be in the cemetery near the grave early, for fear of missing his victim, and Hortense had a long walk to get in position as his back-up round the other side of the cemetery. After watching him disappear through the tall gates, she left the house too, pushing their two bicycles. She made her way all round the Philips factory, past the Parkpoort, down the hill behind the factory, and then back up along the footpath above the railway line until she was walking under the back wall of the cemetery. At this point the wall is very high, nearly nine feet over the path and runs for several hundred metres unbroken between one corner of the Philips factory and the houses at the end of Bierbeekstraat, which runs off the bottom of Pleinstraat. Georges and Hortense had decided that she should go the long way round in case someone on the shorter route noticed her with two bikes and then, seeing her again with only one after the attack, put the two facts together and guessed what she had been doing.

When Hortense reached the mid point of the wall she stopped and leaned the bikes against the wall. Pushing the two heavy bikes round the factory had not been easy.

She had had no time to think about what she was doing, but now she had arrived at the spot behind the cemetery questions began to flood through her mind.

Was she in the right place? She tried to remember where Georges had said she must wait for him, but the wall stretched uniformly in both directions with very little to say exactly where she was in relation to the point Georges had chosen on the other side. She stood on tiptoe to see over the top of the wall, and convinced herself she could recognise the top of a tree. She knew the cemetery so well· from the inside, from helping her mother lay flowers on so many graves over the years. She wondered what Georges was doing. Was he still waiting, or had be been compromised and had to leave quickly? She could just hear the occasional murmur of conversation on the inside as groups passed along the paths close to the wall. Nothing seemed to have happened yet.

Neither of them knew when Jakobs would choose to come and watch Omloop's grave, or even if he would bother that day. The tension of the wait built up for both of them. On the inside Georges had to wait and at the same time avoid the suspicion of the people who passed him. Sometimes he pretended he was seeing a particular grave, at others, he appeared to be simply enjoying the sunny afternoon; but all the time he had to keep within sight of Omloop's grave and the one Stephanie thought Jakobs would pretend to visit.

On the outside, Hortense had no one to fool. The path remained deserted, but she worried that someone she knew might come along and want to stop and talk. It was bound to happen just as Georges started shooting and they would be caught red-handed, recognised and in mortal danger of denunciation. The minutes passed. Suddenly Hortense saw a woman approaching her from Bierbeekstraat, moving slowly along the rough path between the cemetery wall and the railway embankment.

Hortense bent over her bicycle so her face could not be seen and made as if to blow up the back tyre. She silently urged the woman to walk faster, to go by and disappear before anything happened on the other side of the wall.

'Good afternoon,' Hortense muttered at the woman's standard greeting, greatly relieved to see she was a stranger. The woman passed.

Hortense settled down to wait again, carefully watching the fields on the other side of the railway cutting in case anyone was out for a walk, or for German patrols taking a short cut back into Louvain along the path which circuited the old abbey, whose spire she could see beyond the fields, to cross the railway on the little footbridge at the back of the Philips factory.

Abruptly the calm peace of the afternoon was shattered by an explosion of shooting, coming it seemed to Hortense from right above her on the other side of the wall. The first volley of shots was followed by a moment of silence. Then another two shots rang out and at the same time she was disgusted to hear people shouting and screaming further inside the cemetery.

'He's there! He's running over to the wall. He's trying to escape.'

Hortense was furious that these people, her fellow Belgians, were doing their best to give Georges away to the Germans.

But where was he? It seemed to Hortense that he was taking a very long time to get over the wall. In the suddenness of the attack, in the frustration of waiting to play her part, each second seemed to last an age. Had he been caught?

Hidden behind some trees, Georges had spotted Jakobs crossing the cemetery, alone. He had gripped the pistol in his pocket and eased off the safety catch of his pistol with his thumb. He watch Jakobs walk past Omloop's grave and surreptitiously check to see if there were fresh flowers. He looked past Jakobs and saw he was not being followed by SS bodyguards and then casually walked out of cover along the path towards his target as though enjoying the afternoon air, until they were only a few yards apart. Jakobs was of medium build with heavy jowls and thick black eyebrows. There was no doubt about his identity. Georges pulled out the pistol and opened fire in one smooth movement, giving his victim no more chance than Jakobs had given the victims of his denunciations in the past. The man's natural suspicion had alerted him at the last moment, too late to avoid the fusillade of bullets, but some had gone wild. Georges was oblivious to everything except the need to complete his task. He was quite unaware in those few seconds that nothing else had changed in the cemetery. In a strange suspension of time, no one moved as Georges stood over the badly wounded body of Jakobs who was attempting to crawl away, and finished him off with two carefully aimed shots. Then he looked up and started to run. At once, people started to shout and some began to chase him. Others ran for help towards the cemetery gates. In the cemetery offices the superintendent heard the shots and lifted the telephone. Regardless of his sympathies, he had to report the incident or he would be in trouble.

Georges sprinted towards the cemetery wall and jumped on to a large tomb he had spotted during his earlier reconnaissance of the site. Without a moment's hesitation he flung himself over the wall, dropped nine feet to the path below and sprawled on the ground with the force of his landing. He looked up to see Hortense staring at him.

She never forgot the wild look in his eyes, mad, fierce and burning with the heat of action. He hardly seemed to recognise her. He grabbed his bicycle, started shoving it down the path and leaped aboard when already several yards away and running fast.

For a moment she watched him go, crossing the little footbridge over the railway and growing small in the fields towards the abbey. Then the commotion inside the cemetery galvanised her and she followed his example, pedalling furiously in the opposite direction, up the path beside the wall to Bierbeekstraat. Her legs began to shake with the effort as she tried to get away before someone thought of looking over the wall to see where the assassin had gone.

When she finally turned out of sight at the corner of Bierbeekstraat she was exhausted and had to stop. She got off the bike and stood trying to control her breathing, walking a bit to make her legs work properly. To her horror an acquaintance came out of a house across the street. At once Hortense seized her pump and began to fiddle with the back tyre as though she was checking for a flat.

'Hallo, Hortenseke,' she said. 'Did you hear those shots a moment ago?'

'No?' Hortense felt the woman's curiosity burning into the back of her neck.

'Yes, just now! I think one of those blackshirts has been shot.'

'Oh? I didn't hear anything. I've just come over from my aunty's,' Hortense explained. She was sure the woman knew her aunty lived in Tiense Steenweg, not far from Professor de Vleeschauwer's house.

'I see. Well, you'll catch all the fuss by the cemetry gates when you get home,' the woman replied, as Hortense declared her tyre all right and stood up again.

Hortense biked home more slowly. As she cycled up Pleinstraat she saw several GFP trucks and a black Citroën drive at speed across the top of the street towards the cemetery gates. By the time she reached the house the square was full of people. German soldiers had closed the gates, refusing to let anyone in. She could see Belgians who had been inside when the shooting took place being questioned by plain clothes SD. Typically the SD had separated them into two worried-looking groups, the men on one side of the gates and the women and children on the other. One by one they were hustled out after interrogation and identity checks.

'Is Georges all right?' Stephanie whispered as Hortense came into the house. She watched her daughter slump down in a chair in the small kitchen.

Hortense nodded and said, 'Yes, Mama. He got away.'

Stephanie Daman quietly brought some ersatz coffee to her daughter and said no more. The tension flooding through Hortense was blatantly clear to her mother who knew precisely what she had been doing.

One can hardly begin to understand what Stephanie Daman had felt as she watched her daughter push those two bicycles away earlier that afternoon; as she stood at her flower stall and watched Jakobs walk into the cemetery; when she heard the shots ring out from the far side of the cemetery; and while she fussed about the shop during the long wait until Hortense reappeared from the other end of Pleinstraat. But this was one day of a lifetime of worry in which she and her husband so brilliantly concealed their fear of the future behind a solid wall of support for their daughter and son.

Hortense was absorbed thinking about Georges, wondering if he had managed to get right away. She glanced up. Her mother was looking out of the window at the scene by the cemetery gates. An ambulance had arrived. Both women knew the Germans had reacted very fast. Clearly they had been prepared for an incident in the cemetery. They had been waiting not far away to arrest the person Jakobs intended to catch bringing flowers to Omloop's grave. The two women were cheered by the thought that the SS had arrived to a quite different outcome.

The Partisans counted the attack in the cemetery a success. One more person who supported Hitler's regime had been eliminated and could no longer threaten the lives of those in the Resistance. Betrayal, denunciation, collaborators and Belgians recruited into the SS were their constant threat.

Throughout the Occupation, the Belgian Army of Partisans attacked 1392 collaborators, killing 1137 of them (compared with 1017 German soldiers killed and 962 wounded). This number of attacks on traitors, high as it may seem, did little more than dent the problem. There were, it seems, an endless number of people prepared to assist the invaders for a wide variety of reasons. Over 100,000 people were accused after the liberation of Belgium in September 1944. Special courts were set up to try collaborators and 87,000 were brought to trial. Of these 10,000 were acquitted. Sentences of death were passed on 4170 but only 230 were executed: 3193 of these death sentences were for military collaboration. These statistics do not compare with the unofficial 'purge' or private vendettas which took place in France after the liberation, when more than 10,000 were summarily executed (the official figure; in fact as many as 100,000 may have died). The huge numbers involved give some idea of the extent of the danger facing the Resistance.

As always after a successful BAP attack, the Germans responded quickly, arresting suspects on the slenderest of evidence. By the end of 1943 only the merest suspicion of complicity was sufficient to be sent to prison or deported to a camp in Germany. German patience was exhausted. Himmler's efforts to replace von Falkenhausen's military government with a civil regime controlled by the SS had been unsuccessful, but, ironically, the increasing efforts of the Partisans supported his claim that von Falkenhausen's military government was incapable of suppressing local Belgian resistance. The SS pressed ahead with their own solution to the problem.

All Resistance groups were under pressure. The commandant of the Underground Belgian Legion, General Jules Bastin, was arrested in November 1943 and replaced by Colonel Jean Gerard. Gerard did not last long before

German efforts to catch him forced him to flee to Britain. The escape lines managed to continue despite being harried by the Gestapo. François Daman maintained his contacts with the Belgian Legion, the escape lines and the Partisans and succeeded in avoiding arrest. However he was well known to the GFP and SD in Louvain. And so was Hortense.

All policemen and security forces, then and now, admit that their best intelligence comes from the 'terrorists' or 'freedom fighters' themselves. The SS were no exception to this rule. Their best information came from Partisans themselves, and, in Louvain, they had their best coup just before Christmas 1943 when they picked up a man called Frans Vleugels, a Partisan code-named 'Firmin'.

Vleugels was nearly forty when he was arrested on 21 December. He was immediately interrogated and tortured, and he talked at once. All those who have been questioned by unscrupulous interrogators agree that it is unhelpful to maintain a stoic silence. Most would say it is impossible to remain dumb without inviting disaster. The British army teaches the standard response advised by the Geneva Convention, that a captured soldier need only give his name, his rank, his army number and his date of birth. These replies are known as the Big Four. This teaching is simple for captured troops to follow but ignores the plain facts. An interrogator without respect for the Geneva Convention will not throw in the towel when all he hears is 'Big Four'. All countries have developed their own characteristic techniques for obtaining information from prisoners, and ex-prisoners assert that some answers must be given when the pain gets too much, whoever you are and however brave or well-trained you think you are. The pain limit varies, but the real question is what to say at that point, and how much? There seems to be a clear difference between saying something to stop the torture for a moment, and telling all. There is no doubt at all that the SD interrogators took no notice of the Geneva Convention. Equally there is no doubt that Frans Vleugels, though he was a career soldier in the Artillery with François Daman before the war and the BAP battalion commandant in Linden, told them everything he knew. With unseemly haste.

Christmas in Louvain looked bleak. The Damans had heard through the BAP's own sources of information that something was being prepared by the SD, but they had no idea of the scale. They did not have long to wait. It was a considerable shock when, on 23 December, only two days after Vleugel's arrest, the SD arrested dozens of men and women in the area. The traitor had quickly given more than 250 names in his initial statement on sixteen pages of closely typed A4 paper. The SD stenographers and typists had to work overtime to keep up. The detail in his denunciation is chilling, including accounts of all the actions he had been involved in, and giving the real names, code-names, addresses, safehouses and tasks of everyone he could remember.

The SD dossier on François Daman was confirmed. His name appears on the second page (and in numerous other places), listing him as an intelligence and liaison officer and in contact with General van Overstraten and with van Gortenberg, so establishing him as an important link between the Partisans and the underground Belgian army. Pierre Hermans or Georges was also listed several times as a company commandant. Hortense's sweetheart Jan Sprengers appears on the first page even though he had not been seen since earlier that year. Hortense featured twice, listed as 'Daman, Hortensia', a corps courier. The net was closing fast.

Christmas and New Year 1944 was a busy time for the SD and GFP in Louvain. The more people were arrested, the more information came through. Not all folded as completely as Vleugels, but interrogations cross-checked and produced further reports leading to more arrests.

This seasonal snowball effect was punctuated by the grim news beginning to seep out of Partisans and helpers being executed or deported to camps.

Vleugels himself did not escape. The SD used him, extracted every last scrap of information he offered and then sent him to the camps as well. If one can feel any sympathy for an individual who has so thoroughly betrayed his people, one might wonder what went through his mind when finally, later in 1944 in Neuengamme concentration camp in Germany, he was cornered near the latrines by some Belgians wearing the red triangle which designated them as 'political prisoners'. Without a word they seized him by the arms and legs and tossed him repeatedly up and down, beating his body on the ground without compunction until he expired.

François Daman could avoid capture, being on the run, but his family could not move out of trouble. After the first arrests the Damans knew the Louvain Corps of Partisans was at risk, but they felt they had been sufficiently careful not to be indicted. In retrospect this seems short-sighted. However, the family lived in a close-knit community where it was very difficult for strangers to learn what was going on. Vleugels, whom they quickly identified as responsible, was from another district. The Damans felt their tradecraft had been as good as it could be. Vleugels had never been to the house in Pleinstraat, and they hoped he had not named them.

In fact the SD, who had their names, held off them because they wanted François more than the rest of the family.

François could see the risks more clearly and discussed the options with his parents. They could stay and carry on with their work, taking extra care, or they could leave. However leaving their home for the second time in the war was perhaps too big a step to take. Jacques Daman and Stephanie balked at the consequences of putting the whole family on the run, including Hortense's younger sister Julia, now thirteen and not at all well after meningitis.

Hortense was by now scrupulous in her efforts to be professional. Gone were the days when she had endangered everyone with understandable, but stupid and dangerous girlish impulses. She now believed she would survive the war without being caught. She continued as a courier between Gaston in Louvain and Louis van Brussel in Brussels. She took more care than ever before, often arriving more than an hour before her contact was due, to watch the area and check no one else was interested. Frequently she would abort a meeting or refuse to go to a safe house because she felt something was not as it should be. François and Gaston always supported her decisions.

Her animal instincts for something amiss were highly tuned to the unusual, so much so that when in early January two men came into the shop she was immediately suspicious.

'Good morning,' she said cheerfully and moved directly behind the counter in a businesslike way as though to serve them. Standing next to her mother she warned her at once, by moving her foot out of sight under the counter and pressing it against her mother's foot.

The two men were well dressed in heavy overcoats and wore wide-brimmed felt hats. They made a gesture of asking for some groceries and then one of them said, 'Have you seen Godefried Dreesen round here? He's a mate of mine and I heard he'd been staying in Louvain for a while. Thought you might know of him, seeing as you run this shop. I expect you know most of what goes on around here.'

The story was plausible, and it was true shopkeepers knew their local area well, especially handling everyone's ration cards. But the men were too well dressed, too well-fed, too polite and too inquisitive. Hortense was sure they were Belgian SS and, judging by their accent, from Northern Belgium. Flemish is a difficult language and the Gestapo depended on their Flemish-speaking volunteers.

Her mother knew very well the SS would not send these men unless they knew something already and that to deny Gaston's existence altogether would be a mistake. Instead she agreed Dreesen had been about, coming and going, but that she had not seen him for a long time. Stephanie and Hortense were both cheerful and convincing, but gave the two men no chance to prolong the conversation. They thought they had successfully dealt with them when a shadow closed rapidly over the door to the street. The door opened briskly, ringing the bell on the frame above. Godefried Dreesen, codename 'Gaston', commandant of the Louvain corps, stood framed in the doorway against the weak January light.

Hortense stood helpless behind the counter with her mother. For a long moment no one moved. The men looked at each other.

'Good morning,' one of the SS said to Dreesen, casually and very polite.

'Good morning,' Dreesen replied carefully, realising something was wrong. 'Madame Daman, M'selle,' he added formally, nodding at Hortense.

The two men hung about by the door, delaying their departure, and when Dreesen spoke again, asking for some bread, Hortense noticed them stare at him closely. She served him with mindless automatic gestures, watching the two men. They caught her look, abruptly left the shop, turned up their broad collars against the sharp wind, and walked briskly away past the factory towards Parkpoort.

Hortense was in no doubt that the two men had recognised their quarry. Gaston had an accent like theirs, from the area of Limburg in the north. Gaston had been arrested by the SS in Limburg, interrogated and imprisoned. None of them recognised the two men among the Belgian SS in Louvain and he agreed with Stephanie and Hortense that they had come looking for him from Limburg.

After this incident, Stephanie reminded the Partisans closest to them about the Vigor soap advertisement sign hanging in the shop window. If it hung at an odd angle in the shop, then no one was to come inside. It was the danger signal.

A timeless favourite of police is to watch the wanted man's family, assuming that one day he will visit, or one of his close relatives will visit him. It is not clear whether the SS bothered with refinements like this when they had the assistance of the information from Vleugels and all the fruits of the subsequent arrests. However Madame Dreesen, Gaston's mother, visited the Daman shop shortly after the two SS had been nosing about for him. The old lady was brought down from Limburg by Dreesen's aunt, and came to the Damans' corner shop on the pretext of buying flowers to put on graves in the cemetery. In fact she wanted to thank Stephanie Daman for being a mother to her son.

Hortense was deeply moved by the old woman's sincere and tearful speech. Not until later did it cross her mind that the two women's visit had been logged by SS men occupying the guardhouse of the Philips factory, providing them with just the sort of confirmation they wanted.

The SS knew Hortense was involved. But they wanted her brother, François Daman. For some time they had been using an empty office in the guardhouse as an observation post on Pleinstraat. With care, no one would notice a few more Germans and it was an ideal place with a fine view of everything that happened in Pleinstraat, especially at the corner shop at the top. All they had to do was wait.

# 8

# St Valentine's Day 1944

'Terror? Never. It is simply social hygiene taking those individuals out of circulation like a doctor would take out a bacillus.' Benito Mussolini.

In January 1944 the Partisans struck back at the Germans, to prove they were still in the game. There were twenty attacks in the month and the effort continued into February averaging one a day until the 10th, when there were four. That day two more collaborators, Irene Ickx and Buellens, were shot; a patrol of Belgian SS were ambushed with three killed and one wounded, involving Pierre Hermans and 'Freddi' Desiron, a remarkable man who later escaped from a concentration camp in Germany and walked all the way back to Louvain; and the railway station at Korbeek-Lo was attacked, throwing the lines out of Louvain into chaos.

These actions infuriated the SS, particularly when they thought they had delivered the Partisans a tremendous body-blow with the dozens of arrests they had made with the help of Vleugels's denunciation. Typically the SS did not hesitate to take reprisals and shot several prisoners in Breendonk the same day, 10 February, including Eugene Haesaerts.

The Partisans had certainly proved they still had the

capability after the arrests, but how much real damage they caused to the German war effort is a matter of debate.

This vicious riposte to setbacks is copied by modern groups like the IRA, the PLO and the Basques' ETA. An example is a series of IRA attacks on British army personnel in Germany in the summer of 1988 after they lost three killed in an SAS ambush in Gibraltar. However, real change is seldom brought about by the violence of a few.

During the war Partisans throughout occupied Europe, especially in the East, diverted sometimes large numbers of German troops to enforce internal security, but the great Allied armies were still required to battle their way into the centre of Hitler's Thousand Year Reich to destroy it, and they had a long way to go. At the start of 1944 the British and Americans had landed in Italy but were bogged down at Anzio and below the heights of Monte Cassino. The Soviets had retaken the Crimea and started their offensive at Leningrad, but they had still not cleared the Germans out of Russia. The D-Day landings were in preparation but there was no guarantee of success. The Wehrmacht continued to fight tenaciously on all fronts.

SS police units had been equally thorough in counter-attacking the Partisans. After a little over a year they were in a position to strike back hard and they had learnt it was important to ensure the security of their operations. Perhaps they had taken even longer to realise their plans were at risk from spies inside the police than the Partisans had taken to appreciate the dangers of collaborators; but by the end of 1943, if not before, the SS knew. Marcel Van den Borght, whom Hortense had been visiting for months, was one of the names which Vleugels had given away.

After the spate of attacks the SS lost patience. This time they took care that no clue of their plan was apparent in the Louvain Kommandantur or the gendarmerie. While the Partisans rested over the cold February weekend after the action of the week before, a massive operation was being prepared using GFP and SS from units in Brussels and towns well outside Louvain. More than 700 men were placed on alert and briefed ready to converge on Louvain.

Monday, 14 February was St Valentine's day and passed without incident. The sky was overcast, the temperature below freezing, discouraging all activity. Hortense's father Jacques returned as usual from the shoe factory in Brussels at about eight o'clock and Gaston came across the street from the Storckels' house for supper with the Damans as he always did. Taking off his coat he sat down with Jacques and Hortense while Stephanie and Julia put food on the table. Their small mongrel dog Timmi lay curled up beside the fire which warmed the small kitchen against the bitter night outside. They chatted as they ate, relaxing in the homely atmosphere, enjoying the company of those they trusted and loved and turning their backs on the oppression and winter cold outside. They were unaware of the terror which was closing in on them.

Under cover of the black night a convoy of Wehrmacht trucks eased slowly along the Boulevard and braked gently to a halt under the rustling trees. Their headlights, narrowed to sinister slits in blackout conditions, cast a yellow glow over rows of GFP soldiers sitting under the canvas canopies in the back. They waited silently for orders to move, their steel helmets gleaming dully. SD officers in black coats and peaked caps with the death's head insignia moved swiftly round to the back of the trucks and issued a rapid series of commands in low tones. The soldiers climbed down trying not to rattle their equipment, stiff with cold after the hour-long journey from Brussels, and holding their rifles across their chests, immediately filed away into the darkness to positions on which they had been briefed earlier that day in their barracks. Within minutes Pleinstraat and the fate of the Daman family was sealed. The corner shop was surrounded on all sides. A black Citroën staff car moved slowly towards Pleinstraat under the trees past the factory.

Inside the house Hortense enjoyed the last minutes of the family life her mother and father had taken so much trouble to protect as a haven of calm in the years of Occupation. Under the tremendous pressures of her life as a courier Hortense had always been able to turn to her parents and family for the loving support they had unfailingly provided. She was too young to appreciate the secret terror which Jacques and Stephanie experienced each time she left to carry messages for François, Gaston or Louis van Brussel, or to understand the true cost of their encouragement; but she had watched her mother feeding many young, homeless Partisans on the run and loved her all the more. Abruptly, her home was destroyed at the flick of an officer's wrist outside in the dark.

The doors crashed in back and front at the same time. Black-uniformed soldiers stormed into the kitchen and shop, kicking over the furniture, shouting and striking out with their rifles.

'Run!' Hortense screamed at Gaston, knowing he was the man the Germans most wanted to arrest. A picture of the two Belgian SS who had visited the shop in January snapped into her mind. Then she was knocked to the ground. Strong hands seized her by the hair and pulled her back to her feet. She saw her mother punched and shoved against one wall, while another two soldiers grabbed her father and began to beat him with their fists without mercy. The kitchen seemed to be full of soldiers and plain clothes SD, smashing chairs and crockery until the floor shook with the violence of the attack. The uproar was swelled by the hysterical barking of Timmi until, to Hortense's horror, one soldier smashed his rifle

191

butt on to the little dog. It stopped moving and he kicked the body into a corner under the stove. Hortense found herself shaking with shock and she felt sick.

Gaston had disappeared and for a moment she thought he had somehow managed to escape. After a few moments he was dragged inside the house by three GFP, his face cut and bleeding badly. They held him by his arms and repeatedly banged his head on the wall, all the time shouting 'Terrorist, Schweinhund!' in his ears.

The chaos eased when the officer in charge walked into the kitchen. SS Sturmbannleiter Robert Verbelen looked with disgust at the struggling family whose lives he had shattered. Since the start of 1944, SS-General Jungclaus had put him in charge of a newly formed unit called the 'Veiligheidskorps' (the VK) whose purpose was in theory to protect the SS and evacuate their families in the face of the Allied armies. In practice, Verbelen's VK was a group which terrorised the population without restraint and with the full support of Jungclaus.

He shouted at a Gefreiter to put a stool near the Flemish dresser. Hortense watched his actions with mounting disbelief. Without hesitation, he stepped on the stool, reached about on top of the dresser and brought down a heavy package with a sneer of satisfaction. The package contained all the Damans' savings and had been hidden in the secret compartment. Jacques had decided money was safer hidden in the house rather than placed in a bank, the assets of which might at any time be raided by the German military government. In the event the money would have been safer in a bank for they never saw those savings again.

The loss of the money was bad enough, but Hortense and her parents stared at Verbelen for quite a different reason. How had he known exactly where to look? Surely only the closest of their friends had known about that money? It could not have been Vleugels. Hortense thought that even if he knew of their connection with the Partisans, he could not know about the money as he had never been to the house in Pleinstraat. There was no chance to think any more about it then.

The Germans ransacked the house, smashing and trampling round everything like maddened bulls, and dragged the family about like rag dolls as they worked from room to room. A large GFP soldier held Hortense by her long blonde hair in a twisted grip and pulled her up the stairs to look into the bedrooms where he frenziedly tore the beds to pieces and threw clothes from cupboards and drawers. As they passed the top of the stairs she saw Verbelen looking at a large map of Europe on the wall. Her father had kept the map up to date with the events of the war, using flags to pin in positions of the Allied and German armies. He had always been careful to place the pins to accord with the official German news bulletins, just in case someone in the shop saw up the stairs, although he listened to the real position on the BBC. Hortense watched Verbelen move several flags to positions reflecting the true situation and then he screamed for her father.

'All terrorists like you listen to the Jewish BBC,' he swore. 'So you'll be charged with keeping a map to record the lies they tell.'

In Nazi thinking the Jews were always to blame and the BBC had been reported to be heavily influenced by Jewish commentators in the collaborationist newspaper *Le Pays Réel*. The paper was founded by Léon Degrelle, then serving with the Waffen SS, 'Viking' Division, at Cherkassy on the Russian front. Degrelle was one of Belgium's best-known Nazi sympathisers. His commitment to National Socialism had made him volunteer for the Russian front where he was promoted through the ranks from SS private to SS Sturmbannführer (Major) and was awarded the Oak Leaves to the Knight's Cross of the Iron Cross, Germany's most coveted decorations for valour in the field.

Verbelen's accusation was deliberate since there was no specific charge against Jacques Daman. Under the Hostages Order it was good enough for the SS that he was related to suspected Partisans.

For the second time in the war the house was destroyed by Germans, this time piecemeal. When the GFP were finally satisfied, Hortense, Gaston and her father Jacques had just time to grab their coats before they were shoved into the street and crushed together on to the back seat of the large black Citroën with a plain clothes SD officer on either side. Verbelen got in the front. He snapped an order and the driver took off at speed. He drove fast across the Boulevard, through Tiensepoort to the Kommandantur in the centre of the town.

Hortense and the others had no chance to come to terms with their sudden savage arrest. The SD shoved them up the steps of the Kommandantur and along seemingly endless corridors, shouting all the time, their boots stamping and echoing on the hard floors. Somewhere Hortense was aware of Gaston being taken in another direction, but she hardly had time to notice before she and her father were flung into a large hall. More SS began screaming at them to join two lines, one for men and the other, opposite the first, for women.

Hortense was mortified to find herself standing directly opposite her father, every one of whose bruises she could see quite clearly. Next to her she recognised a schoolfriend her own age and then realised the girl's father was standing next to her own. She lowered her head to avoid seeing the men's humiliation, and immediately gasped in pain as an SS man behind yanked her head back with a handful of her hair.

The uniformed SS swaggered up and down the two ranks shouting and lashing out with whips and sticks without warning or excuse. Hortense looked along the ranks of dejected and terrified people. She knew many of them but she was careful to give no sign of recognition.

Everyone was shivering with cold and shock. Many of the men and women were wearing only the house clothes they had on when they were dragged out of their homes. The hall was unheated and Hortense was appalled when one Belgian SS man began to move down the line of men roughly tearing their braces with a dagger from his belt, letting their trousers fall to the floor. The SS behind him bellowed at the men to remove their trousers and then kicked them away. When they came to Jacques Daman they pushed him about shouting with laughter to find he was the only one wearing long-johns. Hortense dropped her eyes again, mortified to see her father made fun of like that and very much embarrassed by the sight of the men taking off their clothes. She realised the SS intended to strip all the men to the skin, including her father.

In spite of herself she lowered her head again. At once a savage blow smacked the side of her head making her stagger and she cried out in surprise. Again the SS behind her yanked her head back by the hair. The man opposite, the father of the girl next to her, shouted at the Germans to stop hitting Hortense. It was a brave act. Almost casually, an SS policeman walked over, whipped his hand round from behind his back and stabbed a long needle into the man's genitals. His scream echoed round Hortense's mind long after she was finally taken from the miserable scene in the hall and flung alone in a cold cellar beneath the Kommandantur. The man who had spoken out for her did not last long. He died shortly afterwards in Breendonk.

Jacques Daman watched his daughter being beaten and dragged away without any thought of his own fate. He did not care what the Germans did to him. His chief concern was for his family and he was in torment as Hortense was shoved out of his sight, her arms gripped hard by two SS. Standing naked in line with the other men in the cold room increased his sense of helplessness, as it was intended to, and he prayed for Hortense. Fortune was at least kind that he could not know what else she was to suffer for her decision to resist the Nazis, three and a half years ago.

Hortense was badly frightened in the dark of the cellar. She felt water running on the walls and there was a stale smell in the dank air. She imagined she could hear rats moving about, waiting for her, about to run over her feet. She was bruised and hurt and felt sorry for herself. She wondered what would happen to her next and as her fears spiralled down on her, she began to cry.

The tears flooded her eyes but she could see nothing anyway in the total blackness. She walked hesitantly forward, bending over and reaching out with her arms to feel ahead. Her hands touched a large stone slab. It seemed to be a sort of table. She climbed on to it, thinking that the rats might not be able to get at her, and curled up, hardly bothering to wipe her tears. Some time later she cried herself to sleep in the dark, exhausted in the aftermath of a series of shocks any one of which was enough to shake the balance of an adult twice her age.

'*Raus! Raus!*'

The heavy door of her cellar crashed open and four SS in plain clothes marched in and grabbed Hortense before she was properly awake. Two of them were Belgian SS who had been present at her first arrest a few months before. Born on 23 July 1919, Lambert Janssens was slim with thin hair slicked back from a central parting, a beaked nose and fleshy lips set in a perpetual sneer. On 10 November 1945, a year after the liberation of Belgium, he was sentenced to death for his crimes by a court in Louvain. Fernard Faignaert was two years his junior, born on 10 December 1921, an ordinary clean-looking young man like any other, but he was sentenced to death by the same court after the war for helping the Germans to torture, maim and kill fellow countrymen and women. Their sentences were not commuted. Hortense was to get to know them very well in the next weeks.

## St Valentine's Day 1944

They seized her tightly by the arms, shoved her upstairs, along corridors and outside into the freezing night air. The early hours are always the coldest and February is arguably the coldest month of the year. Hortense immediately began to shiver. The SS pushed her into a car and shoved in beside her. Being crushed between their sweaty and rough serge coats was little comfort. The journey was short, up Bondgenotenlaan-straat, which led from the centre to the railway station, right into Justus Lipsiusstraat and right again into Maria Theresiastraat. The car stopped outside the tall stone walls of the main gate to the Little Prison of Louvain.

This women's prison was used as an overflow of the main Central Prison, which was across the Boulevard from Hortense's house in Pleinstraat and where the sixteen pistols had been stolen. The Little Prison had, and still has, three solidly built red-brick wings standing out like spokes of a wheel from a central hub, each three stories high, tall and narrow, like warehouses, with lines of small windows set at regular intervals, each slightly vaulted and secured with three thick iron bars. The design dates back to the 1830s when the Belgian Inspector General of Prisons, Ducpetiaux, was favourably impressed with the octagonal system, also known as the Pennsylvania system, in which only a few guards in the centre were required to monitor hundreds of prisoners in the wings. All the cells could be seen by simply glancing up the long corridors or galleries lined with steel doors in each wing on each floor.

Another principle adopted by Ducpetiaux was still operated in the 1940s. Prisoners were to be kept apart from each other, minimising contact including speech. Criminals had shown themselves unfit for society and it followed they were patently unsuited to exert their anti-social influence on each other, and worsen their characters by spending time together. The only people who were allowed communication with prisoners were the prison officer, clergy and religious instructors. So it was that nuns ran the women's section of the Little Prison in one wing, the first on the left on the way from the main entrance into the central hub.

Hortense knew nothing of prisons, not then. She was pulled out of the car and pushed through the wicket gate in the stout timber doors under the Gothic arch of the main entrance. Inside she hardly had time to notice the office on the left, where the Mother Superior presided, before she was led through an octagonal hallway covered in glass, through a massive oak door and then a barred gate into a long passage leading into the central hub of the prison. Here Janssens shoved her to the right, into one of the men's wings, and pushed her along with blows on her shoulders until she was standing bemused in the middle of the long block, staring at the rows of metal doors ranged on either side. A shout far above made her look up to the vaulted ceiling high above the floor. On the second floor up, on a steel balcony which ran round the wing like a gallery, she could see two SS men leaning over the wrought iron railings.

A moment later Hortense was shocked to see the face of Gaston thrust over the railings next to the SS man who was gripping him by his hair. High above her on the second floor, she hardly recognised him so badly was his face beaten and bloodied. He jerked and struggled and she realised he was still being hit by another man she could not see on the balcony behind him. She saw something falling, and heard it land on the stone floor, quite close, like a grape bursting. She looked down and saw it was blood.

'Is this the bandit?' the SS screamed in Gaston's face, pointing down at the girl two floors below them. He punched Gaston in the face, opening cuts again. More drops fell. 'Is she part of your group?'

Hortense stared up in disbelief, thinking that all the time she had been asleep in the dark cellar under the

Kommandantur, the SS had been torturing Gaston to make him talk.

'This is what'll happen to you if you don't tell us everything we want to know,' Janssens shouted suddenly in her ear.

Blood fell steadily, spattering on the black and white flags as the SS laid into Gaston again, unsatisfied with an answer Hortense never heard. They had got Godefried Dreesen at last. The dull thud of each blow and his screams echoed and bounced round the empty vaulted wing and followed her when Janssens and Faignaert shoved her back across the central hub into the little passage towards the women's section. Their heels snapped along the flags, beating a harsh metal din. Hortense noticed that even the smallest sound, like the rustle of Janssens's stiff leather coat, echoed like a clash of brass cymbals inside the prison.

The SS stopped at a steel door in the short, narrow passage and rang a bell. They waited a long time until eventually an elderly nun opened the door. She said nothing. Janssens pushed Hortense forward. The nun motioned her to step past her inside, and, without a word to the two Belgian SS, closed the door in their faces. She led Hortense deeper into the women's wing, which opened out into a much smaller version of the men's wing she had just left. There were only six cells on the ground floor. Hortense was taken up narrow spiral stairs on the left of the block to a cell on the first floor. The nun closed the door, slamming the steel against the stone reveal, and left Hortense in darkness.

Hortense listened to the echoes ringing round the lofty hall outside as she heard the sharper sound of the key moving in the lock. A shaft of pale light fell into the cell as the nun removed the key and slipped softly away. Hortense Daman was in prison.

She stared at the door long after the sounds had died away and silence fell on the women's block. Then she felt her way to the steel ribbed cot she had seen on one side, fell on it and went straight to sleep.

In the morning she woke in the pale light from the barred window high in the outside wall at one end of her cell. She saw the dark shadows of the bars through the glass, which was grimed with dirt. She looked round. Her cell was about six feet wide and twelve long. The walls were brick and bare and under the window there was a large pipe running across the room at floor level. She put her hand on it and was pleased to find it provided a little heat. The cell door dominated the other end. It was made of iron and studded with rivets. There was a circular trap set in the wall on one side of the door for the nuns to pass food inside in a swivelling drum without having to come in themselves, and they could spy on the occupant through a small round hole in the centre of the door. Beneath this was a trap hinged at the bottom which could be unlocked to drop outwards into the passage. Hortense was to find this was used to allow fresh air into the cell and sometimes to communicate with the prisoner without opening the door. In the corner behind the door was a single tap protruding from the brick wall. Under this was a pisspot, a metal tin about fifteen inches high and ten across with another bucket inside. The lid had a lip to it which fitted in a channel round the edge to stop odours escaping from the inside, but it still smelt. Her cot bed was built like an eighteenth-century railway bridge, square and solid, of cast iron with steel straps to support the hair mattress. It was in three parts, hinged so that the end could be folded over twice on to itself and made into a table with a square flat piece of wood placed on top, a procedure which had to be carried out every morning.

On her first day of captivity, however, Hortense had no idea what to do. She was a long way from the experienced prisoner she was to become, hardened to conditions beyond the imagination. She sat on the cot with her feet on the pipe under the window and felt miserable.

She discovered the Germans had left her with her rosary, which she had managed to keep in her pocket. She pulled it out and began to play with it. The familiar sensation calmed her and she found herself praying.

Noises in the hall roused her. The sound of banging and clattering quickly filled the empty space. People were approaching. The feet stopped outside her cell. A key struggled in the lock, the door opened and the hubbub in the hall filled her cell. It was time for the daily morning cleaning routine. A sister appeared with a bucket of water.

'Here,' she said, not unkindly. 'This is for washing yourself. This is for cleaning the cell, and some of the other prisoners will come and take your slop bucket.'

Later a woman prisoner arrived, as the sister had said, and changed the slop bucket. Another woman gave her two slices of hard black bread and a cup of weak ersatz coffee.

The women were rough and ready, obviously used to prison life. Hortense realised that they were 'real' prisoners, who had committed 'ordinary' crimes like theft, or even, as she was to find out later from the nuns, murder. They wore prison clothes and some had been in the Little Prison for years. The idea of being locked up for so long terrified Hortense, but she pulled herself together with the thought that she would be released when the Nazis were defeated. She never lost her confidence that England would again rescue Belgium.

She looked more closely at the bread. She tried a bit. It was disgusting, but she ate some eventually. She could not help thinking how well her mother cooked, even with the constraints of rationing. These thoughts made her more miserable. She wondered what had happened to her mother and to Julia her little sister, and how many more Partisans had been picked up.

Still later in the morning her door was opened again. The Mother Superior stood framed in the light falling through the glass roof lights in the hall behind. She was an old lady and had been the warden in the Little Prison for a long time.

'Hortense Daman?'

'Yes, ma'am,' Hortense replied politely, standing up.

The Mother Superior knew of the Damans through Stephanie's grocery business, but she introduced herself and then said, 'My Order runs the women's section of the prison, and there are women here serving their sentences away from society for all kinds of crimes. Some have done the very cruellest things. In your case I have been told by the Sicherheitsdienst that you are a terrorist, a bandit, and that you must be accorded no special privileges. As far as I am concerned you're a political prisoner. I hope you will learn to behave here.' She glanced at the rosary hanging from Hortense's hand, and added, 'Pray, my child, for God's support.' She paused as she turned to leave the cell, and said, 'But don't wear the beads out.'

The SD were busy after so many arrests and they did not waste time with their interrogations. Another sister came later in the morning and fetched Hortense from her cell. They went back down the winding iron spiral to the ground floor and along the narrow passage which led to the men's section and the central hub. The nun opened the small door which was the entrance to the women's wing through which Hortense had come the night before and she saw Janssens and Faignaert waiting for her.

They grabbed her and flanking her on either side, walked her out towards the main entrance. They passed through the octagonal glass-roofed hall and the wicket gate into the street outside. Hortense had not been in prison for a full twenty-four hours but was amazed how the sight of a normal street, one she knew well, heartened her.

Her amazement continued when, instead of shoving her into a car, the two SS turned right out of the gate and marched her down the pavement. She could not understand why the Germans should run the risk of walking about with her in broad daylight. She thought perhaps they wanted to make an exhibition of her, as they had made no effort to keep the street clear of other people.

They turned into Justus Lipsiusstraat, going towards the centre of town as if to the Kommandantur, but just as they approached the statue of Justo Lipsio himself – professor of Louvain University before the Great War – Janssens pulled her to the left, into Leopold I straat. Only a few yards down this street, Janssens and Faignaert stopped her at the door of a house on the right, to all outward appearances a rather smart four-storey residence in the typical vertical Flemish style.

This was the Gestapo's interrogation centre, where Eugene Haesaerts had been tortured. The door was opened by an SS policeman, Hortense was shoved inside and propelled quickly up the stairs into a room on the first floor. Off-balance, she stumbled through the door, and met with a bunched fist which swung out of nowhere and struck her full in the face.

'Sit down!' SS Stafleider Max Gunter screamed at her, rubbing his knuckles. He pointed at a one-legged stool on the floor between Hortense and a large desk in the centre of the room and again screamed, 'Sit down!'

Three other SS stood round and bellowed at her, as close as they could, deafening her.

Reeling from the blow, Hortense tried to do as she was told. She found it hard to sit on the stool which kept slipping off balance on its one leg, as the Germans intended it should. They continued to shout, firing questions at her one after the other, without giving her a moment to answer, trying to beat her down and terrify her.

Since the raid on her home, Hortense had been through the mill. Prison was a new and frightening experience and the last hours had been a shock to her confidence.

She had always thought all of them in the family were good enough to survive the war without being arrested. She had not counted on denunciation. In the clear mind of a seventeen-year-old the truly unpleasant effects of treachery cannot be easily grasped. Someone who knew the Daman household well had helped the SS. How else had Verbelen known exactly where to find the family's savings? But she had been arrested before, and had been questioned on numerous occasions in the street by German patrols. By this time her German was really fluent. The pointlessness of the frenzied verbal attack began to annoy her.

'Hold on, hold on,' she cried out. 'One at a time. Who am I supposed to answer first?'

'What?' shouted Gunter, astonished.

'In any case,' Hortense continued, 'I'm not deaf. If you ask me questions I'll do my best to answer them, but there's no need to shout.'

Gunter came round behind her, grabbed her ear and twisted hard. Putting his face close to her head, he screamed at her. When Hortense lost her patience and told him he was 'a very rude man', his reaction was typical and set the tone of the endless interrogations that followed. Swiftly he turned and picked up a chair standing against the wall behind her. Something warned Hortense, who was about to turn her head.

'Face your front,' Gunter bellowed, swinging the chair high across his shoulder. Then he smashed it down over the slight frame of the girl sitting with her back to him.

The chair broke apart. Hortense was catapulted forward, her chest crashed into the heavy desk, breaking three ribs, and her arms were flung out across the top, scattering pens and inkwells. In a moment the wide leather surface, files and papers were covered in a sticky pool of red and blue inks. Gunter completely lost his temper and ordered the Belgian SS to remove Hortense at once.

The interrogation was resumed later and it was immediately apparent to Hortense what the main theme was to be.

'Where's your brother?'

'I don't know?'

'When did you last see him?'

'I haven't seen him for ages.'

'Liar! Your father's told us he has been round to your house recently.'

'I'm sure you must be mistaken.'

'No!' They all began shouting again.

'Anyway, my father works all day in Brussels, so I don't see how he would know whether François has been home.'

'We know he's been to see you recently.'

'Well, he may have been. If he came when I wasn't there. Maybe I was out, delivering groceries for my mother.'

'You know we've arrested your mother?'

'What've you done that for?'

'She's a terrorist, like you. She's been feeding and helping you terrorists.'

'You must be joking,' Hortense replied, her bruised face a picture of surprise. 'I've never heard such a story.'

'Do you deny that she's been sheltering a wanted terrorist?'

'Of course. What d'you mean?'

'The man we arrested with you in your home, who's been staying with you for ages.'

'You mean Godefried Dreesen?'

'Of course. He's a terrorist.'

'I don't believe it! Surely he's not a terrorist? As far as I know he's a nice man who works somewhere in Louvain.'

'Where?'

'I don't know.'

'Why's he been staying round at your house?'

205

'I don't know, but my mother is well known for helping all sorts of people, and giving them a little extra if they come buying things in the shop. Including German officers, like the one from the factory,' she added, personalising the conversation.

Hortense had had no formal training in how to cope with interrogations, but instinctively adopted a style which was as close to the truth as she could make it without giving anything away. It was true to say that her mother helped people, but unnecessary to say that included the Partisans. She could say she had not seen François for some time, without saying how long, or that her father was not aware of what was going on at home because he was in Brussels all day, even though in practice it would have been strange if he had not known what went on in his own house. She gave her answers credibility by admitting what she could, but always sliding past the real point of Gunter's questions. She naturally appreciated that it would have been folly to have refused to answer questions or to have made some attempt at a cover story, as that would have been taken as a full admission and encouraged more beatings followed almost certainly by swift execution as being of no further use. She pretended to be wholly pliant to their questions but always managed to avoid the main issue, and she played constantly on her youth and sex. Young girls were not expected to be given much responsibility in those days, and had no voting franchise until they were twenty-one.

Hortense was taken back to the Little Prison in the afternoon by Janssens and Faignaert. They walked again taking the same route up Justus Lipsiusstraat and right along the prison walls to the main gate. Inside they halted at the little door in the passage to the women's section, pressed the bell and waited impatiently for several minutes for the elderly sister to open the door.

Without a word the sister took Hortense back to her cell on the first floor, and locked her in. Hortense fell on her cot and began to cry. She was bruised and ached all over. The pain was especially bad round her chest. She felt terribly alone.

The evening meal began with a cacophony of trolley wheels rolling over the white and black tiles, ladles clashing in and out of metal tureens, dropped lids, the softer beat of the prisoners' spoons in their pewter bowls and an overpowering smell of cabbage. Hortense looked at the soup with lumps in it and more black bread. She was feeling sorry for herself and ate little. She was not yet conditioned to eat anything she was given, let alone scavenge for scraps on the floor.

Shortly after, the light outside faded, the sisters turned out the gas lighting in the hall and quiet descended on the wing. Then Hortense heard a scuffling noise on the balcony. Very softly, the key turned and a sister opened the door.

The nun came into Hortense's cell. Speaking very quietly she told Hortense to stop crying.

'I want you to be very brave,' she continued gently, 'because your mother is here. Promise me not to cry, or the other prisoners will hear.'

Before Hortense could really take in what was happening, the nun motioned her to be silent, with a finger over her lips and to follow her. She led Hortense along the balcony, across a wrought-iron bridge over the hall to another cell on the same floor, No. 13. The door was open. Hortense went inside and was shocked by what she saw.

Stephanie Daman was sitting on her cot, terribly battered round the face, with a great gash across her cheek. The cut, the result of a swinging blow from Gunter with his heavy ring, was hanging open. Her lips were swollen, her eyes dreadfully puffed and her flesh bruised yellow and green.

In the emotional embrace of mother and daughter, Hortense was swamped with feelings of relief at seeing her again, but filled with rage at the Germans' treatment of her. She stopped thinking of herself. As they talked she saw her mother's teeth had been knocked out. The nuns had tried to do what they could to administer first aid but they had to be careful their help was not obvious or the Germans would have noticed. Like the Gendarmes, they continued their job after the German invasion but quickly learned to make a difference between ordinary criminals and resistance fighters.

She told Hortense that she had been left in the wreckage of her house after the GFP had driven off with her husband, daughter and Gaston. Julia had run over the road to the Storckels' house at No. 124 Pleinstraat. Anna Storckel was a close friend of Hortense's and Stephanie felt Julia would be safer there than at home. In the morning Stephanie had adjusted the Vigor soap advertisement at an angle in the shop window in case any of the Partisans came by. Her father Pierre Van den Eynde came to give his support but everyone in the street was terrified and kept well away. Only Pierre Hermans had tried to visit. As he bicycled slowly up to the house, he checked in the window for the Vigor soap sign. At once he saw it at a crazy angle.

'Get away, Pierre!'

Hortense's grandfather came out of the front door as Pierre passed.

'Get away,' the old man whispered urgently. 'They've arrested Jacques and Hortense and they're still watching us.'

This was all the warning Pierre needed. He accelerated off without hesitation. He turned sharply round the corner and along a path through the trees, keeping as far as he could from the guard room at the factory. Abruptly a man in a long trench coat with collar upturned against the cold and wearing a felt hat stepped out from behind a tree where he had been hiding. He ran at Pierre reaching out his arms to grab him off his bike, but Pierre

# Tie Rack

Terminal Three International Departures
Heathrow Airport
Hounslow  Middx TW6 1JA

| Item code | Description | Total |
|---|---|---|
| 3545540000013 | WOOL ARGYLE SOCK | 3.99 |
| 3550121200010 | CTN ARGYLE SOCKS | 3.99 |
| 3550080800016 | CTN ARGYLE SOCKS | 3.99 |
| | SOCKS MULTI-BUY | -0.98 |
| | Total: | 10.99 |
| CASH | | 11.00 |
| | Change: | 0.01 |

18/02/96 10:06:13-10:06:32   Branch:0007
Clerk:29 GURDEEP KAUR SIN Jrnl:01/068831

Tie Rack adds colour to your life !
Head Office No. 0181 230 2300
VAT Reg No. 443 942 147

managed to swerve round him. He bounced over the grass and kept going, fighting to keep his balance and gain speed. The Gestapo agent faltered and watched his quarry pedal furiously away towards the Boulevard. He glanced over at the factory and went back to his post behind the tree. Pierre Hermans had escaped capture, but Stephanie Daman was easier prey.

The nuns in the prison were well used to the rough conditions and with dealing with the thieves and murderers put away by society, but they did what they could to help Hortense and Stephanie Daman and the other women once they realised they had been arrested for helping the Resistance. The warden of the prison chapel, Gustaaf Legrande, had told them about the arrests. At great personal risk he acted as a secret courier through whom the prisoners passed news to their families. He lived in Pleinstraat and regularly met Hortense's grandfather, who in turn told François. One day he smuggled in to Hortense a photograph of her sister Julia with Michel Berges, her eldest sister Bertha's son of whom she was very fond.

The Mother Superior rearranged the cells so that the normal criminals were relocated on the top floor and all the political prisoners were installed on the first floor. After the routine of the day was over the sisters opened all the cells and the women were free to visit each other or congregate on the open floor space which covered one end of the first floor over the little passage to the men's section. The Germans would not have liked this so everyone was sworn to keep as quiet as possible. The danger of stool-pigeons among the other criminals could not be discounted. The sisters even oiled the locks and hinges so the doors could be opened silently.

The Germans were not allowed inside the women's wing and this gave the nuns time to conceal what was going on. Hortense learned that Sister Augustine, the elderly nun who had sole responsibility for opening the little door in the passage from the men's side had been deliberately chosen, for she was very deaf and more than a little blind. She always took an age to open the door when the SS banged to be let in.

The reunion with her mother gave Hortense strength. Seeing Stephanie's wounds made her realise her own situation was by no means the worst and stopped her feeling sorry for herself. But she needed all the strength she could muster, for the SD gave her no peace.

Every day for thirty days until mid-March, she was called for by the SS, who waited at the door in the passage. Very often Janssens and Faignaert marched her down the street to the plain building in Leopold I straat. At other times she was taken by van Avondt, whom she had met on her first arrest, or Frederick Dirickx, Gerardus Paenhuysen, Gustaaf Clement, Albertus Beelen, Robert Poot and others, all volunteers in the Belgian SS.

Day after day the men in Leopold I straat persisted with the same line of questioning. Day after day they resorted to sudden beatings, screaming and kicking their young victim for hours on end. She left the Little Prison in the morning after breakfast at six o'clock and often she was not brought back until the early hours of the following day, bruised and exhausted. The irony of her route escaped her captors. Every day she passed the statue of the famous Justo Lipsio, whose very name and reputation were the antithesis of the SD and their brutal techniques, yet whose marble back was turned on the sufferings of this daughter of the town which had so honoured him.

During the worst of her interrogations Hortense never wondered why these men, all Belgians, could treat her so cruelly. To her they were the enemy. She supposed it was natural they should act that way, though she despised and hated them for it. They wanted her information and she refused to give it. She had been for so long a courier for her brother, with whom the SS were obsessed, for Louis van Brussel and for Gaston, that she knew literally hundreds of people's names and addresses. Her detailed knowledge of the local Resistance, both Partisan and the escape lines, was colossal. However at no stage did she contemplate telling them a single fact. This was not a conscious decision, as might have been made by an older person or a trained SOE agent or SAS soldier operating in occupied Europe, so much as an attitude which stemmed from the example of people she knew had been tortured and kept silent; men like the Commandant Lambert, Nijsen, Seymens and Haesaerts. Their examples and those of others who had given their lives for Belgium, like Camile van Acker and Baron Jean Greindl or Nurse Edith Cavell in the last war, fortified her against the blows. Her sense of duty to her people and her country, which had stirred in her as a young girl learning history at school, had hardened in the last tough years of Occupation into a powerful force within her. With all the clarity of her youth, unseduced by the uncertainties and compromises that come with age, it never crossed her mind to talk.

Every night she and her mother would meet, giving each other strength in their shared suffering. They sat together in one cell or the other, side by side on the cot, grey shadows in the dim reflection of the gaslight in the hall outside, their hair in unkempt wisps round their heads, like soft haloes, and they talked. Hortense had already been through a great deal with her family over the years of the Occupation, but she found she was beginning to learn things about her mother which she had never before known. They began to build a special strength of their mother and daughter relationship, and the link they forged was all the stronger for being hammered out of adversity. The value of this bond was inestimable as it was to be an invisible lifeline for both of them, each taking turns to pull the other from a miserable decline.

They discussed why Hortense, and a few times at the beginning Stephanie, had been walked daily to interrogations. Why did the Germans take the risk, even over so short a distance? Was it to see who recognised them in the street? Several times Hortense had seen people she knew but she had not given the slightest indication of this to her SS guards. Once she had seen Pierre Hermans bicycle past, and for a brief moment of elation she wondered if the Partisans would attempt to rescue her. In the end, she and her mother decided the SD were hoping that was exactly what would happen, and that François Daman would be in the forefront of the attack. This idea gelled one day when Hortense noticed Janssens look up as they walked down towards the statue of Justo Lipsio. Discreetly she followed his glance and saw a face at a window. The face nodded a signal. She became convinced the GFP waited in ambush every day hoping to catch her brother, and this was why she was guarded with seeming indifference by the few Belgian SS who accompanied her. Certainly her interrogators left her in no doubt how keen they were to 'speak' to François.

Near the end of the thirty days of interrogation, Hortense was waiting in the octagonal hall by the Mother Superior's office near the main gate, when a noise behind made her look round. Faignaert hit out, but not before she saw her mother behind her. On this day, the only time it happened, the two women were marched together from the Little Prison and slowly down Justus Lipsiusstraat, separated by some twenty metres. Both were by this time convinced of the reason for this walk and prayed François would not fall for the bait. Nothing happened.

On another occasion, several weeks later, Janssens came for Hortense very late one night. He made her put on another woman's coat and took her by car to a hall called the Metropole, which the Germans had commandeered as soldiers' quarters. There she waited for hours sitting in a chair near the entrance while the SS stood around smoking and talking. She was guarded by a Wehrmacht soldier who asked her what she was doing there. When Hortense told him, he bit his lip and said nothing more. He had just heard that the SD had taken over the Wehrmacht's intelligence service, the Abwehr, and he wanted nothing to do with politics and the SS. By 1944 even von Falkenhausen was under investigation.

The Metropole was extremely busy. Soldiers and GFP ran up and down the stairs in full equipment. Hortense could see there was a big operation in progress and wondered why she had been brought to watch. Abruptly the reason sank in, and she felt her energy drain away. Clearly the SD hoped to arrest François and planned to confront him with his sister immediately. She waited for hours in suspense. Finally the two van Avondt brothers, René and Albrecht, both in the Belgian SS, angrily took her back to the prison. Back in the safe-keeping of the nuns she collapsed exhausted, with her mother in her cell. She dared not say she thought they might have caught François.

The rigours of clandestine life had left François Daman thinner than ever. Belgium suffered badly from rationing and food shortages and those on the run had even less to eat. What made it worse for François Daman was the way he controlled and bottled up his feelings. His whole family was torn apart. His parents' house in Pleinstraat had been wrecked and was boarded up. His wife Elisa had been living in the woods for over two years with his boy Jacques, who was eight, and she was suffering from pneumonia. He knew very well that the GFP were hoping to catch him, using his sister and mother to bait the trap. Out of frustration he threw a brick through a window into the Kommandantur with a message wrapped round it threatening retribution if anything happened to his family. There was nothing more he could do. Much as he wanted to attempt a rescue, the harsh fact was that the Partisans could not afford to risk the lives of twenty-odd men to satisfy the emotions of one man. Those emotions can only be guessed at. His family had always felt anti-German but he tortured himself wondering how deeply they would have become involved in the Resistance without him. He had been on the run since October 1942 and had become adept at avoiding the Gestapo and SD. His parents and favourite sister had sat it out at home until they were beaten up and arrested, ironically on St Valentine's day, and he was tortured with guilt. This self-criticism was justified for the Gestapo had filled out his father's prison record with the words, 'Hostage for his son'.

One day Hortense was returned from interrogation to the prison early and during the afternoon she was disturbed in her cell by a sister who brought another prisoner.

'We've got no room. This woman's got to share your cell,' she explained shortly.

Hortense said nothing. She watched the woman come in and sit down on the cot next to her.

'Been here long?' the woman said conversationally, scratching herself. She was ordinarily dressed, as though she too had been arrested as a political prisoner. Hortense did not recognise her.

Hortense did not reply. She stood up, crossed the cell and knelt in the corner by the pipes.

'Our Father, which art in heaven, hallowed be thy name,' Hortense began muttering, and fingered her rosary.

'It ain't that bad surely,' the woman said, amused.

Hortense ignored her and went on with her prayers. The woman looked at Hortense's back and said, 'Maybe it would help to talk about it?' There was a faint note of impatience in her voice.

There was no reply, just a murmur of familiar prayers. The woman tried several more times to chat without success. After only an hour she lost her patience completely and banged on the door for the sisters to let her out. Hortense never stopped praying on her knees in the corner till the woman had left, but she smiled to herself. The woman was a stooge.

After a week or so the Gestapo made another attempt. This time the woman lasted longer, through the afternoon till evening. She seemed able to withstand the constant droning of prayers, which she tried to halt periodically with subtle overtures to conversation, but when Hortense suddenly went over to the slop bucket and made a most atrocious smell she too banged on the door for release.

It is academic to speculate what might have happened to Hortense if the life of the Little Prison in Louvain had continued. It was not to be. The war outside raged on. By the late spring of 1944 the Germans were in retreat on the Russian front and well aware that the Allies were planning a massive invasion of Europe in the West. Only the site of the landings was still unknown to them. Many Germans supported their Führer's view that the invasion was sure to come across the shortest sea passage, into the Pas de Calais. No one was surprised therefore when some of the innumerable squadrons of bombers which had streamed over Belgian soil to pummel German cities were diverted to attack targets inside Belgium itself.

In the afternoon of 12 May 1944 twelve bomber crews of 419 Squadron at Middleton St George in England met in the briefing room to hear the details of a raid to take place that night. This was the Canadian Squadron to which Williston and Arseneau had belonged, and the room was where they too were briefed for their fatal mission to Cologne, when they had to bale out over Louvain.

Among the Canadian crews who gathered in the briefing room were two who sat up and took particular interest when they heard that the target of that night's bombing mission was in Belgium. They both had relations there. The young pilot and captain of Lancaster KB718 was Art de Breyne. He was a first generation Canadian whose relations still lived in Belgium. His father had emigrated from there in 1906 and his mother, who was English and came from Durham, a year later. He had already done several ops to bomb targets in Belgium, in Ghent, St Ghislain, and at Bourg-Léopold where the attack on a German army camp at 2 a.m. caused 2000 casualties as they lay in their beds. His bomb aimer, Sergeant Jack W. Friday, was concerned when the Operations Officer pointed at the map and revealed that the aim was to destroy the railway marshalling yards in Louvain. Jack Friday had relations in Louvain. He said nothing and tried to concentrate on the job in hand, noting the bearings to the target area and the altitude for release, a mere 7000 feet and well within the range of the German 88mm anti-aircraft guns, but essential to ensure reasonably accurate bombing. He tried to put out of his mind the fact that the great church of St Peter in the centre of town was only about 1100 metres from the railway station and that the area around the railway yards was heavily populated. Art de Breyne kept thinking of the old university buildings packed into the narrow streets. Neither man could have known that a young blonde girl and her mother who had helped Arseneau and Williston, their predecessors in the squadron, were held in the Little Prison for women, no more than 250 metres from the railway.

Late that Friday night the peace of the countryside around Middleton was shattered by the roar of the engines of twelve Lancasters taking off. De Breyne and his crew had bombed marshalling yards in Ghent and Boulogne on Monday and Tuesday nights and were tired. The long dark journey down the length of England passed without incident and they started the run in to the target at twenty-two minutes past midnight. De Breyne looked out of the Lancaster window to the east at the yellow glow of explosions five miles away and 7000 feet below. He assumed this was another target and ignored it. Ten minutes later they arrived over Louvain and he could see golden circles of explosions and burning fires far below on the ground, but he identified no target-marking indicators, called T/Is. These T/Is were essential to show the bomb aimers exactly where to release the bombs. De Breyne turned the huge four-engined aircraft round in a single orbit over the target area searching for the T/I, his eyes sweeping over the chaos of fires and explosions beneath. It seemed to him the whole area was blazing and once more a picture of the old town filled his mind, the university colleges and libraries interspersed along the streets among high, narrow residential buildings. He imagined people cowering in cellars while the aircraft thundered overhead. After another circuit, constantly checking with his navigator, Flying Officer Body, and other members of the crew to see if anyone could spot the target markers, de Breyne decided to abort the mission. Whether he was unconsciously biased because of his connections with Belgium it is impossible to say, but he acknowledges he felt uncomfortable about dropping his bombs on the town without indicators. He was sure he had saved the life of a friend by ordering the return to England. He noticed how pleased Jack Friday sounded when he told him the drop was aborted, but it was not until they returned to Middleton that the bomb-aimer told him about his relations in the town.

The Squadron Operations Record Book describes the mission as 'a particularly unfortunate night, as Aircraft 'J' (Art de Breyne) was an abortive effort . . . [and] two of the Squadron aircraft were missing from this sortie. Weather conditions were good . . . with the exception of the visibility which was considered poor . . . Enemy opposition encountered seemed to be moderate. The target marking was . . . just fair. The results of this mission are not expected to be good.'

They were not. Louvain was devastated. Bombs dropped all over the town, which had not seen such a bombardment since the fighting in 1940. In the Little Prison the nuns came running as soon as the first bombs fell on the railway yards just outside the walls. A cacophony of slamming and rattling began as they opened all the doors. They shouted at everyone to go down the stairs and a mad rush started into the cellars. The noise was deafening, with the nuns shrieking, guards shouting and the roar of explosions echoing round in the empty space of the vaulted prison wings. Several times the prison itself shook with the impact of 500 lb bombs streaking out of the dark sky from the Canadian Lancasters 7000 feet above. There were no lights in the prison but the blazing fires outside threw ghastly patterns across the arched ceilings and lit faces with sudden flashes of manic colour. Hortense did not see her mother during the frightening dash into the basement passages under the wings of the prison, when men and women prisoners all jostled together. She was pushed with a mass of others into a large cellar where the air was thick with dust. The cellar door slammed shut and was locked by a German guard. Hortense looked round. The first thing she saw was what seemed to her a quite immense bomb, hanging out of the ceiling where its plunge earthwards had been finally stopped. The cellar had received a direct hit, but by some miracle the bomb had not exploded. In shafts of light coming through the broken ceiling the huge metal nose seemed to float about in the swirling acrid dust and to point directly at her. The bomb dominated the whole room.

She stared at the menace above her, aware of the locked door, and wondered whether the bomb would explode. Even down in the cellar she could feel the prison shake as the Canadians released tens of thousands of pounds of high explosive over the railway yards less than 300 metres away. The danger she was in hardly seemed realistic. She was already a prisoner of the Gestapo, interrogated, tortured and constantly at risk of execution, which was the expected fate of most arrested Partisans, and now she was beneath a vast, primed but unexploded bomb. The bomb did not seem to make matters any worse. If it exploded their lives would evaporate instantly in a cloud of red steam but until that finality she lived a prisoner at the mercy of the Sicherheitsdienst.

A familiar voice called out behind her.

'Hortense?'

She turned round, searching the dirty air for the face of a friend.

'Marcel!' She spotted the grinning face of the gendarme under the layer of grime which covered his skin. They were all filthy but she easily recognised Marcel Van den Borght. They pushed over between other prisoners and clasped each other in a warm embrace, delighted to see one another safe and alive. The bomb was forgotten as they began to exchange a flood of questions and answers about what had happened since the day of Hortense's arrest three months ago.

Marcel had seen all the arrests, several hundred being picked up by the end of February, and realised his own position had become extremely delicate. He was suspected and finally arrested by his own gendarmes. They placed him on a civil charge in order to put him beyond the reach of the Gestapo and the SD. The SS dealt only with crimes associated with state security and resistance to the Occupation.

To her enormous relief, he told Hortense that François was still free, though the SS had made a tremendous effort to catch him. He always managed to keep a step ahead and had not slowed in his work with the Partisans or with the escape lines. This news cheered her very much. She had survived the interrogations partly from the satisfaction of believing that her brother was continuing his struggle, and hers, against the Germans. The news gave her confidence. She could not wait to tell her mother when she had an opportunity after the raid.

219

The distant sound of explosions faded but it was some hours before the door was thrown open and the prisoners were herded back to their cells. The prison had been badly hit, especially the women's wing. A stick of bombs had landed on the other side of Justus Lipsiusstraat, and the prison wall had been flattened. The laundry, cookhouse and mortuary buildings around the women's wing were also seriously damaged, all the roof-glass had been blown out and debris littered the floors everywhere inside. The following morning the women prisoners were put to work helping the nuns clear up the dust and rubble and restore what order they could. Hortense was relieved to find her mother unhurt after the raid. When she was sure no one was listening she passed on Marcel's good news about François.

The attack had caused appalling chaos in Louvain. A diarist of the time recorded that he had watched the bombers release flares and witnessed a dog-fight between German aircraft and the British planes, perhaps accounting for the two missing Lancasters. The devastation was widespread around the town including Marshal Foch Square, right in the centre next to the church. Residential areas and many university buildings were hit and burnt out, among them the Fonteyn Library, the Institute of Physics and the Institute of Zoology in the Rue Namur. The Kommandantur, the old pre-war Palais de Justice, where Hortense and her father were humiliated the night of their arrest, had itself suffered rough justice: by morning it was no more than a burnt out shell. The diarist noted also that the railway marshalling yards round the station were damaged but not put completely out of action. The target was certainly hit but the railway was working again in a matter of days. However the enormous damage to the rest of the town, some of it a long way from the station, took years to rebuild, and innocent lives were lost.

All this damage was done by only a handful of aircraft,

and raises the controversial question of how effective
such bombing raids were during the war. Was it really
necessary to use so much explosive and scatter it about
so inaccurately? That night over Louvain there were
certainly nine Lancasters, and possibly the two which
were brought down managed to release their bombs first.
We know that Art de Breyne did not release his. Each
aircraft carried seventeen 500 lb high explosive bombs,
so that at least 76,500 lb of high explosive was dropped
all over Louvain. Leaving aside the consequences of this
mission on Hortense Daman's life, that night cannot have
been much out of the ordinary for the Canadian bomber
squadron. The experience was typical, and thousands of
these raids took place, with hundreds of thousands of
pounds of explosives tearing great holes in the ground in
Germany and occupied Europe. The enormous number
of casualties, for example over 6000 Belgian civilians
killed by Allied bombing, has been described by more
qualified commentators as a sad evil which could not
be avoided. The bombing was a strategic effort to end
the war by destroying the enemy's industrial support
and taking the battle into the heartland of the Third
Reich. The moral aspects of the bombing and whether
it achieved its aim have been discussed elsewhere, but
in relation to Hortense's experiences as a Partisan and
to other clandestines in occupied Europe, the value of
such attacks seems unimpressive. In 1943 Pierre Hermans
left Hortense's home in Pleinstraat and used some 4 lb
of plastic to blow the line south of Louvain, killing 285
German soldiers. No civilians were harmed. In all, the
Belgian Army of Partisans carried out 1268 attacks against
railways, put out of action and damaged 641 locomotives
and over 10,000 pieces of rolling stock. SOE in France
used only about 3000 lb of plastic in the entire war and
put ninety factories completely out of production. These
agents and their civilian helpers used well under half the
explosives that one Canadian Lancaster bomber carried

on a single night over Louvain. Clandestine agents on the ground carried out the attacks and placed the explosive exactly where it could do the most damage to the target, and incidentally where it did the least harm to the civilian population. Nor do the losses compare. In the course of the war Bomber Command lost about 55,000 extremely brave men, a figure over four times the total strength of SOE; while the American bomber crews lost nearly 80,000, mainly in daytime raids.

Most important in war is the financial cost, arguably more so today with the increased cost of aircraft and support systems than in the Second World War. The price of Bomber Command's losses was immense in machines and equipment. For example, in four and a half months in 1944 Bomber Command lost 1000 aircraft destroyed and 1682 seriously damaged. The losses of the subversives, disguised and grubbing about in their dangerous secret world in the streets and safe houses of occupied Europe with a few satchels of plastic explosives, whether trained like SOE agents or untrained like Hortense Daman, were minute in comparison. But their losses were in some way more telling in human terms. Louvain alone lost over fifty Partisans and the number of families which were split up and destroyed bears no thinking about. Their commitment was none the less fierce, their bravery equal but of quite a different sort to that of the young aircrews. The striking difference is the means of achieving the aim. One might ask what groups like the Partisans might have done had they had regular supplies of equipment, the equivalent of a few 500 lb bombs, instead of having to barter pistols and explosives from other more fortunate Resistance units.

These comparisons demand that staff officers preparing for the next war (and their masters, the politicians) look very carefully at the means and benefits of harnessing the local population, or of using more unconventional special forces to develop SOE's cost-effective example. After all, the Russians have allocated no less than 22,000 Spetsnatz 'diversionary' troops to fight in West Germany alone, where small patrols armed with the Kalashnikov assault rifle (a derivative of the Wehrmacht's MP44, incidentally) and plastic explosive will cause havoc in the rear echelons of NATO forces.

If the bombing failed to destroy the Germans morale and willingness to fight, which has been claimed, it certainly did raise the morale of people everywhere in the Resistance. François and Hortense knew their efforts alone against the Germans were not enough, and the bombing proved to them far more convincingly than any carefully phrased radio message that the Allies meant to defeat Hitler. When people heard the deep drone of bombers flying overhead in the dark sky, they would lean out of their windows to catch a glimpse if they could and wish them luck. Shouted warnings by German street patrols to shut the windows and not show a light meant nothing. People were delighted that Germans somewhere would get a pasting that night. In the prison Hortense and her mother were not in the slightest put out by the raid, only pleased to be alive.

Art de Breyne and his crew returned from that mission unscathed, but only a month later, on 12 June, after fourteen operations with 419 Squadron, their Lancaster was bounced from below by a Luftwaffe Junkers 88 while they were attacking Cambrai railway marshalling yards in Northern France. De Breyne could not hold the stricken Lancaster, which plunged into a corkscrew dive. He managed to straighten the plane as they passed 3000 feet and immediately ordered his crew to bale out. He held the Lancaster steady as his men left one by one, terribly slowly, it seemed to de Breyne, who kept glancing at the altimeter and finally abandoned his aircraft at about 700 feet above the ground. His parachute had hardly opened before his feet slammed into the ground. Unknown to him, a drama continued in the rear of the plane above him. Warrant Officer Andy Mynarski had seen that Pilot Officer Brophy, who was rear gunner, could not turn his turret to get out and jump. He went down the belly of the falling Lancaster and spent precious minutes trying to force the turret mechanism to move round, fully aware that they were losing altitude all the time and that he could have escaped himself in plenty of time to use his parachute. Finally Brophy persuaded him it was useless and this brave man jumped from the plane. He had left it too late and his parachute never opened.

Assisted by the efforts de Breyne had made to keep the Lancaster on an even keel, the plane glided down in a nearly perfect landing-attitude. One wing was ripped off by a large tree and the Lancaster broke up as it hit the soft French fields beyond. By some miracle Brophy, still encased in the perspex turret, was flung out and landed unharmed. The French farmer who picked him up and spirited him away still finds it incredible that he emerged without a broken bone. Four of the crew, Art de Breyne, captain; Pilot Officer A. R. Body, navigator; Warrant Officer Kelly, wireless operator; and Pilot Officer G. P. Brophy, rear gunner, returned to England via the escape lines. Once home Brophy was able to report Mynarski's extraordinarily brave attempt to save his life and, because the citation was reported by an officer senior to the dead man, Mynarski was awarded a posthumous Victoria Cross. Jack Friday, for all his family contacts in Belgium, and flight engineer Sergeant R. E. Vigars were unfortunately picked up by the Germans searching round the wreckage and spent the rest of the war as prisoners in Germany.

In the chaos of the morning after the raid on Louvain Hortense was busy sweeping up shards of glass on the black and white diamond-shaped tiles when she saw a nun walking over to her. The nun silently motioned her to step to one side and follow her. Hortense followed down a short passage leading off the women's wing which led towards the nuns' private kitchen area (now the prison laundry). The nun turned and spoke to Hortense in a soft whisper.

'There's an old man outside who keeps calling your name,' the older woman said. 'You can't see him from inside here, so you can come with me, if you want to. But you must promise not to run away.' The nun's straight clear-eyed gaze demanded honesty.

'Of course, Sister, I promise,' Hortense replied, intrigued.

The prisoners were normally permitted one period of exercise every day, in a small walled enclosure next to the nuns' garden. During the time Hortense had been held in the prison she had only been allowed to exercise outside once, and the simple act of going out of doors was a special occasion. When she saw who was outside, however, she did not even notice the privilege.

At the little door they used to go into the garden the nun pointed. The garden, like the wall beyond, was no more, buried under a pile of broken brick where the prison wall had collapsed. Hortense could see plainly into Justus Lipsiusstraat over a rubble barrier to her freedom no more than a metre high. The bombing had breached the prison perimeter wall.

Her attention was riveted, not by the chance of escape, but by the sight of her grandfather Pierre Van den Eynde, standing on the other side of the rubble shouting to her.

'Hortenseke! How are you?' The old man was clearly very agitated and overjoyed to see his granddaughter.

'I'm fine, Bompa! So's Mum,' she called back. He was so close, only 30 metres away, on the pavement outside.

'Come on, come with me. You can get away!' he called to her, waving his arms and hopping about on the edge of the pile of rubble in the gap in the wall. 'You can get away!'

Hortense looked back. To her surprise the nun had gone inside. There was no one to stop her escaping.

She was on her own. She began to walk towards her grandfather, longing in that moment to go home with him and enjoy his company again in peace in front of the fire. The gap between them closed. She was close to the broken prison wall. She could see the devastated houses beyond, in the direction of the railway station.

Then she thought of her mother still inside the women's wing. What would the SS do to her? How could she manage without support? And her father. What of him, also a prisoner somewhere? Might not the SS take some revenge on them for her escape? How could she leave her parents to suffer while she ran away? The thought made her pause.

'Come on' her grandfather called urgently.

After no more than a moment's thought she knew she could not escape. It was a mad decision, in retrospect, which runs contrary to all the best rules of escape and evasion, which dictate emphatically that prisoners should never hesitate to seize the opportunity to escape. Even if some are left behind it is better that one gets away, given the chance. In Hortense's case the chance had been given providentially by the same Canadian Squadron that she had helped earlier.

But she stayed.

Her grandfather saw her stop and knew instinctively what she was thinking.

'Courage! Be brave, Hortenseke,' he cried out, his voice ringing with encouragement. 'Don't forget, be brave!'

He glanced up the road. She heard shouting and the sound of vehicles. She realised the Germans were alerted and turned to go inside, in case they accused the nuns of risking her escape. She did not want to get them into trouble. She took a last look at her grandfather, who stared fixedly at her as the German soldiers began to shove him away with their rifles. It was the last time she saw him.

# St Valentines Day 1944

She walked slowly through the door into the nuns' kitchen and down the passage into the wing. She met the nun who had brought her out coming the other way with her mother. The nun had had complete confidence that Hortense would not break her word and had gone to find Stephanie Daman. It was too late. Hortense explained what had happened and the two walked back into the wing. Stephanie was pleased her father had not been hurt in the bombing but sad not to have seen him. She never did see him again.

The opportunity of escape is rarely presented, often passes unrecognised and is easily missed. Hortense had chosen. She was in the hands of the SS, an agency far more ruthless than mere fate. She and her mother turned back into the prison, unaware of the horrors which awaited them in the future.

# 9

# Into the Cold Inferno

'Effective and lasting intimidation can only be achieved by capital punishment or by means which leave the population in the dark about the fate of the culprit.' Field Marshal Wilhelm Keitel, Chief of Hitler's General Staff.

For Hortense, the raid on the night of 12/13 May 1944 marked the beginning of a lonely spiral into hell. The Little Prison was no longer secure and only two days later, on 15 May, the SS came to the door in the narrow passage to the women's wing and rang the bell for admission. As usual, Sister Augustine took a very long time to answer the summons and the SS were in a bad temper when they eventually shoved their way down the little corridor into the women's wing. They began to call out names and the nuns opened the cells to let the women go downstairs to muster in front of the Germans.

Hortense and her mother Stephanie stood among a group of some forty-five others, all political prisoners like themselves. Most had been arrested at the same time. Most, like the Damans, had been denounced by men like Vleugels.

The SS consulted a typewritten list and shouted out names. The women were hustled out of the women's wing down the narrow passage.

'Van den Eynde, Stephanie,' screamed the SS, and Hortense's mother stepped forward. The Germans followed Flemish custom and identified her with her maiden name. Stephanie walked slowly out of the wing and glanced back at her daughter. She did not know what would happen and had little confidence she would ever see Hortense again.

Hortense watched her mother walk out of sight through the small iron door she had come to know so well, passing through it every morning for a month for interrogation. She concentrated on every detail of her mother's form. Then she was gone.

When thirty women had left, they turned to the remaining group of fifteen and marched them out of the women's wing to the courtyard entrance to the prison where a German army truck was waiting.

With armed guards in the back, the truck turned out of the tall gates of the Little Prison and Hortense guessed the direction they took was towards Brussels. After an hour they were driving between the high Flemish-style apartment blocks in the southern approaches to the capital near the Gare du Midi, the main railway station for all routes to the south. The truck turned off and in a few minutes halted in front of the white stone castellated façade of St Gilles Prison. The less showy and more practical brick-built prisoner blocks loomed behind.

St Gilles is Brussels' main prison, built about the same period in the nineteenth century as the Little Prison in Louvain, but much larger. There are five huge wings, three storeys high, radiating from the central hub. During the Second World War these were crammed with prisoners. Apart from the run-of-the-mill criminal population, the prison was over-crowded with political prisoners, the victims of German oppression. There were men and women who had been in the Resistance, others suspected of Resistance work, hostages for friends and relations who could not be caught, who had done nothing at all, and Allied servicemen who were held there for weeks before finally being shipped off to prisoner of war camps in Germany. Williston and Arseneau had been held in St Gilles after their betrayal and arrest, before being moved by train to their Dulagluft (POW camp for airmen) in Frankfurt. During the Occupation St Gilles was run by the German Wehrmacht and not the SS.

The truck rumbled through the gate past the guard-house lodge and Hortense looked out through the back for a last glimpse of the streets outside prison. She watched the massive timber gates grinding shut behind her and then the truck stopped in the courtyard. The Germans shouted at the women to get out. They immediately separated Hortense and a girl called Gisella from the group, dragged them out of the courtyard up some steps and shoved them down a long corridor which led into the heart of the prison. It was a vast cavern, the small cells like bare stone caves standing off narrow cast-iron galleries rising in tiers above the hard tiled floor. The prisoners lived like so many troglodytes in lofty, vaulted tunnels which rang constantly with the sound of steel and smelt sickly of cabbage and urine.

Gisella was a white Hungarian, a nurse, who lived in the same street in Louvain where she had been imprisoned, Maria Theresiastraat. She was worried that her home had been hit by the bombing. She had been denounced and attended a trial set up by her SS interrogators during which she was sentenced to death. She had told Hortense that she had had no idea she was to be tried and had no opportunity to defend herself or answer any accusations. The trial was a farce, no more than a rubber stamp to satisfy the obsession with tidy documentation which seems to have reached even into the most hellish activities of the Nazi regime.

When Hortense was marched to her new cell on the first floor, half-way along the iron walkway, she discovered she was not to be afforded the luxury of a trial. A panel was fixed to the door, clearly marked in bright red letters, 'Ter Dood Veroordeeld' ('Condemned to Death'). A skull and cross-bones painted above set the seal. The guard pushed her inside, slammed the iron door and locked it.

Hortense had graduated. Only a few weeks from her eighteenth birthday, she was in solitary confinement under sentence of death in her country's main prison. In Louvain, she had been walked to the Gestapo offices in Leopold I Straat every day for a month and suffered brutal interrogations. But every evening she had been brought back to the women's wing where she had had the support of her mother, through the courtesy of the nuns.

Also, there had always been a little news of the outside world through the verger in the chapel. In spite of the shock of her arrest and savage questioning, her introduction to prison life there had had some compensations. In Louvain, her home town, she had been surrounded by friends. In St Gilles she was alone in a harsh adult world.

Hortense was badly shaken to see that stark message on the door of her cell, but she had always assumed that capture meant death. François had told her that from the beginning, and she knew of enough cases of men and women in the Resistance who had been executed.

Like so many Partisans and victims in all the occupied countries, Hortense Daman was held without trial, without legal representation and unable even to present her own defence. She doubted there had been more than the briefest discussion about her, and assumed one or two SS officers, probably Max Gunter or Robert Verbelen, had sealed her fate by a casual stroke of the pen. The SS had tired of their attempts to persuade her to give information about her brother or to use her to trick him into making mistakes so that they could arrest him, and had literally written her off. As a courier for the Partisans, among the groups most hated by the Germans for its links with Communism, there was never any question but that the

SS would eventually dispatch her into the twilight world of 'Nacht und Nebel'. The Nacht und Nebel order had been made on 7 December 1941 and, by the time Hortense was condemned to death in St Gilles many thousands of victims had disappeared without trace into the system of anarchy set up by Hitler and Himmler's SS. Like a dog, Hortense had no idea what her captors would do to her next, but she never for a moment thought twice about her own commitment or doubted that the Allies would defeat the Nazis and liberate her country.

Her cell was much the same as the one in the Little Prison, but the ceiling was higher and the walls were plastered. Only five paces long and three shorts paces wide, the cell was barely furnished. There was the same sort of cast-iron bed, which folded three ways into a table during the day, and a chair, an *armoire* fixed to the wall by the cell door, a tap in the other corner behind the door with a bucket underneath, a piss-pot and a pewter mug and bowl stamped with the block letter and cell number. The window was set high in the outside wall, six feet above the floor where again a central heating pipe ran across the cell. The three panes were filthy and the window frame, which was hinged at the bottom, could not be opened more than a fraction at the top to let in a little fresh air.

Prison routine revolves around food. Today the regimen in St Gilles is controlled by a woman director and the food is considered – by the prisoners themselves – the best in Belgium's prisons. There is even a menu. Under the Wehrmacht the situation was rather different. 'Breakfast' was a weak, grey ersatz coffee, which tasted especially foul as the Germans dosed it with a strong solution of bromide to control the sexual drive of the inmates. Prisoners could look forward to this slop at six, after which Hortense had to fold her bed, clean her cell and wipe the floor. The main meal of the day at lunchtime was served amid the usual cacophony of clattering trolleys, spoons, metal bowls, the rattle of locks and slamming doors, always accompanied by the smell of boiled vegetables which permeated every corner of the prison. A gruel of soup was normal, with mashed potatoes, but the kitchens might send up anything including lumps of raw fish. Hortense was always disgusted but she wanted to survive and decided early on to eat what she was given. Her experience in prison so far made her realise that she could not afford to be choosy about the food. The din of metal and the nauseating smell washed out of the kitchens in fresh waves again at four in the afternoon, filling the vaulted wings and focusing the prisoners' minds on a meagre ration of black bread, which was generally brown and covered with mould.

In the evening, after this issue the guards came to her cell and she had to strip naked for the night. Hortense was always embarrassed standing naked in front of the soldiers as she handed over her bundle of clothes. They were clothes she had been wearing since the day of her arrest, but she considered herself fortunate that the weather was improving through May and the nights were not so cold. All the same there was little comfort on her straw mattress. It was about two inches thick if she shook it carefully to spread the straw about and keep her off the metal slats of the bed. Then she curled up under a thin blanket, her long blonde hair bright in the grey gloom, a small figure only half covering the seven foot iron bed that had been made to accommodate her country's worst and largest criminals.

At seven o'clock every night someone would open 'Radio' St Gilles. '*Écoutez-moi les gars!*' a voice would shout, echoing easily round the high-ceilinged wings. '*Ici Radio St Gilles! Ici les nouvelles de Londres!*'

And after a few days, she heard, 'The British have captured Monte Cassino in Italy and are marching on Rome.'

Others would take up the cry if they had news to tell or, if the German officer on duty sent guards from the central hall to quiet the prisoners in one wing, someone else would start up in another.

Though incarcerated, the prisoners were exceptionally well-informed. Newcomers with up to date news were frequent, and every day men and women were taken out for interrogation by the Gestapo in their headquarters in the Avenue Louise. The rule of thumb was that the higher up the seventeen-storey building a prisoner was taken, the worse the interrogation would be, so that people on the street could not hear the screams. In between sessions with the SS, they were held in cells in the basement, which had air conduits leading to grilles set in the pavement. Friends and relatives would risk their own freedom to walk past the hated building and drop tiny balls of screwed up paper down the grilles. They desperately hoped the messages on those little pieces of paper would reach their loved ones who had been arrested. These messages echoed round the darkened wings of St Gilles prison every night.

'For Michel, Anne-Marie and the baby are all right,' or 'For Joel, your mother's out of hospital.'

Any news was good news. Radio St Gilles was encouraging and Hortense always listened carefully. She hoped to hear news of her father. She was not to know that Jacques Daman had already been condemned without trial, like his wife and daughter, to obscurity under the Night and Fog order, guilty as 'hostage for his son' and under 'the collective responsibility of members of families of assassins and saboteurs'.

Jacques Daman's interrogation in Louvain had been almost cursory and he was trucked to Breendonk within days of his arrest. There he suffered the privations of a regime which he described as far worse than anything else he experienced. The Commandant SS Major Johann Schmidt enjoyed making life as miserable as he could for the prisoners, including the free use of torture in a small concrete room, which he installed with a drainage sump in the floor to take away fluids. He had the full support of his staff, Prauss, Vermeulen, Wyss, de Boodt and other Belgian SS. The last three had beaten up and buried alive a young man of eighteen, almost the same age as Hortense. When the boy's head was all that could be seen, he cried out for his 'Mummy!'. De Boodt laughed and kicked sand to fill his mouth and block his nose. This last desperate cry was but one of a huge volume of screams uttered for all the unspeakable things which were done there to over 3500 people, both men and women. The scale of the atrocities implies that Breendonk must have been a massive place, but the prisoners lived in claustrophobic underground passages stinking of sweat and urine, sixty to a room on bunks three tiers high, where talking was banned altogether and food a meagre 225 grammes of bread a day with soup. They were forced to back-breaking work moving earth from above the fortress in a day which began at 4 a.m. and ended at 8 p.m. Every minute was controlled by the SS. The bronchitic Jacques Daman survived to be taken on a transport to Germany on 6 May. After two days in a cattle truck he arrived in Buchenwald concentration camp where he was numbered 48576 and continued his struggle to live.

Nor did Hortense hear anything of her mother although Stephanie Daman was also taken to St Gilles after the bombing in Louvain. She was kept in the great prison in Brussels for only a week until 23 May when the Gestapo sent her by train, in a cattle truck full of other prisoners, to Vught concentration camp in Holland. *En route* their transport was attacked by Allied planes and the prisoners were kicked and herded by the SS into underground bunkers. Once the women realised they were not going to be shot out of hand, there was some small comfort in the thought that the attack showed how strong the Allied air force had become over German occupied territory. However, comfort was decidedly not a feature of Vught. Stephanie Daman was given number 1049 and forgotten.

Personal messages were not the only 'transmissions' on Radio St Gilles. Often a prisoner would shout out that a handful of English pilots had been picked up and were 'keeping us company in B Block'.

Everyone assumed that an Allied invasion of Europe was going to take place. Even the guards, most of them older soldiers in the Wehrmacht, accepted the inevitability of invasion from England backed by the logistic strength of the Americans. Though aircrews of all nationalities were fighting with the Allies, they were all called 'English', since in Belgian eyes it was the English who had so often come to Belgian aid in the past. Now, the invasion to liberate Belgium again would come from English shores.

Messages were also passed along the pipes using the Morse code. Hortense was not trained in Morse, but she had picked up a certain amount and passed on words as best she could from the cells on each side. After a very slow start she managed to open a conversation with a man two cells away and, assisted by Radio St Gilles, he told her he had been arrested in Liège for having no identity papers. He expected to be released soon and she asked him to tell her family she was all right if he got out. In the event, this man was released and he passed the message to Hortense's elder sister Bertha.

In the last week of May she was sitting in her cell when a light flashing on the dirty window panes caught her eye. She looked up and noticed the light flickered on and off her window in a regular manner. Someone was signalling to her in Morse, sending the SOS signal.

She glanced at the solid iron door of her cell. She never knew when one of the guards might chance to use the peephole to peer inside. She could hear no one outside on the landing so she stood up, took the chair and, after some time finding the right technique, succeeded in balancing the legs of her chair on the fat heating pipe below the window. She clambered up and reached to the window frame. Hanging on precariously she was just able to squint round it through the narrow slit of light which was as far as the window would open. She searched the barred windows of the cell block opposite for the tell-tale flashing which had attracted her attention. The light started again. She thrust her hand through the gap and gave the thumbs up sign. Then over a period of several days her unknown ally gave a tremendous boost to her confidence. By dint of hand signals and sign language she quickly learnt he was a pilot, and he gave her to understand that there would be many more like him coming soon and the sky would be filled with parachutists. Repeatedly he turned his hand over to show a parachute and pointed at the sky. Then, after pointing at his watch, he opened his hand out slowly three times to show all five fingers and Hortense became convinced something was going to happen in fifteen days time.

On the evening of 6 June Radio St Gilles had hardly finished the first sentence before the prison was in an uproar.

'*Les Alliés sont venus!*' the cry went up. The invasion had started. '*Vive les Anglais! Vive la Belgique! Vive la France!*'

The shout was taken up in every cell. Every prisoner began cheering and singing. Throats became hoarse singing the Marseillaise and anti-German songs. The sound was deafening, magnified tenfold and ringing round the high vaulted ceilings in each wing.

In the centre the German soldiers screamed for silence and were ignored. The officer on duty called out the prison guard and the din was increased with the crash of boots on the tiled floors as soldiers ran up and down the landings beating on doors and threatening prisoners with solitary confinement. Finally Hortense heard the Germans firing their rifles in desperation.

Eventually the prison settled down, but beneath the uneasy silence ran an undercurrent of triumph. Not a prisoner went to sleep that night without the magnificent feeling that the Germans were at last on the run. Hortense was thrilled her airman informant in the block opposite had been right and she slept in peace, with the certainty that Belgium would soon be free.

Within a week the old soldier who was her guard told her she was to be moved into Germany. He risked punishment telling her, but he was a veteran of the Great War and had a family of his own. The techniques of the SS were not his. Coming so soon after the invasion, this news upset Hortense who expected the Allies to be in Brussels any minute. After some while thinking about it she decided to tell her friend opposite. She arranged the chair carefully on the pipe and struggled into position to see through the window. She had kept her own sliver of mirror from the Little Prison, with one or two other personal effects, and began signalling SOS to attract his attention, counting down the line of barred windows in the block to find the right cell.

There was no response. Normally her airman was quick to reply and she was immediately suspicious. She stopped flashing and got down swiftly off her chair.

Her cell door crashed open and two officers stormed in shouting triumphantly, 'We've got you now!'

They grabbed Hortense by the arms and she was shoved and pushed down the narrow cast-iron stairway to the prison superintendent's office, a glass-sided room just off the central hub. As she was propelled inside she noticed four men standing to one side, their hands in manacles. One wore a baggy sheepskin jacket typical of aircrew clothing.

The superintendent in charge went berserk. He began screaming at Hortense who was standing only a couple of feet away.

'You're nothing but a terrorist! A saboteur! A criminal bandit! You've always denied you had any contact with Englishmen, but now we've caught you talking to one.

We've caught you red-handed!'

Hortense had survived a month of the SS in Louvain and had become thick-skinned to this sort of treatment. After several minutes of frenetic shouting, every detail of which could be heard by the prisoners outside the glass-walled office, she waited for a lull and said very quietly, 'Herr Commandant, I'm not deaf.'

'What!'

'Herr Commandant, you're completely wrong. I'm not a terrorist and I don't know anything about Englishmen.'

The German calmed himself and demanded an explanation. 'Then what were you doing at the window?'

Hortense continued in a quiet tone and told him that her father had been arrested with her, for no reason, and that ever since she had been in prison she had wondered what had happened to him. She said, her voice echoing her real feelings, that she had worried about him all those weeks, not knowing where he was.

'Get on with it,' the German snapped irritably, but Hortense saw his anger had evaporated.

She told him that the previous evening she had heard someone coughing and the sound had been carried through her window from one of the cells nearby.

'My father's not well. He's got bronchitis, and the coughing sounded exactly like him, Herr Commandant,' she said, fixing him with a look of young innocence in her wide blue eyes. 'Put yourself in my place. I had to see if the person coughing was my father. Even if I'd known that you were waiting outside my cell yourself.'

There was a long pause as the German stared at her.

'Nine days bread and water,' he ordered finally, and the old guard marched Hortense out of the office.

As she passed the group of four with their hands manacled, she opened her eyes wide in a signal of caution and pursed her lips to indicate they should say nothing. At least she knew they must have heard every word of her interview with the Commandant.

'Oh dear, Hortensia,' her elderly guard admonished her like a nanny, quite upset by the affair. 'What have you done now?'

He shut her up in her old cell and came back within the hour to escort her down to the *cachots*, the solitary cells. She was marched again down the spiral cast-iron stairs, past several checkpoints at grilles in the corridors and finally pushed into a cell with double doors. The second door was extra security on the prisoner and gave no chance to escape. Even when a prison guard came in to feed or water, the inner door was always locked on the prisoner. The window was a tiny opening near the ceiling nine feet from the floor, so Hortense thought her cell was below ground, but prisoners in the solitary block were not intended to see out and her cell was actually on the ground floor. Nor was she allowed any possessions, day or night. She was ordered to undress, her clothes were taken from her and she was locked in.

Her cell was ten feet by five and the ceiling was arched, giving the feeling of being inside a tomb. There was no movable furniture. Her bed was a raised stone box in one corner, on which was a rolled-up mattress even thinner than her first, and a stone lavatory seat was built in the other corner, with a bucket under the hole which she could not get at. A guard came to remove the bucket by letting himself into the narrow space between the double doors, and at mealtimes he passed her bread and water through a trap in the inner door. At no time was it necessary for the guards to enter her cell.

She spent a week there. Strangely, she found this period more comforting than her life in the cell on the first floor. She was away from the constant noise of the main prison and free of its routine. Even the bread and water was supportable compared with the unpalatable mush served upstairs. She looked forward to her ration of three slices of black bread a day and made each crumb last.

Hortense was much changed in the time since her arrest. Her original determination had helped her through the worst interrogations; her unswerving conviction in her cause had hardened after the SS failed to break her; and all the time she was buoyed up by the strength of youth. On the practical side, she was fast learning the tricks of an old con, picking up the art of survival in prison. So much had happened to her in the last months that these few days seemed a peaceful break for her and, almost in a religious sense, she went into retreat.

Outside, the invasion had not gone as well as the Allied commanders had planned. Two weeks after D-day 629,000 soldiers had been landed on the Normandy beaches and the Mulberry harbours were bringing ashore 6000 tonnes of supplies a day. The Germans had not expected the invasion to be in Normandy, but the Wehrmacht reacted quickly, mustered its forces – meagre in comparison with the vast numbers of German troops engaged on the Russian front – and fought back hard. In spite of this resistance, the Gestapo and the SD began to take special measures to maintain the misery of the occupied peoples of France and Belgium. Prisoners of Himmler's SS were not to be allowed their freedom. As the Allied divisions started their advance across Europe the SS filled endless transport trains with prisoners, usually crammed into cattle trucks, which became the trademark of their suffering, and deported them deep into the heart of the Third Reich.

On 16 June they came for Hortense.

In the early morning the prison guards were meticulous in giving her her clothes, the dress, coat and other things she had worn since her arrest. She was marched from the solitary block to her cell. Shortly afterwards the soldiers came again, this time with iron shackles which they fitted over her wrists and ankles. All the chains were linked together to a single ring in the middle. She found it difficult to walk with them hanging round her legs and was afraid she would fall as they led her down the steep spiral stairs to the ground floor.

All the time she had been in St Gilles she had seen no one else she knew. When she reached the prison yard outside she saw one or two familiar faces from Louvain, but she was careful to say nothing. She was never sure who might be listening or who might have been a stooge planted by the Gestapo. Many of her innumerable friends and contacts had avoided arrest and fought on. She was well aware that the Resistance could still be harmed by the careless talk of prisoners.

She was trucked with the other women to a large railway station in Brussels. The SS did not choose the Central passenger station where people could see what was happening. They took their Nacht und Nebel, or NN, prisoners to the backwaters of the loading yards used for the commercial and market areas. Hortense clambered down from the truck, her chains catching on the tailgate. SS soldiers shouted at the group and she shuffled forward, her chains rattling and dragging awkwardly on the concrete. She and fourteen others were separated from the main group and made to stand in a line on a platform facing a long train. The SS was there in force, a mass of black and grey uniforms. Shining black jackboots and everywhere the death's head emblem gleamed on cap-badge and collar. The officers, among them SS Lieutenant-General Richard Jungclaus, SS Major Robert Verbelen and SS Staff Officer Max Gunter, stood about in nonchalant groups, chatting.

Cattle trucks stretched along the line as far as she could see, packed with women. She could see their faces peering out of the narrow slits at the top. The word went down her line that the train had come from France, bringing women prisoners from the south and from Fresnes Prison in Paris. The cattle trucks were authorised to carry eight horses or thirty men, and troops were often carried this way. Hortense guessed that some of the trucks had as many as sixty people inside and there were more Belgian women waiting to be loaded on. Not all the rolling stock was trucks. In the middle of the train, opposite the place where Hortense and her little group were standing, there was one ordinary third class carriage with an SS soldier standing on the running board at either end.

Hortense looked about her at the other Belgian prisoners on the platform, in the hope of seeing her mother. She was not to know that the SS moved literally millions of prisoners across Europe during the war, hundreds of thousands from France and Belgium, and that the chances of her seeing her mother were slim indeed.

She recognised Verbelen and Gunter and saw them talking to Jungclaus, whom she knew by his rank. He detached himself from the group and sauntered slowly along the platform in her direction. As he drew level with the motley crowd of scruffy women he turned to Hortense and stood right in front of her. He was a tall, good looking man, immaculate in his Nazi SS uniform with the silver oakleaf collar, insignia of a general, black breeches and high jack-boots. He confronted the slight figure of the young Belgian girl standing manacled at her slim wrists and ankles, her long fair hair falling about her shoulders over clothes which were looking decidedly shabby.

He threw up his arm in a stiff Nazi salute and said conversationally, 'Well now, Hortensia, have you changed your mind?'

'What d'you mean?'

Jungclaus was about to continue when the SS began shouting again and he stepped back a couple of paces to let his soldiers get on with their work. Several SS went down the line of women with Hortense and loosened their shackles. Then they shouted at them to get on board, shoving them towards the third class carriage. Hortense struggled up the steps from the low platform, holding up her chains, and was pushed into a seat just inside the carriage at the end. The SS came on board behind her and immediately locked her chains to the ironwork of the wooden bench she was sitting on. Shackled hand and foot, she could hardly move except to wriggle about on the seat. Standing up was impossible.

After a few moments Jungclaus got into the carriage. He was sure his rank and presence would awe the young girl. He knew she realised he had the authority to make anything happen. Or stop it happening. He stood in the gangway and said, 'I'll give you one last chance.'

'I don't understand?'

'I'll give you a last chance,' Jungclaus almost smiled as he repeated himself to emphasise his words. 'I'll give you your freedom, set you free, if you tell me where I can find your brother?'

'I can't help you,' Hortense said.

'Can you hear what I'm saying to you? D'you understand?'

'I've nothing to say.'

Jungclaus looked down at the girl. Like the worst of his unscrupulous staff he was an experienced interrogator and he knew what Gunter, Verbelen and the others had done to the girl in Louvain. He knew where she was going and what would happen to her, when and if she got there. He knew how men and women reacted to such treatment and he had come to know much about Hortense Daman and her obstinate terrorist family. He looked at her open, fair face and recognised in her wide-spaced blue eyes gazing up at him more than just an attempt to pretend innocence. She was certainly not innocent but he saw a clear, unblinking faith in her commitment to fight him. He had long lost his belief in the integrity of other men; he had seen too many fold up at once and blurt out everything they could to save themselves, but this young girl had displayed a conviction he could respect.

244

'A pity, Hortensia.' He stepped back a pace, snapped his heels together and flung his arm up again in a smart Nazi salute. He paused and added, 'I wish you had been a German.'

He turned and marched out of the carriage, his boots clicking over the wooden floor, and went down the steps.

His words gave a tremendous boost to her confidence. Her chains were starting to rub and cut into her flesh, and the sight of other women shackled to benches all down the carriage, slumped dejectedly in their torn and shabby clothes, like bags of dirty laundry, was enormously depressing. She was a prisoner, bound hand and foot, condemned to death and waiting to be sent to oblivion in Germany, but Jungclaus's remark told her she had won. More important than that, his words told her that François was still free.

She needed all the strength she could muster to survive that train journey. Hour after hour for four days and nights the long transport rumbled slowly across Europe. The women were left manacled in their places on the wooden benches and soon the carriage stank as everyone shamefully succumbed to relieving themselves where they sat. All round the carriage women lolled about in their mess trying to sleep. Occasionally SS guards walked up the centre gangway to check the prisoners. There was no food or water.

The train jolted slowly eastwards along steel tracks polished with the wheels of similar transports. Occasionally they halted to replenish the steam engine with coal and water and the jolting stopped for an hour or two. Engineers checked the wheels and the SS stretched their legs alongside the cattle trucks. During one such stop she was surprised to see a group of SS bring a prisoner from the train over to a water trough to drink. The man wore a sheepskin jacket and walked with a distinct limp. She thought he looked very like the airman she had been signalling to in St Gilles.

The route led into Holland and near the end of the first day the train stopped in Vught concentration camp. There women were standing dejectedly in squads on the side of the track. Hortense could not see much but she heard the SS shouting at them to climb in. She looked through her window, which had partly misted up with the dank atmosphere of her carriage, and saw men working in fields beyond the rolls of barbed wire piled up to make fences. They were quite a distance away but all the same they seemed to be thin as sticks inside the grey striped clothes they wore and she wondered why their movements were so slow.

The warm June sun beat down on the roof of the train and the air became unbearably foetid. Hortense felt truly alone, closed in by her reluctance to talk to fellow-prisoners, who were strangers, and by the sheer misery of the journey. She tried to sleep, to find oblivion and shut out the smell, the wet filth of sitting in her own excrement, the sharp pain of the irons at her wrists and ankles, the stiffness and sudden cramps. Parched in the hot atmosphere, she retreated into a semi-conscious state in which the hours merged and the days blended with the nights in one long nightmare.

On the second day they crossed the Dutch-German frontier into the Third Reich. The stations they passed were drab. Everyone seemed to be in uniform including groups of boys Hortense saw on the platforms. She guessed some of them were no older than she had been at the beginning of the war. They were Hitler Jugend, Hitler Youth, scrubbed clean, their faces alight with pride in their uniforms and the guns they carried as they watched their enemies pass. Their dark eyes had seen more than was good for such youngsters and the hate in their faces and gestures convinced her they knew precisely the nature of the cattle-truck transports.

The train passed fields of pale green corn ripening in the warm sun. Hortense looked through the dirty window and could not help thinking of her walks in the fields around Louvain in the summer, the soft grass brushing her legs, the birdsong and the smell of hay. A series of sharp noises broke the cocoon of her thoughts and, with a weird detachment that surprised her, she saw a group of Hitler Jugend firing at the train. They were standing some way from the railway line in the greenish-yellow cornfield by the track, and she could see puffs of smoke at the muzzles of their rifles. Then the image was gone.

The train reached Berlin. It seemed to Hortense entirely natural that she would eventually be taken to the German capital though she had had no idea how long the journey would last, or what would happen next. The train inched through suburbs showing extensive bomb damage. Houses and factories were wrecked and rubble had been swept up in piles in the streets. The train finally stopped in a siding in a large marshalling yard. Night fell and Hortense dozed again, shutting her mind to the rank condition of the carriage.

She was woken by explosions, vast and recurring, destroying the blackout with curtains of light and noise. Through the window, over the silhouettes of broken buildings, she could see broad fingers of soft light from the searchlights and the sharper lines of tracer bullets punching up in deadly swinging curves to find the bombers which could be heard droning overhead. She wondered why the Allies bothered to bomb Berlin any more. She had seen nothing but devastated towns and cities all across Germany and Berlin seemed to her the worst hit.

The SS guards had vanished. She assumed they had run for shelter when the raid started and left the train unguarded. There was little she could do, being tightly manacled to her bench, and a great sense of the inevitable overtook her. The whole train, packed with 2000 helpless prisoners, stood on the dark siding in Berlin, unprotected and vulnerable to the sticks of indiscriminate rage which dropped out of the sky.

The following day, 18 June, the SS returned in the early dawn and the train started slowly out of the city. It stopped and started interminably as bomb damage was cleared off the track or troop trains passed, claiming higher priority. After a long hot day being shunted from siding to siding, they stopped again when darkness fell and Hortense realised they were still in Berlin. Once more the calm of the compulsory blackout was shattered by the British bombers. Again the SS left the train unguarded and the prisoners spent another night crushed together, listening to the menacing sound of the bombers in the blackness and waiting for the whistling scream of one small cargo to plunge on to them.

In the morning the train moved out of Berlin for the second time, towards Mecklenburg, an old town about eighty kilometres north of the capital. Hortense saw they were passing through flat, sandy and wooded countryside. She glimpsed small lakes between the evergreen trees but the ground seemed rather swampy. Some time during the early afternoon the train pulled up in a station. Hortense paid no attention. The train had stopped countless times. Always it moved on, and on.

This time it was different.

'*Raus! Raus!*'

She heard the solid, unmistakable rattle of cattle-truck doors being flung open. Prisoners were being herded along the platform. She was exhausted, starved of food and water, apathetic and drugged by the monotony of the long journey from Brussels. The sudden hurly-burly of noise and movement was a shock.

SS guards stamped into the carriage, unlocked her manacles and shoved her out down the steps. She stumbled on stiff legs and slid on the mess which slimed the floor.

Outside the sun shone.

# Into the Cold Inferno

Hortense found herself standing on a shallow platform with a group of other women in filthy clothes, grimed and matted from the journey. They were surrounded by SS guards who constantly harried them shouting and hitting out with their rifles without the slightest pretext.

Her column was pushed forward and made to march away from the station down a track past some attractive cottages, which seemed to Hortense to be holiday villas. She saw a woman in her garden with two young children. The little blond boy and girl played together, watched fondly by their mother who glanced up briefly at the column of filthy women prisoners. Hortense wondered how she would explain the frenetic activity of the guards and the disgusting condition of the prisoners to her children; but she seemed hardly concerned. Hortense was to learn that these pleasant houses were the homes of senior SS officers. Ahead, behind the solid grey concrete wall she could see over the heads of the women struggling in front of her, lay the concentration camp they ran.

This was Ravensbrück, a camp for women prisoners aptly called by the French, *L'Enfer des Femmes*, the 'Women's Inferno'.

# 10

# L'Enfer des Femmes

'No enemy who has surrendered will be killed, including partisans and spies. They will be duly punished by the courts' and 'The civilian population is sacrosanct.' Rules 3 and 7 of the German Soldier's Ten Commandments printed in every German soldier's paybook.

The name of Ravensbrück is well known to a generation which suffered the miseries of the Nazi concentration camps. Opened in 1939 with 867 prisoners, the camp was built to hold 6000. Some 133,000 women were sent to Ravensbrück and 92,700 died there. Their sons and daughters heard the echoes of the thousands whose voices were stilled for ever. Perhaps some shut their minds against the volume of unspeakable things which were done, unable to face the sheer callousness of one group of people for another. The deliberate misery of Himmler's concentration camps was such that it is hard to believe it could be forgotten. However time softly grasses over the gashes in a landscape of the worst human experience and it is quite likely that a poll taken now might reveal some strange notions about the reality of the concentration camp into which the seventeen-year-old Hortense Daman was marched in the middle of June 1944.

When she walked through the massive gates of Ravensbrück, she faced exceptional circumstances which would put her spirit to the final test. There are other and many more recent examples of how men and women rationalise their brutality against one another, how they de-humanise their victims, torture and kill them without question, but Hortense Daman, convinced as she was in her cause, was pitched into perhaps the most grisly assault on human values in the modern age.

Ravensbrück was a walled camp. Once inside the gate, Hortense was cut off from the outside world without even a view of the fields beyond the wire. Lines of large wooden huts stretched in front of her, ranked one after the other into the distance either side of a broad and bare grey sandy avenue, called the Lagerstrasse. Here the inmates gathered every morning for roll-call, or Appel, which began at 04.30 in all weathers, winter and summer, and never took less than two hours. Along the Lagerstrasse, many of these wooden blocks were surrounded by dense rolls of barbed wire, particularly on the left side where the camp staff had offices and storerooms. The prisoners dared not cross to that side for fear of being beaten up by the camp guards who worked there. The inmates were housed on the right side in over forty wooden huts. By the time Hortense arrived there were more than 17,000 prisoners and the numbers were swelling all the time. As the Russians advanced from the East and the Allies pushed towards Germany from the West, the SS dragged their prisoners into the centre of the Third Reich rather than allow the enemy to see what happened to them.

Hortense's group was halted in a big square inside the gate. Incongruously, a band standing on one side struck up with forced enthusiasm, beating out a tune of welcome. The players were all women prisoners dressed in the grey and faded blue pyjamas which Hortense had seen from the train at Vught. Like the figures there, they appeared very thin. Some of the SS guards left the new prisoners and went into a solid-looking brick building on the right.

This was the Kommandantur, housing Commandant Fritz Suhren's staff and administrative offices. Another brick building stood at right angles to the Kommandantur, along another side of the square facing the Lagerstrasse and the wooden-hutted camp. This was the punishment block. Behind it was the crematorium. Hortense could see the chimney when she arrived, and she assumed it was for the laundry. The truth was plain soon enough. The tall stack and the stench of burning flesh dominated the camp.

A young woman with a pleasant-looking face and blonde hair sauntered over to Hortense's group. An Aufseherin or supervisor, she was dressed in the field-grey uniform of the women's SS, in black top boots and black cap. She strutted round the crowd of new arrivals and began to poke or hit them here and there with a long whip she carried wrapped around her hand. A large Alsatian dog accompanied her. Fräulein Dorothea Binz was twenty-four years old. She had been posted to Ravensbrück at nineteen and a half. Her first appointment had been in the camp kitchen but within a few months she had convinced her superiors she was capable of better things. She was promoted Aufseherin and quickly developed a terrifying reputation among the prisoners, in which her whip and the dog played an important part. Once she had set her dog on a Russian woman who fell to the ground, and fired up by Binz the dog tore off one of the woman's emaciated forearms.

The SS ordered the prisoners to sit down and wait. Hortense found a space on the ground and wondered what would happen next. There seemed to be no urgency, in spite of the frenzy of shouting that accompanied every order.

Later in the afternoon the SS told them they would have a shower, in the brick building on the right. At once an undercurrent of talk swept the women. The new arrivals had heard rumours back in Belgium of death by gassing. They were not to know that Ravensbrück was not equipped with a gas chamber at that time, but all the women had had treatment from the Gestapo which left them in no doubt that they might be disposed of without a second thought.

Hortense did not join in. She was tired, hungry and miserable in clothes matted with filth and preferred to remain closed in on her own thoughts. Also she was still suspicious of tricks and unwilling to talk to anyone, even women she knew from Louvain or Brussels, in case they might have given away information to the Gestapo. None the less she could not help hearing the terrifying whispers of the other women, that they were going to be gassed. The day passed. The guards took less notice of them, the talk subsided, and they waited, sitting in the open.

They waited for two days before receiving any food and water. Hortense's mouth was swollen and dry. She lay curled up on the ground, faint and exhausted. Then the SS rustled round them again, shouting and kicking, and began to filter them into the building on the right in batches. Hortense was led with several others down a long corridor into a large empty room with a stone floor, tiled walls and gutters along the sides. It was a huge washroom the size of a gymnasium, and shower heads hung from long pipes on the ceiling. The Kapos were waiting for them. They wore red armbands with the word 'Kapo' sewn on it over the grey-striped concentration camp pyjamas. These women were prisoners too, mostly Poles and a few Germans selected for their blind obedience to the system set up by the SS. They were not above a beating themselves but their harshness could be relied upon. They were mostly criminal prisoners who had been in the camp a long time.

One of these, a large woman with black crewcut hair and a voice like a thunderbolt, moved round the new prisoners kicking them and shouting instructions.

'Take off all your clothes!'

Hesitantly at first, the women began to strip. Garment by garment, they reluctantly shed these last vestiges of their individuality. Filthy as they were, Hortense took off her clothes reluctantly, somehow aware it was for the last time. Her coat had once belonged to her father. Bertha, her older sister, who worked in *haute couture* in Brussels, had turned it into a coat like one worn by the famous movie actress Deanna Durbin. She undid the soft suede shoes her father had made specially for her, dropped her dress, then her petticoat, which her grandmother had knitted for her. One by one she discarded these pathetic links with her family and let them fall on the pile. Finally she took off her gold necklace, which had been given her on her confirmation, a small gold wristwatch and a ring with her initials 'H.A.' engraved inside it. So far the Germans had returned these trinkets to her, even after her spell in the solitary block in St Gilles. Now they glittered dully in the folds of soiled clothing. She stood naked holding the photograph which Gustaaf Legrande had smuggled in to her in the Little Prison in Louvain, that of her young sister Julia and her nephew Michel Berges, as a baby on a rocking-horse. She wanted to keep this small fragment of her home. The fat Kapo appeared suddenly in front of her.

'Get on with it!' she bellowed. She spotted the photograph. Her hand shot out, and cursing Hortense, she flung it on the pile, which she swept up in her arms and marched away.

Other Kapos cleared the other clothes and the prisoners were alone in the shower room. Hortense was the youngest. She was appalled by the shapelessness of the other women and embarrassed by the sight of people she knew, whom she would have called 'Madame' at home out of respect for their rank and position. Naked they were all levelled to the same status. The smell in the room was overpowering. They waited, and Hortense found it impossible not to notice some of the women watching the shower heads with undisguised fear. Abruptly, the pipes shook, knocked against the tiles and cold water gushed out of the showers.

'See! It's water, it's water!' the women cried, their relief turning quickly to practical urgency as they set about scrubbing themselves vigorously to clean off the caked faeces and the dirt of the journey.

Hortense cleaned herself as best she could, grateful for the opportunity, and wondered what was in store for them. She knew something of SS methods from her interrogations but she quickly saw that in Ravensbrück they did nothing without shouting and used any excuse to hit out at the prisoners. Still naked and dripping with water, she was herded with the others out of the shower room and the SS began to call out names.

'Daman, Hortensia!'

Following directions, Hortense went into another room where a number of Kapos stood behind a long line of bare wooden tables. Naked prisoners stood in front of the tables. Some watched Kapos sifting through their clothing which had been dumped on the tabletop, others sat on stools while a Kapo none too gently cut off all their hair. The floor was covered in little piles of wet hair. Hortense saw a space and found herself facing the fat Kapo with the black crewcut and thunderous voice.

'Name?' the Kapo snapped.

'Hortense Daman.'

Hortense had been listening to the other prisoners and gathered that if the bribe was sufficient this Kapo might let her keep her long blonde hair. While she wondered what could possibly satisfy such a person, the woman fetched a bag and up-ended Hortense's clothes on the table.

'Now, what've you got? Or your hair goes.' With practised movements, she checked the tacky garments and pocketed the gold chain, watch and ring. Hortense picked up the photograph of Julia and Michel.

'Please, can I have this?'

'No!' The Kapo's voice boomed back across the narrow table. 'Who's the boy anyway?' She stabbed a fat finger at the baby.

'My nephew.'

'No photograph!' She tossed it back on the pile.

'Well, can I have my shoes back?'

'No! You'll have to wear other shoes.'

'I can't,' Hortense said, hoping to persuade the woman she had to wear special shoes. 'I can't wear any others. My father made them for me.'

'You can't have anything,' screamed the crewcut Kapo. 'You're a terrorist! Get out!'

This was the last time Hortense saw her clothes, but she had saved her hair, at least for the time being. Another woman, an opera singer from the Ukraine, was not so lucky. She went completely berserk when her hair was swiped from her scalp. Afterwards she slumped into a state of docile acceptance but she never recovered her sanity. On Appel, when the entire camp assembled at dawn for roll-call and thousands of women stood in silence, heads bowed, in grey ranks, block after block, down the full length of the Lagerstrasse, this woman's beautiful voice could be heard above the screaming of the SS guards, running up and down the operatic scales, the notes pure but insanely jumbled.

Hortense was ordered into a small ante-room, incongruously but unmistakably a doctor's surgery. Four doctors in SS uniform were waiting for her. One told her to get on top of a solid table in the centre of the room and proceeded to examine her intimately. Hortense, with her Catholic upbringing, had never before experienced exposure such as this, either of other people or herself. Although now used to being told to strip off for one reason or another, her embarrassment had never faded. Mortified with shame, she lay on the table trying to control her thoughts about this German doctor's probing fingers and shut out the impassive faces of the others. She

256

was relieved to see him step back and join the watchers on the other side of the room. Suddenly, a brilliant light was shone on her from the ceiling and she felt a scorching, burning agony down her left side.

The SS doctors offered no explanation and made no attempt to calm Hortense, who had burst into tears with the pain and shock.

One of the doctors motioned to a severely upright woman immaculately dressed in the starched uniform of a matron, complete with lace cap on her head. This was Ravensbrück's hospital Oberschwester, Elisabeth Marschall, a professional nurse and Nazi Party member of fifteen years standing. Hers was a punishment posting into Ravensbrück for a breach of SS regulations at the Hermann Goering works in Brunswick, where she had given food to two French slave workers. The gesture was not typical of her behaviour in Ravensbrück. She listened while the doctor said something to her and then went over to Hortense, who sat on the table shaking with fright.

'You're a terrorist, a *Schweinhund*,' she spat at the naked girl by way of explanation.

'That's the second time I've been called this,' Hortense replied at once, automatically reacting to her pain and fear with irritation. 'If I translate this into Flemish, it's meaningless. A pig-dog? I ask you! What does that mean?'

The senior doctor present, with the collar tabs of an SS Surgeon-General, started laughing. Karl Gebhardt was Himmler's own doctor and his particular interest in examining the female prisoners in Ravensbrück, a thoroughly unsanitary place at the best of times, arose from his instructions from the Reichsführer SS to find a suitable and swift means of sterilising women. Nazi ideology dictated that certain women were beyond the pale. They had to be written out of the Nazis' scheme for the future to prevent them contaminating true Aryan stock. Gypsies, German women who co-habited with

Jews, Jewesses and political prisoners who had been condemned to death were all to be sterilised. Gebhardt, who was President of the German Red Cross at the same time, was assisted by another doctor, SS Colonel Viktor von Brack. Brack concentrated on the technical aspects. They were still perfecting the techniques.

In a letter to Himmler, Brack wrote:

> If any persons are to be sterilised permanently, this result can only be attained by applying X-rays in a dosage high enough to produce castration with all its consequences, since high X-ray dosages destroy the internal secretion of the ovary . . . Lower dosages would only temporarily paralyse the procreative capacity . . . The necessary local dosage for women is 300–350 Rontgens.

He went on to describe some of the disadvantages, for the SS scheme and for the victim:

> As it is impossible unnoticeably to cover the rest of the body with lead, the other tissues of the body will be injured and radiological malaise will ensue. If the X-ray intensity is too high those parts of the skin which the rays have reached will exhibit symptoms of burns in the course of the following days or weeks.

Hortense never knew it, but the man who was laughing at her comment about German oaths had just sterilised her with a violent dose of X-rays from a machine hidden in the table she was sitting on.

'Where'd you learn German?'

'I've picked it up since you all arrived in Belgium.'

'Well, that's very good, Hortensia, but on your papers it says you're a terrorist.'

'Maybe that's what it says on my papers, but I've never done anything wrong to anybody.'

'You helped English pilots.'

'I've never seen an English pilot in my life,' Hortense

replied with her most innocent expression. 'I've never seen an Englishman. The Gestapo kept asking me that, and I told them. . . .'

'Oh, the Gestapo, the Gestapo,' the doctor interrupted with an air of superiority sometimes typical of his profession. 'They don't know what they're talking about.'

He half turned to the others, who treated him with great deference, and said, 'This girl is my case.' He went on to explain in a grim warning to Hortense, 'I want to make it plain to make sure you understand you've been sentenced to death but that the sentence has not been carried out. Yet. So be a good girl in the camp and do as you're told.'

It was clear that the brief interlude was over. The doctors had enjoyed their little chat with the pretty young girl sitting nude on the table. They were surprised and delighted to find she was more than an inanimate laboratory specimen, with a voice and feelings. However she was still a terrorist and condemned to death. To all intents and purposes she was no longer a part of the human race.

She was taken without ceremony into another small examination room, sat on a chair and, without preamble, given an injection in her left thigh by one of the other doctors, Dr Rosenthal. This too was extremely painful, but neither he nor the matron made any attempt to ease the hurt or even explain what they were doing. Elisabeth Marschall led her into the corridor immediately.

'Here's your number,' Marschall said tonelessly, handing Hortense a piece of paper on which was written '42742'. 'From now on you've no name. Just this number.'

Hortense was shoved into another room. Someone gave her a big grey-green dress with a coarse and open weave, on which a large grey cross had been sewn front and back. This cross designated one condemned to death.

She now continued along the route with other new arrivals, going from room to room and being given

259

something in each, moving inexorably into an environment designed to reduce her to a nameless, characterless non-person.

She collected a needle and thread, a patch of white material with her number printed on it, a red triangle and a black 'B', and sat with the other women in a large hall on the stone floor, sewing on their numbers. Hortense had to sew the red triangle, one flat side uppermost, on her left shoulder, with the 'B' in the middle of it. The red signified she was a political prisoner and the 'B' that she was Belgian.

All prisoners were categorised with coloured triangles. Red signified all political prisoners including Communists, partisans and resisters from all the occupied countries, east and west. Mauve was for religious fundamentalists, usually pacifists, blue for emigrants, brown for gypsies (Zigeuner), black for the mentally deficient (Asozial) and prostitutes, green for criminals, and rose-pink, typically, for homosexuals. Ravensbrück was filled with prisoners of all these categories. Most were women, but there were a few men for especially heavy work.

Jews wore a yellow triangle, point up, but since Ravensbrück was not specifically for Jews there was never more than a small number until the end of the war, when prisoners of all categories swelled the inmates to 36,000. Besides, Jews were marked for harsh treatment and did not last long. Either they were transported to death camps, there to receive what the Germans oddly but accurately called Special Handling (Sonderbehandlung), or they were killed when Fritz Suhren had the extermination plant built at Ravensbrück at the beginning of 1945.

The political prisoners and the criminals were the largest groupings. Some Communists had been in the concentration camp system since 1933, when Hitler was elected to power in the Reichstag and banned all other parties. Often by the time war broke out they had managed to reach positions of leadership within the camps, like 'trusties', and the SS left much of the day to day organisation to them. This was particularly the case in Buchenwald, where Hortense's father Jacques had been since May. The Communists' leadership could make the conditions no less appalling, nor prevent atrocities by the SS, but they could sometimes ameliorate the camp administration by bringing some order into the deliberate, manic chaos of the SS. There is no record of any similar prisoner power-base in Ravensbrück but there was certainly an underground network of political prisoners, mostly Communist or socialist, which passed on information at the least. Prisoners were routinely posted to help in all the camp offices, such as the hospital and the administrative office, and though there were few opportunities to alter the fate of those to be transported to death camps, they read the records and kept tabs on what was happening in the camp.

After she had sewn on her triangle and number Hortense was taken back to the shower room and some Kapos came in with armfuls of clogs which they threw on the damp floor. Hortense selected a stout pair with solid wooden soles and strong leather uppers, thinking of her father the master shoemaker.

By this time she was feeling rotten. The weather was warm but her skin was inexplicably hot all over. In a warm daze she joined a group and was marched out of the new arrivals buildings and along the wide sandy Lagerstrasse to Block 7. This block was used to house new prisoners and the Blockälteste recorded their arrival. A Blockälteste was a prisoner with a red armband, but without the word Kapo sewn on it, and was usually chosen for her brutal and blind support of the SS. They wielded enormous power over the inmates in every detail of day to day matters, but Hortense never saw this woman hit anyone in Hut 7.

When Hortense walked into a room in the centre of the

building, known as the knitting room, she was horrified. Gaunt emaciated women, most with bald heads, sat round the walls staring at her, their eyes huge and dull above sunken grey cheeks. Some were knitting socks which were sent to the German army. They lived in the block and did no hard physical labour, staying close to the single stove in the centre of the room, but later as numbers increased these knitters were the first to be sent on death transports. Either side of the knitting room were two large barrack rooms which seemed to Hortense to stretch away into a gloomy distance without end. It was like peering into a catacomb. Each barrack was filled with lines of cots stacked up in twos, side by side, tiered right to the ceiling and pushed end to end to form four continuous wood structures with narrow alleys between them, which ran the length of the room. There were over three hundred women allocated to one barrack room and considerable numbers were sitting among these dingy bunks. When they heard the noise of the new arrivals they stuck their heads out of their bunks into the narrow alleys to see what was going on, like insects disturbed in an underground nest. Hortense was frightened by the noise of women crying and screaming, sounds which came from deep within the stack of dirty wood bunks. Looking down the alleys between them she saw several bodies lying quite still on the floor, and although the day was sunny and dry and there were no panes of glass in the windows, the rank stench of human sweat and urine stung her nostrils.

A group of women shuffled up to her and reached out their skinny hands to touch her, their nails encrusted with black grime.

'No! Get away!' Hortense cried out and cringed back, terrified by their contagious, alien appearance.

There was no room on any of the bunks. Already six women were sleeping in two bunks, side by side. Hortense, the youngest, and twenty others who had come with her from Louvain, had to sleep on the floor in the knitting room. On one side the barrack room was full of Belgians, and the other, on the far side of the latrines and entrance corridor, was full of Frenchwomen.

Her first night was miserable. She pulled the grey dress round her and tried to shut out the sounds of the hundreds of women stacked in their bunks. The following morning she watched a fine dawn break on Appel at 04.30. They had been allocated no work detail so after two and a half hours at roll-call, they waited again in Block 7. It turned into a lovely warm June day but Hortense began to feel seriously ill. She had a blinding headache and her head was spinning. She decided to lie down but the smell inside the hut drove her to sit outside on a wooden bench by the door, in the camp street which ran between the blocks. Her left side, where the pain had started on the table in the doctor's examination room, had come out in a rash, and suppurations had broken the skin of her face and neck and down her arm to the elbow. With her head buzzing, she thought in a detached way that the hot sun would cure the rash. Worse, her thigh had begun to swell and discolour where she had been given the injection.

She walked gingerly over to the women she knew from Louvain to tell them how she was feeling, in the hope they might have some idea what to do to help.

'Go away,' one woman snapped rudely as she noticed Hortense approaching.

'We're busy talking and we don't want little girls listening in,' said another.

'I'm ill,' Hortense whispered rather feebly, her head pounding. She tried to make her eyes focus on the women.

'That doesn't look very nice,' said the first woman, pointing at the red rash on Hortense's neck; and Hortense collapsed. She wanted to answer but she found she could not speak.

The women picked her up, took her inside the hut and found a space for her on a top bunk near the ceiling, where they hoped to hide her from the guards. One of them was a Polish doctor. Another was a fine Belgian woman called Claire Van den Boom, a qualified nurse. They both worked in the hospital, which the Germans called the Revier. Inevitably the name was ironically translated to 'Riviera', though there was simply nothing in common between the Revier at Ravensbrück and the rich man's resort on the south coast of France.

Claire stayed with Hortense a while and another woman gave Hortense a small lump of sugar to suck, which tasted of mint.

Hortense stayed on the top tier and swayed in and out of consciousness for a day. Various women checked her from time to time. She wanted to help herself but was hardly able to speak.

Finally she heard a voice in German, the Blockälteste, saying, 'She can't stay here like that. She'll have to go in.'

Conditions in the camp were bad, but the situation in the hospital was worse, not better as might have been expected. Prisoners did their utmost to avoid having to go to the Revier. They worked with temperatures as high as 104 degrees rather than report sick. They could expect nothing but short shrift from the German hospital staff.

The camp doctors were Trommer, Percy Treite, Rolf Rosenthal, a woman Hertha Oberheuser and the dentist Hellinger. They were all medically qualified but their actions were far removed from the ethics of their Hippocratic oath. Treite was half English, giving the lie to those arrogant Englishmen who believe that the Nazi camps were somehow exclusively a German problem. His English mother, who christened him Percy, had married a German and her son had received a good education. He was tall, good looking, and in any other situation would have been considered charming. Even at his trial in Nuremberg after the war, some former inmates were prepared to see some good in him. He was involved in choosing the names of women who were to be executed and cremated but distanced himself from actually oveseeing the selection. He was not a thug like his brutal colleague Rolf Rosenthal or the camp guards, but was callously disinterested in the atrocious conditions of the camp and his hospital. Trommer and Rosenthal were simply bad doctors with brutal minds. Rolf Rosenthal had on several occasions kicked and beaten sick women waiting in line for treatment, and admitted at his trial that he gave lethal doses of morphine to sick prisoners. He thought that was easier than curing them.

The doctor's attitude was echoed and magnified by the German nursing staff who enforced the regulations with a severity which often led to deaths of inmates. The matron, Elisabeth Marschall, often made women attending sick parade stand outside in the pouring rain for hours, after which there was always an increase of pulmonary diseases, and she took an active part in selections. Women did not report sick without good reason.

Hortense, however, was barely conscious. She could not stand for any length of time and was clearly unable to hold her own in the harsh life of the camp. Claire and the Polish doctor took her on a stretcher to the Revier on the other side of the Lagerstrasse, opposite the courtyard near the main gate where she had waited after her arrival. They put the stretcher down outside the hospital and Claire pulled Hortense to her feet.

'Stand up! Don't for God's sake let me down. If you can't stand, we're both for it.' Claire knew that stretcher cases were not admitted. There was no point. 'I know what you've done to be sent here,' she continued, bracing the feeble young Belgian girl who was collapsing against her. 'So stand up!'

Hortense was hardly conscious of the argument Claire had with one of the German nurses to let them inside the Revier.

'The place is full,' said the nurse flatly. 'The wards, even the corridors are full. There are beds everywhere. You'll have to take her away.'

'She's very sick.'

'What's wrong with her?'

'I'm not sure but she needs help badly.'

'Well, there's no room for any new patients, especially if no one knows what's wrong with her.'

Claire Van den Boom had been a nurse for many years. She was not tall but had a forceful personality. She brushed aside the other nurse's protests and found the matron. Marschall watched Hortense carefully while Claire explained the situation. Finally she agreed to find her a space. She alone had the authority to organise extra bedding and arranged a cot in a corridor at the end of a wooden block in the back of the hospital complex. At least Hortense had somewhere to lie down, but the spot was hardly ideal. On one side of the corridor were outside windows, which were glazed. The windows overlooked a small inside courtyard. On the other side were the doors to the contagious wards for people with typhoid, typhus, venereal diseases and extreme cases of dysentery.

Many would not survive. A Norwegian inmate, Fru Salvesen, said, 'The sick were all lying on the floor, which was crowded, so much so that I had to step over them . . . If you arrived in the Revier with typhus and you survived and were discharged, you very soon came back with some other disease picked up while you were there.'

Hortense lay at the end of the passage, with a window on one side and, not three feet away, the door to the end ward on the other. The doctors consigned hopeless cases to this ward and more dead patients emerged on stretchers than came out alive. An Italian girl called Lydia occupied the bunk at her feet and in time they made friends. Hortense had no idea what was wrong with her. She seemed quite cheerful though she was covered with sores.

A few hours after Hortense was installed in her bunk,

wearing a thin hospital gown, Marschall appeared in the corridor.

'We're going to operate,' she announced bluntly.

This was a shock but by now Hortense had a raging temperature and could not feel her legs at all. Marschall lifted up her left leg and showed Hortense what had happened. The flesh was vast, absolutely black and had swollen to a foot in diameter.

'They'll have to amputate this,' Marschall went on ignoring the shock in her young patient's eyes.

Without preamble she arranged a stretcher. Later in the day they came back for Hortense when she was barely conscious of her surroundings and carried her into the operation theatre.

She woke up being jolted along the passages on a trolley, back to her cot outside the contagious wards. Elisabeth Marschall gave her a biscuit. When Lydia saw them coming she burst into tears.

Matron's severe features split in a laugh. 'It's all right,' she said. 'Your little girl is still in one piece. We decided not to cut off her leg after all.'

Hortense was put in her cot. She was helpless. Only a few short days before she had arrived in the camp exhausted, filthy, but in good health. By the time the surgeons Trommer and Treite had finished with her she had an abnormally high temperature and was unable even to lift her arms to feed herself. In a concentration camp it was a dangerous condition to be in and she depended completely on the selflessness of other prisoners to help her. The nurses, especially Claire Van den Boom, came to care for her when they could and the Italian Lydia spoon-fed her until she recovered some strength, in spite of her face being covered in black scabs from her rash.

Her left leg was in a terrible state. The bandages were paper. There were no linen, crepe, or even cloth bandages to waste on outer dressings. The paper became sodden with the suppurations and blood which oozed from the wound and needed changing often. Claire used to come in at night and gently change these paper dressings and give Hortense little bits of extra food to supplement the meagre milky slop which was all patients received in the Revier. All the prisoner nurses came along the ghastly passage to the contagious wing to chat to Hortense and cheer her up, but she grew most attached to Claire and called her, 'My little mother.'

From time to time Treite and Rosenthal came on their hospital rounds to see what progress Hortense was making. Every five days she was wheeled into the operating theatre for the dressings under the paper to be changed. Dr Oberheuser was usually present to assist Rosenthal. They had filled the wound itself with yards and yards of gauze, to soak up the endless suppurations of pus, which needed lifting out and changing. These sessions terrified Hortense and she persuaded the German nurses to let Claire accompany her. They laid her on the operating table, covered her face with a cloth and then prised open the nine inch long gash they had cut in her leg. Then they began to slowly pull out the stinking strips of gauze. Hortense usually fainted with the pain. Her flesh inside the wound stuck to the gauze which dragged across the nerves bared to the open air. The German doctors had cut her thigh to the bone.

In addition to a camp doctor at Ravensbrück, Oberheuser was an Assistant Physician to SS Surgeon-General Karl Gebhardt at the Hohenlychen Institute, the SS orthopaedic sanatorium eight miles from Ravensbrück. This bleak-faced, stout woman generally assisted with Hortense's examinations. She had masculine features, her straight black hair was cut like a man's, and she wore a shapeless grey skirt and thick grey socks as part of her SS uniform. In the madness of Ravensbrück Hortense was never sure whether this doctor was a man or a woman, though she came to establish a certain rapport with her over the months; and Oberheuser may have been impressed by the sufferings of the young Belgian girl, even if she was a condemned terrorist. Hortense never knew that Oberheuser's real interest was to see how her young patient coped with the massive infection of gangrene that Rosenthal had injected in her leg on her arrival.

She would not have believed this possible of a doctor. She thought the swelling was connected with the injection, but imagined that the needle had been infected. Brutal as the Gestapo had been to her, and unpleasant as the camp had appeared in the short time she had been a part of it, the idea that there were qualified doctors who would deliberately infect a patient never crossed her mind.

Experiments on humans however were not a localised aberration of certain doctors' minds. The Nazi totalitarian system sanctioned this treatment. In May 1942 Hitler had said:

> . . . in principle, when the well-being of the nation is at stake, experiment on human subjects is permissible . . . those detained in concentration camps or prisons ought not to remain completely unaffected by the war while German soldiers are being subjected to almost unbearable strain, and our native land, women and children are being engulfed under a rain of incendiary bombs.

This was Hitler's justification, and good enough for the SS. There were numerous experiments in various camps. The gangrene tests were excused by the lack of sulphonamides and penicillin available to German troops wounded in battle. Gebhardt also believed that the death of Reinhard Heydrich, SS Obergruppenführer, Chief of the Security Service and one of Himmler's favoured protégés, was a factor. Heydrich was attacked and died after fourteen days from gangrene infection in his wounds, which the German doctors, including Gebhardt, who flew to Prague to see him, could not prevent. All this provided the impetus to experiment.

Doctors Oberheuser, Rosenthal, Fritz Fischer (an SS Sturmbannführer and assistant at Hohenlychen) and Schiedlausky (senior medical officer at Ravensbrück until transferred to Buchenwald camp at the start of 1944) had been present when the experiments had been started at Ravensbrück camp. Rosenthal and Oberheuser maintained a clinical interest in subsequent subjects. There were other cases in the Revier apart from the Belgian girl. Several Polish girls who had also been used as human guinea pigs used to hobble along the corridor to see Hortense because she had the same symptoms. They were always cheerful and did their best to encourage her. They were content just to be alive. All these girls had had their legs amputated and did not appreciate why.

The weeks passed and Hortense's recovery was painfully slow. Occasionally Treite and Rosenthal passed her cot to go in the room at the end. Treite would flick her on the top of the head and say conversationally, 'So! Still with us, little Hortensia?' The doctors and German staff were genuinely surprised that the teenage girl had lasted so long.

On several occasions orderlies struggled past the cots with stretchers, on which lay women barely alive. Hortense could reach out and touch them. She asked Vera why these patients were always carried out again dead. Vera was a well-built German girl prisoner and a Kapo, who was a nurse in the Revier. She treated Hortense fairly and told her to forget all about what happened in the room at the end of the corridor. It was much safer not to ask questions. Occasionally when Treite or Rosenthal went into the ward Hortense heard the most tragic screaming. After these visits the hospital porters always came to carry out dead women on stretchers.

Once again, Hortense and the other patients never realised the extent of the degeneration of their medical staff. Rosenthal and the charming Treite both administered lethal injections of phenol or morphia to exceptionally sick patients in that end ward.

On 12 August Hortense had her eighteenth birthday. There was little to celebrate, except life itself. She lay in her cot, unable to move, though she found she could feed herself better now. She listened to Lydia singing Italian folk songs of the mountains where she lived.

Two days later she began to itch. Her skin seemed alive and she wondered whether it was a sign of recovery, the scabs healing. She could not easily move herself and only managed to reach down under the single blanket to scratch with the utmost difficulty. When she brought her hands back, she was shaken to see her finger covered with blood. When Lydia saw her fingers, she panicked and began to shout for the nurses to come at once. She was terrified that Hortense's wound had haemorrhaged and her friend was bleeding to death.

Lydia was alarmed when the first person to answer her shouts was Elisabeth Marschall. The matron swept up the corridor in a crackle of starch, past the line of sick lying under the windows to the end, and stood over Hortense.

'She's bleeding to death,' Lydia said, almost hysterical, but Marschall was well-used to grim sights in the Ravensbrück Revier, some of which she had caused herself. Once, five Jewesses were brought to the hospital, each dumped helplessly sick in a wheel-barrow. Marschall refused to allow anyone near them and they stayed outside all night. The following morning all were dead of exposure.

She was a severe figure indeed, looming over the two girls in her pressed uniform, glaring down at the sticky red mess on Hortense's fingers and inspecting the cot. Suddenly, she bent over and briskly pulled back the blanket to investigate.

'This isn't serious,' she said and to the girls' astonishment she began to laugh. 'These are creepy-crawlies! And they're going to eat you all up unless we do something about it.'

Hortense looked down at the sheet wrinkled up round her body. It was seething with bed-bugs, gorged on her blood, and large numbers had split where she had been scratching, staining the cot and straw mattress dark red.

'We can't leave you like this,' Marschall continued. 'It'll all have to be changed.' She marched off to issue orders and very soon nurses came to take Hortense out of her cot while her entire bed, mattress and sheet was removed for burning and a new one put in its place. Lydia remarked on the surprising speed with which all this was done.

Time passed slowly. Lydia, who was in her early twenties, did her best to keep up their spirits. She had a beautiful voice and Hortense loved her songs from the hills near Naples. They reminded her of sunshine and the simple freedom of a walk in the countryside. For weeks Hortense had had no strength even to feel herself, and later, as she had no spoon of her own, she shared the Italian girl's spoon at mealtimes. One day Claire brought Hortense some soup during feeding time.

'Where's your spoon?' she demanded when she saw Hortense had nothing to eat the soup with.

'She shares mine,' Lydia explained.

'I think someone took my spoon when I fell ill in Block 7,' Hortense told Claire.

Claire said nothing but went off and returned later with a spoon. 'Use this. You're not to share the Italian girl's spoon any more,' she told Hortense quietly so that Lydia could not hear. 'I know you're in the corridor next to the contagious wards. There's no room anywhere else to put you. Lydia, on the other hand, is supposed to be here. The poor girl has an extreme case of syphilis.'

Hortense was unaware of the problems sex caused in the world and hardly knew what syphilis was. She knew venereal diseases were a frightening terror for they had been vaguely alluded to by her priest at school. He had threatened the direst religious and medical consequences for excesses of the flesh. Claire's advice struck her as odd, considering she and Lydia were surrounded by wards full of contagious diseases like typhoid fever, typhus, and gastro-enteritis. The whole place was infested with staphylococci of every sort. All the same she was careful to use her own spoon thereafter, though the Italian girl was quite unabashed. She told her story and Hortense was impressed with her strength of character in such a place. No prisoner in a concentration camp wanted to reduce their chances of survival by being so sick they had to spend time in the camp hospital. Lydia had no choice. She had been a teacher in Italy and involved in the Resistance. Finally she had been arrested, but the ten German soldiers who captured her had all raped her before bringing her to the local Kommandantur. She immediately lodged a complaint to their officers who instituted an inquiry to find the culprits, because, in the words of their Supreme Commander, Field Marshal Albert Kesselring, 'the dignity of the German soldier demands it'. However one soldier had infected her with syphilis. By the time she reached Ravensbrück she badly needed hospital treatment, and had ended in the contagious wing next to Hortense. The irony of her case continued as the investigating German officers found and punished the ten men responsible, even bringing one to Ravensbrück to be identified by Lydia; while at the same time German troops in Italy were destroying and killing large numbers of civilians, again encouraged by Kesselring in a clear incitement to murder and arson: 'Should troops be fired on from any village it must be burnt down and the ringleaders will be hanged in public. Nearby villages will be held responsible for any sabotage.'

Marschall took up Claire's comment about contact with the other patients and personally warned several German girls with venereal diseases further down the corridor not to go near Hortense.

Hortense showed signs of improvement through August but the conditions were not conducive to good health. The corridor in which she lived was dirty, the medicines very scarce, her youthful strength had been terribly depleted and the food lacked the nourishment on which she could build recovery. She spent the days and nights lying in her cot, hardly able to move. The only activity to look at in the passage was when the orderlies brought women into the contagious wards in the passage, or removed their corpses. These unfortunate women never walked out.

Hortense was well enough to be bored. She asked Elisabeth Marschall for needle and thread and began to embroider signatures on a spare bit of cloth. As people came past Hortense persuaded them to sign their name on the cloth and then worked over it with thread. This proved popular and soon she had collected a souvenir from Percy Treite and Rolf Rosenthal as they passed into the fatal end ward, Hertha Oberheuser when she administered the agonising weekly change of gauze in her wound, Elisabeth Marschall and many other Germans on the medical staff. Hortense worked over the embroidery, unaware that the SS doctors and matron who were amused to give their signatures as a memento were responsible for her infections and sickness in the first place.

Inevitably in that corridor, Hortense caught typhus. Her general recovery of condition and the healing of her deep leg wound were immediately set back as she fought off the eruption of pustulous spots and exhausting fever. This time there was nothing she could do to prevent losing her beautiful hair. Sick and undernourished as she was, it all fell out.

Towards the end of August, after two months in the camp, Claire came to see her. She knelt down in the passage by Hortense's cot, took her hand tightly and said very quietly, 'I'm going to tell you something and I want you to be very brave.'

Hortense nodded, wondering.

'Don't cry,' Claire continued softly. 'Your mother has arrived here.'

The tears flooded into Hortense's eyes and poured down her cheeks. Claire held her close, aware that the young girl was horrified to think her mother was to suffer the camp too.

The Germans were clearing out the camps in Belgium and Holland in the face of the advancing British troops forcing their way across northern Europe. Paris was liberated on 25 August and the Germans were in retreat to the flat lands of Holland and the German border itself in the Ardennes.

Claire had learnt that there were a group of Belgians among the new arrivals from Vught, in Holland, where Hortense's train had stopped. Claire found out on the office grapevine who was on the transports and checked the lists for Belgian names. She saw an entry for 'Stephanie Van den Eynde' and recognised the name from Hortense's stories about her home. She went to the arrivals hall to verify that Stephanie was there and later found an opportunity to speak to her. As gently as she could she told Stephanie of her daughter's illness. As she clasped Hortense sobbing to her breast, she sadly reflected that there was no place in Ravensbrück to hide the truth.

Occasionally Fritz Suhren, the Commandant, inspected the hospital on his rounds of the camp. These were regular visits and soon after Hortense had heard of her mother's arrival, she saw Suhren smartly dressed in his SS uniform cross the end of the passage where she lay with a crowd of attendant staff.

'Herr Commandant,' she called out without hesitation. 'May I ask you a favour?'

Marschall whispered something to him as he approached.

'I know you,' Suhren said, having seen the Belgian girl several times in the last weeks. 'You come from a terrorist family. What is it?'

'My mother's in the camp now, and I haven't seen her yet. Would you give her permission to visit me here? We could see each other through the window.' Hortense gestured behind her at the window overlooking the yard used by some of the inmates who were on the nursing staff.

Suhren paused. He looked at the young girl who had dared to ask him if her mother could break the rules. She was wearing a hospital nightdress and it was easy to see how thin she had become, almost grotesque with her bald head. He replied, 'Yes. She can come and visit you.'

Claire brought her. The glazed window could not be opened because of the contagious diseases. Stephanie peered in and knocked gently on the pane. Hortense looked up and saw her mother's face, her grey eyes dark with concern, and struggled up level with the window sill. Unable to fall in each other's arms, to comfort and embrace each other, they stayed either side of the window speechless with emotion, words choked in their throats and tears pouring down their cheeks. Gently Hortense put her hand to the pane and spread her fingers on the glass, and her mother reached out to match her daughter's contact on the other side. They both felt the thin warmth of the other through the glass and saw the little ring of condensation round each finger.

This meeting was vital. Neither could know what hidden strength they each found in that poignant moment through the window, but the invisible force they had created between them in Louvain was regenerated in full measure. They needed it badly in Ravensbrück. They were both strong characters but in the harsh conditions of the camp their lives were at risk as individuals, one seriously ill in the Revier and the other weakened by her time in Vught. They needed each other to survive. The power of their relationship was most effective when they were together and seemed to emanate from one or the other, oscillating back and forth between them. Stephanie was fifty-four when she arrived in Ravensbrück and imprisonment had not improved her health. But she was on her feet and immensely strong in comparison with her daughter. Hortense had not walked since the day she came into the Revier and her medical condition gave little encouragement for the future. Stephanie had the power, and a mother's incentive, to give Hortense a chance to live. Much depended on her.

Weakness was not tolerated in the Third Reich, nor in its concentration camp system, 'the state within a state'. The sick and elderly were simply despatched. In Ravensbrück fifty people a day were shot in the back of the neck by SS Scharführer Schulte and cremated. As the Allies pressed from East and West towards Germany, the SS felt under increasing pressure to eliminate 'useless' prisoners. To survive, the sick had to walk and the elderly had to be able to work hard and run past the doctors, Treite and Rosenthal among them, at inspections, to show they were fit to continue living. The strength Stephanie brought was invaluable. The strength was purpose. Without purpose, women died.

Stephanie came back two days later. This time her face was dark with bruises. Reluctantly she told Hortense she had been stopped by a fat Kapo with black crewcut hair. From the description Hortense recognised the Kapo who had taken her gold cross and chain. The fat Kapo had given her mother a beating for being in the Revier without authorisation before Stephanie could explain that the Commandant had allowed it.

On Suhren's next visit Hortense attracted his attention again. He approached her with the air of a man happy to be recognised as giving out favours and was astonished by the young Belgian girl's first remarks.

'Are you still Commandant in this camp?' Hortense demanded flatly, looking up at him from her cot on the floor.

'Of course,' snapped Suhren crossly.

'Well, that fat Kapo with the black crewcut beat my mother in spite of your giving her permission to visit me at this window here.'

Suhren grunted at this and stalked away. Marschall and Rosenthal followed him looking grim. Later one of the nurses came round to Hortense grinning broadly. It seemed that the Commandant had come across the fat Kapo and kicked her backside.

She recovered from the typhus gradually. But the deep incisions in her leg were slow to heal. The medical treatment from the doctors was rudimentary in the extreme. No records survive the war, if any were kept, but it may be reasonably supposed that the effects of the X-rays on Hortense's internal organs generally reduced her capacity to recover from illness. All she had in the bank was her initial youth and vigour. Even her spirit had become subdued in the hospital, in spite of her mother's arrival. She had become accustomed to being bedridden.

Various nursing prisoners, Poles, French and Belgians, helped her during the weeks she was in the Revier, among them Yvonne, Fanny, Magda who was a tiny Yugoslav girl, and Dr Marie-Claude, an ear, nose and throat specialist from Brussels. One day late in September a German nurse, Martha, gave Hortense a bath. Hortense was carried to the bathroom on a stretcher and Martha took off her nightdress, lifted her up and lowered her into the warm water, coloured blue with disinfectant. Martha was a big woman and held Hortense easily with one hand under her back but Hortense was convinced Martha would drop her in and drown her. Then she was terrified to see black scabs floating off her wounds and covering the surface of the water.

'Stop hanging on so tight!' Martha cried out. 'You're almost strangling me.'

'I'm sorry. I'm afraid you'll drop me.'

'Drop you? You don't weigh a thing,' Martha laughed dismissively.

Later she said, 'You've been in the hospital too long.' The others agreed.

Claire was especially outspoken. 'You've got to go,' she said bluntly.

'But I'm still sick. I can't walk.'

'You haven't tried. Anyway, the choice is yours. You know what'll happen if you stay here.'

Soon after, Hortense watched the Kapos playing their 'game' in the yard outside her window. This was the second time she had seen this particular charade. The Kapos supervising the queues of women from the main camp who were reporting sick brought a batch into the yard outside Hortense's window. On this occasion the Kapo with the black crewcut hair was in charge. These wretched women were so sick they had no option but to report to the Revier and their worst fears were confirmed when they were kicked about in the yard and ordered to undress. The SS guards watched and waited for the fun to start.

'Now we're going to take your temperature,' the fat Kapo bellowed. She screamed at the women to go down on all fours, took a thermometer and stuck it between the cheeks of the first woman's backside, in her anus. With a savage kick the woman was made to scamper across the yard on her hands and knees, like an animal, to the howls of derision and laughter of the SS. This was known as the 'dog game'. Hortense was careful not to be seen and watched by peeking over the window sill. As one naked woman crossed the cold ground an SS guard saw the thermometer fall out over her thighs. He ran over and kicked her savagely in the side and agreed with the fat Kapo amid much laughter that she had to start again.

279

Others, the older ones, were kicked for not crawling fast enough, and by the time the SS grew tired of their sport several women lay motionless on the dirt, too weak to move in spite of the fat Kapo's kicks. They were taken off on stretchers.

Hortense decided it was time to move. In September 1944, about the time Louvain was liberated by the Allies, she was taken out of the Revier on a stretcher. She could not stand for any length of time, let alone walk, but Dr Oberheuser was persuaded that she was fit enough to be discharged from the hospital itself. The nurses carried her stretcher to Block 9 in the isolation compound, on the other side of the Lagerstrasse, where the Appel was called.

Block 9 was a hut similar to the one in which she had spent the first night in the camp, weeks before in June. It was about half-way down the Lagerstrasse from the camp gate where Block 1 started the line. Block 9, 10 and 11 were in an isolation compound on the opposite side of the Lagerstrasse from the Revier and the camp administrative stores. Like the stores, the compound was sealed off from the blocks, above and below and across the camp street alongside, by rolls of barbed wire. The back of Block 8 formed one side of the compound opposite the entrance of Block 9. An SS guard stood at the gate to the compound, which was between Blocks 8 and 9, preventing unauthorised access. There was always a good deal of coming and going in the isolation compound during the day as none of the inmates attended Appel or took part in the daily work details.

With this movement came news of the fighting, passed on by the now continuous stream of new transports filled with prisoners. All the Belgium concentration camps had now been evacuated including Breendonk, and General Montgomery's British 21st Army Group had reached Brussels on 3 September. In the south General Bradley's American 12th Army Group had taken the

Great War battlefield town of Verdun and moved on to Luxembourg, by-passing the Ardennes mountains. These were great successes but the Wehrmacht faced greater odds and more telling losses in the East. Reports of the fighting in Russia came from women Partisans, usually Communists captured harrying the Wehrmacht's stretched lines of communications. At the end of August 1944 Rumania had capitulated, Russian tanks penetrating westwards 450 miles in eighteen days to reach the Danube and the whole of the German 6th Army was lost, totalling twenty divisions. By September 1944 over half a million German troops had been made prisoner on various fronts in the East; while in Normandy only 60,000 were killed or captured in the Falaise pocket which was considered a great Allied achievement. With reports like these, Hortense never lost her confidence that the Germans would be defeated or that she would not spend the rest of her life a prisoner in the camp. Sadly, her health did not match this confidence in the march of world history, and the German reverses made not the slightest difference to camp life. If anything, the SS grew more concerned to liquidate even greater numbers.

When Hortense came to Block 9 on her stretcher she met Mary Lindell, then nearly fifty years old. Mary Lindell, Comtesse de Milleville, had nursed French soldiers at the front for four years during the Great War and when the Second World War started quickly became involved in helping a wide variety of servicemen escape the German occupation so they could continue the fight from Britain. She started an escape line down the west side of France to Spain, and perhaps because she was a fiercely independent, outspoken woman who despised Germans, was caught and condemned to death in Paris. She entered Ravensbrück on 3 September. With her came a young SOE agent, Yvonne Baseden, who had been in the same cell as Mary in Dijon jail and been transported with her into Germany. Mary's nursing skills were recognised and she was put to work in Block 9. Her forceful personality soon made her a figure who could not be ignored.

Mary found Hortense Daman a place near a window. The bunks were stacked to the ceiling with sick women, most of whom had contagious diseases of one kind or another. The isolation compound was a dumping ground for those who could not cope with the rigours of regular camp life. They were excused the Appel, but few could have stood for roll-call even if forced. Hortense soon noticed that a few women were taken out dead most mornings and laid outside on the ground, a little pile of ragged, emaciated skeletons. At night the long room was filled with such screams and tortured yells that Hortense thought in all innocence they might be the evidence of cannibalism. Certainly everyone was hungry enough.

Her mother continued to visit her and bring little pieces of food. Hortense looked forward to the morsels of black German bread which she wolfed down, even though it was rock hard. They met through the window, as before, only this time there was no glass and they could talk more easily, always about home and the family. Her mother was not very well herself at the time and was billeted in Block 11. This block was in the isolation compound on the other side of Block 10 where the mentally sick were housed under the harsh regime of the Blockälteste Carmen Mory.

Hortense grew a little stronger. She could move about with difficulty inside the block, holding on to bunks and the walls, and by October spent a good deal of her time sitting on a three-legged stool at the window beside the door of Block 9, watching the goings-on by the gate into the compound from the Lagerstrasse. On the other side beyond the fence a camp street ran between the rank of huts. One day a prisoner nurse told her there had been a new transport from Belgium and settled her on the stool by the door. Block 8 was opposite the door in Block 9 and was generally used for new arrivals. After a while

Hortense saw movement through the windows of the back of Block 8. She was certain she recognised one or two of them. Then she saw Paula van de Velde, a friend from Louvain, who had been a courier for the Partisans.

'Hallo!' Hortense cried out. 'Paula! It's me, Hortense!'

Several of the women in the group inside Block 8 stopped moving about and came to look out of the window. Paula van de Velde was among them.

'Paula, it's me, Hortense.'

Paula stared at the gaunt figure in a grubby white hospital slip waving in the window of the block next door.

'Paula! It's me, Lisette!' Hortense cried out, using her code name in the Partisans. 'Don't you remember?'

Paula remembered.

'Have you any news of Bertha?' Hortense continued rather desperately, wondering what was the matter with her friend. Paula just continued to stare at her across the sandy yard. 'Is she all right? Tell me!' Hortense had always been worried that the SS would arrest Bertha as well, although she had done nothing against the Germans.

Paula did not reply. She vanished from the window.

'Paula!'

Hortense was saddened and deeply hurt. She and Paula had been good friends. She continued to search into the gloom beyond the windows of Block 8 and saw two or three others she recognised from home. They seemed to be watching her from further inside the hut and pointing.

Puzzled, she saw Madeleine, an inmate and one of the prisoner nurses. She demanded to know what was the matter. Something unspoken in Madeleine's answer, a nuance she tried to keep out, made Hortense ask for a mirror.

'A mirror! Where in a place like this would there be a mirror?'

'Find one!' Hortense screamed, a feeling of sickness rising in her chest. 'I've seen some of the women here with pieces of mirror.'

Hortense made such a noise that someone brought a fragment of mirror. She grabbed it and looked at herself for the first time in months, the first time since she had entered Ravensbrück. The image drifted about in the little piece of broken mirror as her hands shook and then struck at the very root of her soul. It was the image of others she had seen when she first arrived. Gaunt, fleshless, hairless, sick. Now she was one of 'those'.

Hortense spent much of her time sitting by the window of Block 9. Her mother continued her visits; she saw Odette Sansom one day with Madeleine; and there were always fights between women squabbling for food or a cigarette. One day a Ukrainian girl, recognisable from her red political prisoner's triangle, approached the compound gate from the Lagerstrasse and suddenly nipped inside past the guard.

'You! Come here!' the guard shouted in surprise.

'Where's Hortensia?' the Ukrainian girl shouted in German as she ran along the wall of Block 9.

'Here! Over here!' Hortense called out and the girl ran over to the window, threw a long grey and blue striped dress at her, smiled and disappeared round the corner pursued by the SS guard. In the mêlée of the chase round the isolation blocks the Ukrainian girl was able to slip out of the unguarded gate again without difficulty.

The gift was salvation. Hortense had no idea how anyone knew she wanted extra clothing, but she had on only a thin slip which she had been wearing all through the summer in the Revier. With the beginning of the cold autumn weather she had been wondering how she would manage in the winter. Someone had known and found the dress. Somewhere in the camp was an organisation of women, probably Communists and Partisans, who checked the camp records for those like Hortense who had been Partisans too, and then did what they could for them. The dress was invaluable, thicker than her slip, with long sleeves and skirt. Though it had a sinister grey cross on the back which signified someone condemned to death, now she had a chance as the autumn gave way to the coldest winter of the war. `

Not long after, Hortense overheard Mary Lindell talking to another nurse further down the hut.

'If that girl doesn't get off her backside and learn to walk again, you know where she'll end up.' Mary was obviously unaware of the power of her voice, and probably would not have cared had she known.

The remark badly jolted Hortense. She knew what happened to inmates who were considered at an end. She had seen them taken into the ward at the end of her bed in the corridor in the Revier, and taken out again dead. Mary Lindell's bossy tone infuriated Hortense, but she knew she was right. She set her mind against the pain and tried to walk. She staggered down the narrow alleys between the tiers of bunks, to claps and calls of encouragement from the women lying there, women often so sick they would never walk again themselves and knew they had only a short time to live. She suffered raging headaches and occasionally she fainted.

After one of these sessions, Claire stopped Mary from another rude criticism and told her how ill Hortense had been. She lifted Hortense's dress by the hem and showed Mary the left leg, horribly swollen and black. The sight took her a little by surprise and she apologised for being so blunt.

'But I do not apologise for the intention,' she said.

Mary and all the other nurses knew that Hortense had to walk again if she was to survive. Slowly, she began to walk about more and more inside the block. She found helping other patients gave her something to do and she noticed one woman who was largely ignored. The nurses gave her short shrift for Sophia Meyer was German, an overseer, a Kapo from across the Lagerstrasse where she ran a store next to Dorothea Binz's office. She had been sent to

Block 9 to recuperate from a bad bout of illness which the doctors diagnosed as cancer. Surprisingly Hortense did not hate all Germans. She saw the woman as elderly, in her late fifties, unwell and on her own. She decided to do what she could for her. Meyer was a prisoner who usually enjoyed all the privileges of a Kapo and she realised she was unwelcome among the ordinary prisoners, especially in Block 9 where everyone was levelled by sickness. So she was grateful to the young Belgian girl. She asked Hortense to wet her handkerchief and Hortense kept her company quite often while she stayed in the hut.

'Call me Aunty Sophia,' Meyer said earnestly before she left the hut. Neither she nor Hortense seemed to notice anything out of place in the nightmare of the camp at the idea of the young Belgian girl, a prisoner condemned to death, being asked to call one of the Kapos 'Aunty'. Meyer continued, 'You've been kind to me, an old woman, and if there's ever anything I can do for you just ask. I'll do my best.'

Hortense was pleased at the remark, but there was no chance of taking up the offer. Sophia Meyer worked on the other side of the wide Lagerstrasse, in the stores offices and none of the prisoners went there for fear of being knocked over and beaten by Binz or other SS guards. The other side of the Lagerstrasse was decidedly off limits to the prisoners.

There was another good reason. Most of the prisoners tried to keep in the grey background of camp life. Most Kapos and Blockälteste were harsh, brutal women who thrived in the anarchic environment which the Nazis had created to wear down their prisoners. The SS selected and encouraged such women. Their deliberate policy was to destroy the body and reduce the spirit of all concentration camp prisoners. The SS knew from long experience that unpredictable brutality on top of all the other deprivations of food, proper clothing, sanitation or comforts of any kind could break the hardest soul. Even Rudolf Höss,

Commandant of Auschwitz, said of the Blockälteste and Kapos under his command that 'Most were prostitutes with many convictions . . . These dreadful women gave full vent to their evil desires on the prisoners . . . They were soulless and had no feelings whatsoever.' Many of them at Auschwitz had been recruited from Ravensbrück.

Ranking with the worst of these was Carmen Mory, the Blockälteste of Block 10 between Hortense in Block 9 and her mother in Block 11. All the insane women were billeted in Block 10, in a small room about five yards by six, numbering about sixty women or more at once, tiered up in bunks three high and two to a bunk. Carmen Mory had been in the camp for nearly four years. Born in Berne in Switzerland, she had been well educated on courses in Switzerland, France, Holland and England. She had made a dismal attempt to spy on the French Maginot line and then on the Germans on her own account, having also taken a course in journalism at Munich University. The Gestapo arrested her and she was sent to Ravensbrück in February 1941, since when she had not merely determined to survive but ingratiated herself with the SS, become a Blockälteste and joined the ranks of the more feared and brutal camp figures. When Hortense arrived in Block 9, Mory was in charge of Block 10 where she appointed a German criminal to oversee the inmates who were sick with tuberculosis and the women who were considered mad. In spite of her background, Mory had quickly found a niche in the anarchy of camp life. Among her victims was a Polish woman to whom she gave a savage beating and whom she doused with buckets of cold water while she stood naked, spurred on by the fact that this Polish woman was well liked by everyone. The Polish woman died the next day. Several times Hortense had seen sick women dragged on to the stones outside Block 10 by Mory, who repeatedly threw cold water over them, screaming that they had to be clean.

One night in late October Hortense had to go to the toilets. She struggled out of her cot and limped between the bunks to the middle of the block. It was a clear night and while she was there a tremendous din of manic shouting carried across from Block 10. It was normal to hear women screaming out in the night, but this was exceptional. She looked through the open window across to Block 10 and saw there was fighting in the room where the mad women were quartered. She stared through the empty window of the toilets across the intervening space at the one paneless window in the mad women's room. She saw Carmen Mory burst into the room where she began thrashing several women with a heavy leather belt. Hortense crouched down at once, afraid to go back to her bedspace in case Mory spotted the movement inside Block 9. Once she had seen Mory beat a woman prisoner to the ground and then go on until the woman moved no longer. Mory shouted at one of the prisoner nurses who had come with her to fetch some drugs. The girl returned and Mory injected two women who seemed to have been making the most noise. Hortense could hear more sounds of Mory lashing about with the belt and after a while there was silence. Hortense limped back to her cot. The next morning five dead women were laid outside Block 10.

Violette le Coq, a Frenchwoman and artist who drew some harrowing pictures of life in the camp and who had been in La France Combattante, was one of the prisoners ordered to accompany Mory that night and described this incident in her testimony against Mory at her Nuremberg trial.

Stephanie tried to come as often as she could to see Hortense, which meant running the risk of being caught by Carmen Mory as she skirted Block 10, but she was determined to make sure her daughter survived and glad to see her gradually spending more time on her feet. One day after she had gone, Madeleine came over to Hortense.

She stood by the bunk and looked at the skinny young Belgian girl.

'Hortense,' she started, speaking softly and kindly, but there was no compromise in her voice. 'You're very selfish really. You know you're killing your mother?'

'What?' Hortense replied, too shocked to say more. She imagined her mother had been beaten on the way to see her, or something more dreadful had happened that she had not heard about. 'What d'you mean?'

'You're starving her to death,' Madeleine said in a matter of fact way. 'She just brought her own bread to give you, didn't she? She always brings it. She comes as often as she can to give you extra food.'

Suddenly the truth dawned on Hortense, who in her innocence of so much had not realised the sacrifice her mother made.

'Where d'you think she gets it from?'

Hortense had not thought about it. She had spent all the time in the hospital and isolation huts and simply did not realise what life in the camp outside was like. The mass of prisoners in ordinary blocks lived on one kilo of black bread, which was stale, hard and often covered with fungus, between eight women each day. A quarter of a pound each, or six slices of a typical modern loaf. With that went half a litre of weak dirty water which passed for soup, generally tasting of kohlrabi and gritted with sand, which got into everything in Ravensbrück, and half a litre of ersatz coffee each in the morning at about 6.30 after two hours of Appel, and again after the evening Appel.

How her mother came by the bread never crossed her daughter's mind. For Hortense, things happened or they did not. She did not think about them. She lived for the moment. That was a great gift in the camps. Those that thought too much about what they did and what went on around them quickly became depressed. The SS deliberately encouraged pointless and inexplicable brutalities. This was part of Himmler's system and prisoners who wondered why or tried to understand the logic of what was being done to them deteriorated quickly. Defeat and death followed soon after. Survival did not allow the luxury of contemplation. The revelation that her mother had made a sacrifice of such magnitude for so many weeks filled Hortense with shame and concern. The truth also gave her refreshed determination to act for her own survival.

By this time, the end of October 1944, Hortense had been seriously ill in revoltingly unsanitary conditions for four months. The power of her forthright character and her youth had been terribly depleted. Her mother's arrival and subsequent visits had carried her through life day by day. She had never lost her own confidence but she had grown used to her incapacity. She was used to being sick. The doctor, Claude, who caught typhus herself, and the other nurses had pushed her out of the Revier, Mary Lindell had rudely awakened her to the need to walk again although her leg wounds were far from healed, and now Madeleine had made her realise how much she owed her mother for quietly supplying the essential ingredient for boosting her strength: extra food. This was a turning point.

Hortense decided to visit her mother. Her spirit was on the rise again. Her commitment returned, her need to survive, to see her country again, was enough to overcome her physical infirmities.

That first short walk from Block 9 to Block 11 was agony. She took long minutes between each step, standing still to gather her strength, tortured not so much by the pain as the fear of being caught out in the open by one of the Kapos.

Inevitably a voice screamed at her from Block 10. 'You! What're you doing here?' Carmen Mory had seen her.

'I want to see my mother,' Hortense said matter-of-factly, turning to face the Blockälteste with difficulty. Under pressure, as usual, she had found the right thing to say, the right pitch. 'I have to get to Block 11.'

Instinctively she went on the attack with a straight-forward human response which cut across the weakness of her position, at the mercy of someone who might kill her at a whim. She made the conversation sound normal. She did not cringe or babble with fear. She stood and waited for Mory's reply, as if speaking to an acquaintance in the street at home in Louvain. She knew that survival depended on being unnoticed but there were times when Hortense felt she had to act. Swaying slightly on her bad leg, she watched Mory storm over.

Mory faced a rag-thin, crippled girl who gave no sign of fright, and in a gesture of capriciousness typical but rare in concentration camp life, she decided not to lash out but assist.

To Hortense's complete amazement, Mory escorted her personally round to Block 11 to see her mother.

At the start of November, Hortense went back to the Revier to 'report sick'. Although the conditions of Percy Treite's hospital were filthy and the 'treatment' was the antithesis of medical care, there was a system. Hortense could not leave the hospital blocks without authority. She needed clearance from the doctors. She arrived at the Revier, had her temperature taken in the anus as usual, and was finally seen by Dr Oberheuser who had come on another visit from Hohenlychen. Although this masculine-looking and austere woman had assisted in the gangrene experiment on Hortense's leg, seeing her was good fortune. Oberheuser had become used to number 42742, the plucky young Belgian girl, and unsmilingly seemed to admit a slight human regard for her. She agreed to certify Hortense as healthy.

Hortense was sent to Block 15. Nearly five months after entering Ravensbrück, she stood outside at 4.30 in the morning at Appel for only the second time. Life was hard in the main camp but Stephanie had been discharged from Block 11 and the two were together again, sharing a single bunk and giving each other the vital support they needed.

Hortense and her mother started the day with the thousands of other prisoners at 4.30 a.m. when the SS called the roll in the big Lagerstrasse. The women stood in grey ranks, block by block stretching away into the darkness, while Block Leaders and Kapos moved among them shouting and screaming out the numbers. Everything was done by numbers. Over 25,000 people were counted in two hours. Even the dead prisoners had to attend: other prisoners in their block had to bring them out to be recorded present and correct on their last parade. Some others, who managed to drag themselves to Appel to stand up and be counted alive, died before the end, unable to endure even two hours outside in the increasingly bitter morning air. When someone was missing or the SS wanted to punish the whole camp, the roll-call sometimes went on for six hours with counts and recounts. Hortense found standing so long very difficult. As autumn faded and the temperature continued to drop week by week, the sheer pain of being cold was added to this discomfort. The first snows came on 13 November in flurries round the bare legs of the women as they stood at Appel that dark morning.

During the day they went on work details. They were marched to work at a pace which was nothing more than a slow shuffle, but one Hortense found hard to manage. After a twelve-hour shift in workshops they marched back exhausted and stood for the evening Appel before being again confined to the block at 8 p.m. Several times Hortense's temperature soared, her wounds swelled with inflammation, her leg gave out and she could not walk at all. Unwillingly she was obliged to report sick to the Revier, always a risky business, and returned to Block 9 to recuperate. At least there she was spared the stress of Appel.

Mother and daughter stayed together as much as they could, always talking of home and wondering what had happened to Jacques, François, Bertha and Julia. They knew the rest of the family had been completely broken up after the arrests on St Valentine's day in 1944 and worried all the time that François and Bertha had been arrested.

They always took an interest in new arrivals from Belgium, just in case Bertha was among them. One day Hortense was lying in her bunk alone when a friend told her a transport had arrived with Belgian women and there was someone with a name very like 'Daman' among them. Hugely depressed by this news Hortense decided to find out the truth before her mother, as Stephanie was struggling more and more with the onset of winter. Besides she felt sure her sister Bertha would need her help right from the start to survive the rigours of Ravensbrück. Knowing she had family at hand would ease the shock of arrival and give Bertha a great boost. Hortense heard that the new prisoners had already been put in the knitting room, so she assumed they had been through the humiliating process of induction. She hoped Bertha was spared the hopeless medical care she had received which had obviously gone wrong and caused her to become infected. She climbed off her bunk and went into the knitting room.

'Daman?' Hortense called out, looking all round for Bertha. 'Is there anyone here called Daman?'

Hortense moved slowly through the crowd, careful not to bruise her leg as she passed a knot of women sitting on the floor, calling out her sister's name, and something struck her as out of place. Her eyes were playing tricks on her. She had come bitterly to terms with her own appearance. Everyone in the camp looked the same. Inmates looked the same in every concentration camp, she was sure, but several of the women in the knitting room were well-dressed and clean. They looked away as Hortense moved past.

'Duman?' a voice called out from the back of the room. Hortense twisted round to look in the direction of the reply but even when she walked over she could see no one she recognised.

'Daman,' she said again loudly, wondering where Bertha had disappeared to when she had just heard someone call back from that corner.

'No, I'm Dumon,' said an attractive young woman sitting casually at ease on a table close by. Hortense focused on the woman and saw she had made a mistake. In the hubbub of talk and helplessly assuming the worst, she had misheard 'Daman' in 'Dumon'. Hortense apologised with a brief explanation about Bertha. Dumon was sympathetic. Hortense felt tired after the effort of preparing herself to cope with her elder sister and decided to return to her bunk, when it struck her how well turned out this Dumon was. She was even wearing lipstick, stockings and elegant high heels.

Hortense stared fascinated at the young woman. She looked round at the other women and then back at Dumon, at her clothes, surprised at how pretty she looked, how normal. Then the truth dawned on her. She realised why the SS had selected attractive women like Dumon and the others to dress and feed well, why their officers wanted them to look pretty, why the women were taken from camp to camp and what they did for the SS in return for a way of life quite different from the masses in the camp.

Dumon saw the look in Hortense's face and her shoulders lifted very slightly with a hint of apology but her eyes were hard and defensive.

Hortense stumbled out of the knitting room and returned to her bunk in a state of shocked surprise. In spite of her enormous experience of the darker side of men's characters, she was sexually immature. An eighteen-year-old today would find such inexperience hard to believe. Certainly she had seen lesbians in the camp. Hortense and all the other Belgian and French prisoners laughingly described them as women who had not been baptised with holy water. Hortense held strictly Catholic views. She thought she ought to have been angry at finding that there were women prisoners who were prepared to become prostitutes to the SS officers. She had seen practically every other human aberration. Instead she found herself arguing their case. Some young women assessed their situation in the camps with simple and brutal logic. They decided they could not survive as ordinary prisoners, on too little food and a savage work schedule. They knew they would die, so they chose an alternative, which for all but a few must have been as mentally taxing in its way as ordinary camp life was for other prisoners. Hortense found she could not condemn Dumon and her like for their choice, though she was sure that the sacrifice of self-esteem was something she could never bring herself to do, and was certain they would regret it for the rest of their lives, if they survived at all. Dumon did survive. She was a well-educated woman and when she had recovered her freedom she met and married a senior Allied officer.

During their time in Block 15 Hortense and her mother grew even closer. Each had found the greatest respect for the other and at this time in late November 1944 their capacity for survival was about equal. Hortense was growing stronger gradually and her mother was slowly weakening, feeling her fifty-odd years and the rigours of camp life wearing her down. They depended enormously on one another. They shared the same appearance, gaunt, shrunken, tired. They shared a bunk, sleeping head to tail. They shared a bowl and spoon as Hortense had again lost hers. Her mother made her eat more than her fair share and she would say her daughter's recovery was meal enough. The Daman family had always been close-knit, which was their strength.

In November 1944 there was a lull in the Allies' advance on both fronts. In the East the German army had stabilised the Russians' sweep on a line from Prussia to Budapest. In the West the British and American advance had halted, while unknown to them Hitler's divisions were preparing for the Ardennes offensive.

The Nazis had trodden a long and bloody path through their conquered territories towards their stated intention to eliminate 'undesirable' elements. In May 1943 Hitler had declared, 'All the rubbish of small States still existing in Europe must be liquidated as fast as possible.' His extermination camps, with infamous names like Belzec, Treblinka and Auschwitz, had done their best to match the insane dreams of their Führer with the real deaths of millions of people. By the end of 1944 the Russians were coming and Ravensbrück filled up steadily with transports from the eastern camps.

One day after working in the afternoon, Hortense went to see some Yugoslav girls she had become friendly with near Block 4. They had been Partisans with Tito, and were employed in the camp kitchen serving out the cauldrons of soup and coffee from trolleys which they pushed along the Lagerstrasse after Appel. The news was that the SS had put up a large German tent of the sort used in beer festivals in a dip on the far side of the hutted camp, beyond the wooden blocks. As they talked they heard a lot of noise from the direction of the main gate. They looked round the end of Block 4, up the Lagerstrasse to the courtyard by the Kommandantur, where they saw a large group of young children. Hortense guessed there were more than seven hundred children, organised in squads. All the children were handsome, dark-haired, clean and healthy and they carried little satchels. She and the Yugoslav girls were encouraged by their appearance. Such normality was unusual and made them think the war must be coming to an end soon.

The boys and girls saw the prisoners watching them so they waved happily. Hortense and others waved back. She noticed the SS made no effort to follow their usual brutal habits. They treated the children with great care and were obviously taking trouble over them. Everyone said that was a good sign. Shortly the SS began to move them in their squads across the courtyard towards the huts. Hortense and her friends watched these attractive youngsters march down one of the camp streets between the wooden blocks and, following at a safe distance from the guards, saw them installed in the new tent. Some of the SS guards even went round the outside putting sandbags on the edge of the material to keep the draughts out. The sight of such fine looking children was refreshing, and Hortense and her friends agreed to come back the following day.

At Appel next morning Hortense had an awful feeling of death. She could see across the rooftops of the wooden huts that the chimney of the crematorium was unusually busy for that hour of day, belching sparks and smoke. When she went back to see her Yugoslav friends her fears were confirmed. The SS had not been laying sandbags to keep the cold winter air from coming into the tent, but to prevent the gas escaping. The children were Hungarian, and Jewish. It had been a busy night for the SS.

By December there were over twenty five thousand women in a camp built for six thousand. The numbers were swelling all the time with other prisoners from East and West. Shortly before the German Ardennes offensive struck back at Belgium in December, recapturing towns and villages which had only recently been liberated, the SS in Ravensbrück called all the Belgians and the French together and made a selection. Some broke down, convinced they were to be killed.

Everyone in Block 15 was paraded and the SS called out number after number, apparently at random, including Nos 42742 and 47787. Hortense and her mother were marched out of the main gate with the others and moved to another part of Ravensbrück which Hortense came to know as the 'Little Camp'.

# 11

# Pleinstraat Again

'The problems of victory are more agreeable than those of defeat, but they are no less difficult.' Winston Churchill, 11 November 1942.

In Louvain life became more precarious than ever for the Partisans after the mass of arrests in February 1944. Louis van Brussel, Sector Commandant, wrote a secret dispatch to the National Commando on 21 February that the arrests 'were the worst thing that has happened to the Army of Partisans. Five Corps in the Flanders area are affected and might go down as well, though all security measures are being taken.' He and Francois were only too aware that the more arrests the Gestapo made, the more chance there was of a snowball effect. The Gestapo would torture certain key people, like the Corps Commandant Gaston and couriers like Hortense, because they knew an enormous amount about the people, addresses and activities of the Partisans:

There is still great danger of further arrests. I ask you to watch out in these early days until a 'normal' situation is back. Our usual 'post-box' is burnt and must not be used any longer. This is a very serious situation and security is at fault. The whole corps is at risk of complete destruction.

The corps had lost many of its command element, which had to be replaced. Germain de Becker, code-name 'Gerard', took over for a month or two until he committed suicide rather than be captured during a fire-fight with German soldiers on 30 May. Then, at the time of the D-day landings, François took his place. He continued his liaisons with the escape lines and the Belgian Legion, which became the Belgian Secret Army in July; and he was extremely busy organising Partisan operations for the Allied armies' advance. The Louvain Partisans did not let up on their attacks against the occupiers and their collaborators, in spite of suffering considerable losses. They carried out an average of over twenty attacks every month in the five months from April to August 1944, mostly on rail, road and telephone communication lines. Considering the losses of command personnel, couriers and fighters, and having to arrange all these attacks in secret, using new people who ran increasing risks of being caught by the Gestapo, the record is excellent.

June was the busiest month. On the 8th the BBC broadcast a coded message to Underground radio operators, '*Le roi Salomon a mis ses gros sabots!*' (King Solomon has put on his big boots!) This was the long-awaited signal to start attacks in support of the Allied invasion forces which were fighting to establish their bridgehead in Normandy. François organised thirty-two attacks that month. More and more, he depended on the experienced men, like Pierre Hermans and Pierre van Goitsenhoeven, who like him had avoided capture for so long.

The Gestapo continued their search for François to the bitter end, offering a reward for his capture which was published on posters and pasted on walls and notices round Louvain: 'DAMAN, François. Terrorist. Wanted dead or alive. Reward 500,000 Belgian Francs.' The reward was enormous at a time when a pair of workman's shoes cost 140 francs. It did not work. François remained the cunning fox he had been throughout the Occupation and was free to see the British tanks roll into Brussels on Sunday, 3 September and into Louvain a day later.

The Belgians went mad with joy, dancing in the streets and mobbing the English soldiers in the tanks and trucks, and fêting the Belgian Brigade which was their vanguard. Everyone came into the road with flags, banners, music and drink just to savour the sensation of being free again. After more than four years living in fear of a sudden knock on the door in the middle of the night, the Nazi burden was lifted and they celebrated crazily.

François could not join in the delirium of liberation. A part of him was constantly thinking of Hortense and his parents. For a time they had had some news. His little sister Julia and Bertha had not been arrested, and in July a man had visited Bertha to say he had been in a cell close to Hortense in St Gilles prison; Stephanie had been able to write one postcard from Vught before she was transported into Germany in August; and there were fairly reliable reports that Jacques had been seen first in Breendonk and then in Buchenwald. None of the news was encouraging. It was all out of date. Once the truth about Breendonk was revealed after liberation François tortured himself thinking about what they were suffering. He was tortured too by the thought that their arrest and misery was his fault. He admitted that Hortense had always been on a course of her own to fight the Germans occupying her country, but he wondered how much his mother would have helped with supplies for the Partisans and escape lines without his influence. His sense of guilt was most acute for his father, whom he knew had only been arrested as a hostage for himself.

Once he was back in uniform, resuming his career as a regular soldier in the Belgian army, and promoted to Adjutant, he lost no time in trying to find out where his family had been sent. The task was not easy because the

SS had destroyed most of their records before running away, and was frustrating because the Allied armies were taking much longer to batter their way into Germany than he expected. He, Bertha and his wife Lisa visited government departments to lodge search notices for his parents and sister; and of course they went to the Red Cross. In a way, François had come full circle from the time in 1940 when he worked with the Red Cross in the Rue aux Laines, dealing with displaced persons after the German invasion. In September 1944, however, the number of lost people was far greater, and the causes of their despair more varied in a vast catalogue of abuses by the Nazis during the four years of the Occupation. The inquiry about Daman, father, mother and daughter, was one of hundreds of thousands of similar pleas for help. Temporary camps were established everywhere in Belgium housing thousands of homeless of every nationality; let alone those who were lost in the Third Reich's darkest corners.

While the Allied armies continued to fight in Holland, at Arnhem and towards the river Rhine, the transition from Occupation back to democracy in Belgium was not as smooth or as sweet as people had hoped. Certainly those who fought in the Partisans did not expect the bitter wrangling which emerged in the autumn of 1944. Prime Minister Pierlot returned from England without trouble and declared a regency in favour of the king's brother, Prince Charles. After King Leopold III had surrendered to Hitler in 1940 he was kept under house arrest for the rest of the war, and was released by the 7th US Army in Austria on 7 May 1945. However, leaders of the Front of Independence, the political wing of the Belgian Army of Partisans, did not support a casual return to parliamentary democracy with a king as titular head of government. They wanted socialism, preferably of the Communist variety, even though the huge majority of the rank and file in the Partisans, including the Damans, were not Communist, or indeed aware of any Communist connection. Most had no idea that the Front and the Partisans had been controlled by Communists in touch with Moscow.

After liberation these leaders opened the doors to anyone wanting to call themselves a Partisan, to swell the numbers of the Front, and then contested the mandate of the Pierlot government. Food was extremely short in Belgium, and the Communists blamed the situation on the government which had only just come back from England. When they failed at the ballot box, they tried more traditional Communist techniques. The debate became vitriolic and climaxed at the end of November 1944 in a violent stage-managed demonstration outside the Parliament buildings, when thirty-five people were wounded in shooting between Partisans and the gendarmerie. The event was widely publicised, and drew ill-informed letters of outrage from Trade Unions in England, but the stir was out of proportion to popular support for the cause. In practice, far from gaining any influence, the Communists' Nazi-style attempts to gain power were hugely criticised and the Partisans were discredited. The Front was dishonest and cynical to claim that those who had joined after the liberation had been Partisans during the Occupation, merely to lend weight to its political demands. The attempt failed in its purpose but succeeded in tarnishing the Partisans' splendid Resistance record and for ever soured the feelings of those, like François Daman, Pierre Hermans and Pierre van Goitsenhoeven, who had run the risks and made the sacrifices.

The Partisans kept their experiences to themselves after the November débâcle, though most were not the sort of men and women to brag about their exploits. They settled down to living ordinary lives again with their families, no longer on the run, and going out to work. The British army offered opportunities which were readily snapped up by young men as keen to do something to help defeat

Germany as they were to work at all. Civilian labour was badly needed to cope with the massive tonnages of stores being stockpiled for the winter offensive on Germany and depots were established in Belgium, which was close enough to the front. One of these was set up in the Philips factory opposite Pleinstraat.

The Philips factory had seen a succession of soldiers, from the Belgians in May 1940, to the German factory guards throughout the Occupation and finally a British unit which arrived in September 1944, in which Staff Sergeant Syd Clews was responsible for recruiting the local civilian labour. He interviewed various men and was especially impressed by Josef Homblet, not because he showed any particular skill carrying stores but because he had been a footballer at national level before the Louvain Athletic Club was broken up by the Gestapo, when most of the members were arrested. Syd Clews quickly reassessed his depot's chances of winning inter-unit football competitions and employed him on the spot.

Syd did not learn of Homblet's wartime experiences till later, but thought it would be interesting for the Belgian to know that he had been in Louvain before, in the British Expeditionary Force in May 1940. He had joined his local infantry unit, the North Staffordshire Regiment, in December 1939. In Ramsgate, on the way to France in February 1940, volunteers were asked to join the Royal Army Service Corps and he soon found himself supplying shells for an artillery regiment with very old 6 inch howitzers dating from the Great War. When the German Stukas dive-bombed Pleinstraat on 10 May, Syd's unit left Béthune in France, and made best speed towards Louvain against the stream of refugees clogging the roads in the opposite direction. He probably passed the Daman family on the road. The howitzers were put into action during the brief but vicious defence of the river Dyle which runs through the town, and then he was part of the hectic withdrawal to Dunkirk. He was among the fortunate to be brought home across the English Channel.

François saw the British soldiers from time to time when he visited the house in Pleinstraat. The sight of their khaki battledress and cheery manner was certainly an agreeable change but he found these visits depressing. The dereliction of his old family home reminded him of Hortense and his parents. No one had lived in it since the arrests in February, when it had been boarded up for the second time in the war. He had decided that the house and shop must be repaired. He organised the work and came up when he could from his own house in Mussenstraat, where Lisa and their son Jacques were back, thankful they no longer had to hide in the woods. In spite of her pneumonia Lisa had had to keep constantly on the move for fear the SS would pick them up and try to use them to find François.

In the evenings François always tried to get home in time to listen to the radio. The names of people who had been located somewhere in Europe were broadcast nightly and families all over the country who had lost someone waited for these messages, always hoping to hear news of their loved ones. As the British and American armies moved eastwards they released men in labour camps, servicemen in POW camps and a few political prisoners lucky enough not to have been transported into Germany. Every night that François and Lisa sat in Mussenstraat, his sister Bertha and Guillaume Berges, and often her grandfather Bompa, sat in Frederik Lintstraat, also listening to the radio. Sometimes they all got together in Bertha's kitchen to listen intently as name after name was read out in dry impersonal tones. They never lost hope but there was no mention of 'Daman' or of Stephanie's maiden name, 'Van den Eynde'.

François's efforts to trace them through captured German documents had no success. Finally he did hear some news, though it was not encouraging. Jommeke

Vanderstappen's wife had been arrested and sent to Ravensbrück, and in the middle of the winter she was unexpectedly released. So few prisoners were freed from the concentration camp system that the numbers do not appear in the statistics. When she came back to Louvain she brought the depressing news that Stephanie and Hortense were in the camp. Her report increased François's sense of guilt, giving him enough of the story to know that the rest was undoubtedly worse.

# 12

# The Russians are Coming

'Homicidal pleasure has still not been eradicated by civilization in any of us.' A. Mitscherlich in *The Death Doctors*, 1962.

The Little Camp was not walled. It was a collection of wooden huts, slightly smaller than in the main camp, and recently built by prisoners near the factory workshops about half a mile from the main camp gate. The grey, sandy compound was surrounded by an electrified fence of barbed wire. Large guard towers stood on the outside, looming over the rolls of wire, from which the SS could see into every corner of the camp.

Hortense saw that all the women in the selection for the Little Camp were political prisoners with red triangles on their grey and blue striped dresses. At least, she thought, they would not have to put up with the problems of living with criminals, 'asocials' and others who could not be trusted and who had no time for the ideals of the political prisoners.

The group left the main gate, turned left and marched along a track leaving the high wall of the main camp on their left. They passed a smart villa which was known as Himmler's house on the right, and she could see the smoking chimney of the crematorium rising above the wall on the left. Soon they crossed a railway line and

307

were stopped in an open area in front of the barbed wire gates of the Little Camp. The administrative offices for the camp were ahead and she was thrilled to see trees and woods away on the left. Even when they were locked inside the compound it was a change to be able to see the world beyond the electric fence.

The accommodation huts were cleaner than in the main camp, but the work was hard and unremitting. Every day Hortense was marched with all the other women out of the Little Camp, along a track which led between rows of workshops, to Siemens, the huge German electric company, for a twelve-hour work shift. There was no food, unless Hortense brought a little bread with her, and no water supplied. She worked for one week on day shifts and then two weeks on night shifts, on at 6 p.m. and off again at 6 a.m., after which there would be the usual timeless Appel to suffer. Changeover between day to night shifts was always exhausting. The SS allowed no time for the prisoners to catch up on their sleep during the changeover and the women went without for twenty-four hours.

The Siemens factory produced electronic components for German aircraft. Most big German companies producing *matériel* for the war effort, such as I.G. Farben, Zeiss-Ikon and Universelle Dresden, had built facilities at the main concentration camps. The SS had realised in 1942 that the conditions in the camps were killing off too many inmates too quickly. On 28 December SS Brigadier-General Kruger wrote, 'Mortality in the individual camps must be sharply reduced,' because 'work capacity' had to be at 'as high a level as possible.' Prisoner deaths were losing a valuable source of labour which could be used for the benefit of the Reich. Himmler, with Hitler's approval, began what he thought was the most efficient use of camp labour. He obtained a 'legal' arrangement with Otto Thierach, who had just been appointed the Reich Minister for Justice, to allow the SS to work certain prisoners to death. The SS charged industrial companies like Siemens 4 to 8 Reichmarks per day for the prisoners' labour, calculating that prisoners on twelve-hour shifts would last an average of nine months and therefore the SS would gain a figure of 1,431 RM for each prisoner. Included in the category of those to be worked to death were political prisoners.

The logic was stunningly simple. The labour resource was plentiful and could be replaced, so there was no point in wasting food on them while they were quite literally worked to death. There was always a debate in the SS about whether such 'undesirables' should be kept alive at all, and the work camps were a compromise in which the prisoners received less than their allocated share of food to last the nine months. There is no doubt that the SS in charge of buying the rations for the camp inmates did not use all the money for the purpose for which it was intended. Fraud in army cookhouses is a common enough practice in peacetime, let alone in such places as Ravensbrück. When the Russian advances forced the SS to move inmates westwards and swell the numbers in camps in Germany the rationing situation grew steadily worse.

The existence of these factories means that the German population knew a great deal more about the way concentration camp prisoners were being treated than was admitted after the war. There were large numbers of factories near camps all over Germany, about thirteen main camps by the end of 1944 with 500 satellite or sub-camps (work camps) ringed round them. Tens of thousands of prisoners were employed, all on rations as bad as the one kilo of bread between eight in Ravensbruck. All those prisoners were in contact with and managed by thousands of civilians who were not in the SS. It is hard to believe that, at the very least, rumours were not circulated, especially when one knows that the existence of Dachau, north of Munich, was talked about as early as 1933. What is more likely is that a great deal was known but that no one really objected. Nor was it advisable to do so. By 1944 the Germans had been subjected to more than ten years of Nazi propaganda justifying all kinds of criminal acts including murder. Amnesties were offered for these crimes, especially to the Nazi thugs who attacked the Jews. The German people had been indoctrinated since Hitler rose to power, against Jews and also against anyone who said or did anything against the state or the German people.

Hortense was lucky to be in a static job and did not have to use her leg too much. She worked at a loom in the factory which made electric coils, winding wire from six spools on to a spindle with silver coloured insulation paper layered round the coil. When she learned that the coils were going to be used in German warplanes she began to sabotage her output by sticking pins through the wire to bridge the gap of the insulation paper and short circuit the element. This gave her some satisfaction until she was called out by the two civilians who supervised the factory work. One man was short and fat and the other tall and thin. Their characters matched the generosity of their shape. The taller man was miserable. He was the 'Meister' in charge, but fortunately the shorter man had more to do with the direct day-to-day supervision, so it was he who warned Hortense that too many of her coils did not seem to work when they were tested in quality control. He was genuinely puzzled. He thought the young Belgian girl was doing rather a good job.

'I'll do my best,' Hortense assured him. 'Maybe it's because I try to work too fast.'

'Well, it's true you are quicker than some of the others,' he replied. 'But you must be more careful.'

Hortense continued with her sabotage but she cut down on the number of elements she damaged. Even so she had the satisfaction of seeing a good many slip past quality control. Wondering what chaos she was causing on airfields, in workshops or to planes in the air took some of the grind out of the long shifts.

Stephanie Daman, not so 'lucky', was working on one of the machines in the factory. When they were first marched up to Siemens, the two civilians selected women to work on the electronic benches. Hortense guessed immediately that they only wanted young agile women who could easily pick up what had to be done and who still had supple fingers. They selected Hortense but passed her mother by. Hortense spoke up at once. She well knew that the weak and old were taken on special transfers.

'Why don't you take my mother?'

'She's too old,' the thin civilian snapped.

'Not at all,' Hortense said clearly and without hesitation. 'She's fit and intelligent. Well capable of doing whatever I can do.'

'Then she can stoke the boilers,' he decided bluntly.

It was a reprieve. Stephanie Daman spent her days lugging coal into the boiler house and stoking three furnaces. While the chance of being warmer in the boiler house was welcome, the work was hard for a woman in her fiftieth year and she was always very tired by the end of the twelve-hour shift.

The SS did not permit exhaustion in prisoners. Both to and from the factory the guards made the prisoners sing marching songs. Naturally all the songs were in German, and extolled the Teutonic ideal so beloved by Hitler and the Nazis:

> *In meine heimat der blumen die rosen,*
> *In meine heimat der blumen auch das gluck.*
> *Ich will so gern mit meine liebche' ercausen*
> *Ich will so gern nach meine heimat zuruch.*
> *Kom madel weine nicht,*
> *Wenn du von abscheit sprecht,*
> *Gibt mir noch eine kuss*
> *As abscheit gruss.*

In my homeland the roses are in bloom,
In my homeland happiness is blooming too.
I long to be with my loved one
I long to return to my homeland.
Come my beloved, don't cry,
When I talk about (my) leaving,
Give me one more kiss
To bid me farewell.

There was precious little to connect the dreamland German cottage surrounded by roses and flowers with the marching squads of skeletal women at Ravensbrück camp, but Hortense enjoyed the singing however tired she was. The songs were German but the words took her thoughts back to her own home. For a few moments she was able to forget the frightfulness of her life and was transported back to Pleinstraat in Louvain. Doubtless she thought of Jan Sprengers, about hot summer days they had spent together on the banks of the canal. She wondered what he was doing and whether she would ever see him again. She thought of her family, François, her sisters and father. She did not know the orders and instructions issued by Himmler, the statistics of her expected survival or the assessment of her financial worth in the SS industrial effort, but she knew what it all meant in practice. She was just busy surviving and she preferred to be made to sing songs than to have to sit in a cell merely existing or rotting away.

Perhaps it was just as well she enjoyed the singing. Anyone who did not use their lungs with the right degree of enthusiasm was soundly beaten by the guards.

As might be expected, there were alternative lyrics to those the Germans liked to hear. One verse which was very popular with the SS guards was always turned round by Stephanie Daman:

# The Russians are Coming

*Und wir fahren, und wir fahren, und wir fahren,*
*Gegen England!*

And we'll sail, and we'll sail, and we'll sail,
over to England!

Under the persistent influence of Josef Goebbels, perhaps, the SS were either fanatical enough to believe the words of this song, or wise enough to pretend to believe. Perhaps some were still plain stupid enough to credit what was by late 1944 a very remote possibility indeed.

Stephanie Daman turned the lyrics around and sang in muted Flemish,

And you'll drown, and you'll drown, and you'll drown,
You bastards, on the way there!

Hortense was always delighted to hear her mother singing these words. The word 'bastard' was strong language in Belgium and she loved the spirit of resistance in her mother's voice. None the less she always told her off, in case someone in the group of prisoners reported them to the guards, for a little extra food.

If the billets were marginally cleaner the latrines were worse. Hortense and her mother soon realised how their captors really felt about political prisoners.

The routine was hard and hunger was uppermost in everyone's mind. Sometimes dysentery swept through the camp and further debilitated the inmates. Gastroenteritis causes appreciable weight loss in healthy people but these women were already spare. No allowance was made. Rather, the SS guards and officers seemed to relish this extra misery. The latrines were housed in a long barrack hut about 150 yards from the line of accommodation blocks. There was no privacy inside. A deep trench had been covered by a raised wooden bench with holes cut in the top on which the women sat back to back. This was called the 'Altar'. Hortense hated the place. The conditions were unsanitary to a degree that was exceptional in the camp, and the stench was almost tangible. Sometimes when dysentery was rife women fought each other to sit on the bench and often ended by sharing a hole over the ditch.

The SS guards in the towers liked to play tricks on women who were desperate to reach this ghastly place. During the day when the women were away at work, they hid pieces of wood in the sand in the compound, just sticking out of the surface. The sand froze hard at night. In their hurry to reach the latrines the women never saw the wood obstacles. They tripped and the shock of falling made them urinate or excrete on the spot. The guards were waiting for this. At once they switched on the powerful searchlight from the tower which picked out the dark stain on the glistening pale sand, and the sound of coarse male laughter echoed across the compound. In the morning the offending women, and often the whole block, were punished with extra work or standing at attention for an hour or two.

Just before Christmas Hortense was working in the factory at her loom, spinning coils for the Luftwaffe, when she noticed the fat civilian approach her. He often came round to check what the women were doing so she took no notice until he stood right behind her.

Hortense sat quite still, except that her hands continued working. Perhaps he had been watching her surreptitiously from the other end of the work shed and had seen her sticking pins in the coils.

'Louvain is free!' he whispered.

Hortense started and tried to turn around.

'Don't move!' he hissed, leaning over and pretending to inspect the machinery. There were two SS officers on the other side of the line of machines and they were looking idly in his direction. It was plain he was scared stiff of them.

'Very good,' he said loudly and moving away. 'Carry on!'

For the rest of the day Hortense was in a turmoil waiting to tell her mother what she had heard. They knew that the British were fighting closer all the time, and had heard confused rumours about liberation earlier in the autumn. The SS had told them all was lost for the Allies when the German Ardennes offensive was launched. But she was sure the fat civilian would not tell her lies. He seemed to her a more reasonable man than the others, and besides he would not take the risk unless he was certain.

The knowledge that their home was rid of the Germans was an enormous boost to the two women.

They needed it because they faced their first Christmas in the camp. By the end of December the weather was bleak indeed. Day after day the grey skies were heavy with snow and the icy winds came straight off the Russian Steppes, across the flat wastes to the east of Ravensbrück where the Wehrmacht was fighting for Germany's life against the numerical superiority of the Red Army. The temperature dropped steadily. The outlook for prisoners in all the concentration camps of the Third Reich was grim.

Much to Hortense's surprise the SS gave them all a Christmas present, an extra scoop of 'soup' after Appel. The work schedule was the same but on Christmas Eve the women gathered together in their accommodation huts. There was nothing to celebrate except life itself. Even though some were atheists or felt horribly let down by God nearly everyone in the Little Camp came from a Christian background. Whatever they thought about for the rest of the year, they all drew closer that special night. There were girls and women from many nations in the East and the West and they gathered in small groups to sing their own carols.

Two Ukrainian girls with full, rich voices sang a slow melancholy version of 'The banks of the Volga', full of longing, clearly transported by their song to the vast cornfields of their homeland. The other women huddled round for extra comfort against the icy draughts and listened to the singing which carried over the wooden huts and silver sand of the compound on the still night air. One hut after another, one carol after another; every verse, every line, every word of which meant so much more to these women than just the age-old story of the first Christmas. They were thinking of different times, for some of them long years ago, when there was truly peace on earth and they had relaxed in the warmth of their homes at ease with their families, husbands and lovers.

One woman with a lovely voice sang 'Minuit Chrétiens', a very popular carol among the French and Belgians:

> *Minuit Chrétiens, c'est l'heure solennelle!*
> *Le monde entier tressaille d'espérance . . .*
> Midnight, Christians, the solemn hour!
> The whole world trembles with hope . . .

No one spoke. No one could form the words as the tears streamed down their cheeks, hollow and grey with dirt. No one wanted to break the spell that had for a brief moment lifted their hearts out of the ghastliness of Ravensbrück.

At last, inevitably, a voice, finer than the rest it seemed to Hortense, began to sing that most famous carol, written, ironically, in German and more beautiful in German than in all the many languages into which it is translated and sung year after year:

> *Stille Nacht, heilige Nacht,*
> *Alles schläft, einsam wacht*
> *Nur das traute, hochheilige Paar.*
> *Holder Knabe im lockigen Haar,*
> *Schlaf' in himmlischer Ruh,*
> *Schlaf' in himmlischer Ruh.*

316

Silent night, Holy night,
All is calm, all is bright
Round yon Virgin, Mother and Child,
Holy Infant so tender and mild,
Sleep in Heavenly Peace,
Sleep in Heavenly Peace.

The notes rose faultlessly on the cold night air, silver clear like the frozen sand around them, giving no clue to the emaciated body of the woman who sang. Hortense wondered for a moment what the man who wrote that wonderful carol could have found to say if he had heard his carol then, and seen the gaunt faces of those who listened so intently in the barrack huts, their eyes, usually devoid of emotion, set alight by the beauty of the music. Never before had Hortense felt so fiercely and with such clarity of determination that she must survive and go home.

After Christmas the endless routine of the camp went on. New Year's Day 1945 passed like any other and on 12 January the Little Camp received a new officer, SS Hauptsturmführer Johann Schwartzhuber, who was made Assistant Commandant of the whole camp and put in direct charge of the Little Camp. This man came straight from Auschwitz, which had been overtaken by General Rokossovsky's 2nd White Russian Front, part of the Red Army which was sweeping towards Germany. Schwartzhuber brought with him great expertise in concentration camps. He had been in the SS since 1933 and had served his masters well in Dachau, Sachsenhausen and Auschwitz. His speciality was elimination. When he arrived at Ravensbrück the camp held nearly 40,000 women but by the time the war ended there were only 12,000.

As soon as he arrived he began to go through the records of the inmates and selections for Sonderbehandlung, 'special handling', were accelerated. Lists of those to be killed were made up and parties were sent daily to the Jugendlager, a compound in the woods on the other side of the main camp, along the road which passed the Little Camp. There they were shot in the back of the neck by the camp specialist, SS Scharführer Schulte, taken directly into the camp crematorium and burnt. However, this procedure was taking too long and Himmler on one of his regular visits agreed that Commandant Suhren should have a gas chamber built. The work was put in hand immediately to construct the necessary buildings in the Jugendlager. Meanwhile the selections went on, executions continued and the crematorium was kept busy.

Strangely, although the squat, smoking chimney stack of the crematorium could be seen by prisoners in all corners of the main camp, the SS continued various attempts at deception in their programme of eliminations, as they had with the 700 Hungarian children. For a long time Doctors Percy Treite, Rosenthal, the dentist Hellinger and Matron Elisabeth Marschall had been clearing out the wards by picking the sickest patients to be shot and cremated. These wretched women were carried out of the Revier early in the morning, before Appel, so that the prisoners could not see their departure. Patients in the Revier, and prisoners on punishments who were made to stand in the Lagerstrasse an hour or two earlier than 4.30 Appel, knew very well what happened. When Schwartzhuber arrived a new deception was employed. Those picked out on selections were told they were going to the Mittelwerde Convalescent Camp. Certainly this camp existed, but Mittelwerde was in a part of the Reich which had been liberated by the inexorable Russian advance.

Hortense and Stephanie continued to march to the factory and back every day. There were always endless stops for additional roll-calls on these marches and some-times these were used as an opportunity for selections. At the start of the day or even on the route to the factory, the SS would pick out who they wanted to work in the swamp, an area of water-logged ground they wanted to clear. This was cruel work for women so weak. They had to work in pairs hauling a heavy box slung between two poles like a stretcher, filled with sodden earth taken out of the swamp. The ground was very uneven and soft and they had to struggle over planks laid over the wettest parts. The planks were set loosely side by side in such a way that each plank lifted frustratingly under their feet at each step. Just the simple act of walking sapped their precious energies and always the SS were ready with their sticks and fists if anyone stumbled or slipped. On the marches to the factory and back through the trees, Hortense was used to seeing the thin bodies of women on the swampy ground lying where they had fallen. She dreaded this selection. She doubted her leg would last even a single day of such effort.

The SS Offizerin in charge of Hortense's work detail was called Marguerete. Outwardly she appeared and behaved like all the other SS but Hortense noticed she never struck any of the prisoners. It would not be true to say that they became friends but Hortense told her mother she was sure there was an understanding of some sort between them. Stephanie was not so sure. One day in late January Marguerete selected Hortense to stay behind.

'Number 42742, Herr Commandant Schwartzhuber wants the garden outside his office cleared of stones,' she told the ragged Belgian girl standing to attention in front of her.

The order was a surprise but Hortense was delighted. The work was a change of routine and relatively easy.

The Assistant Commandant's office stood directly outside the main gate of the Little Camp, beside the road which curved round into the trees and led past the swamp to the factory and the Jugendlager. Hortense collected the

319

stones and watched all the comings and goings, including several lorries full of elderly prisoners which went up the track in the direction of the Jugendlager and returned empty. By the end of the day she had picked up every single stone she could find. She was tired with being on her feet all day and her leg was swollen and burning hotly. She looked forward to a more static day in the factory. However the garden was spotless. Commandant Schwartzhuber came out of his office as she was finishing and stood there for a moment searching the ground. Then he told her he was very pleased as he could not see a single stone.

The next morning after Appel she was lined up in her squad outside the main gate waiting to be marched off to the factory when she heard her number called out to report for swamp duty. The sound of the order rang in her head. She knew she would collapse. Her leg would not last. Especially after clearing the stones. This simple order was a death sentence.

For a moment she was at a loss. She looked round desperately. Commandant Schwartzhuber was standing by his office, only a few paces from the garden she had so meticulously cleaned up the day before.

Abruptly, she acted.

'Herr Commandant!' Hortense shouted as loudly as she could.

Immediately, the SS guards screamed at her and one of the SS women rushed over with her whip raised high and ready to strike.

'Hortensia?'

Schwartzhuber's bleak voice stopped the SS Aufseherin in her tracks, but she held her whip ready to attack, outraged that a prisoner had dared to address the Commandant. The SS guard Marguerete stood nearby and stared blankly at Hortense.

'Are you the girl who was working in my garden yesterday?'

'Yes, Herr Commandant. Number 42742 reporting. They've put me on the swamp duty today,' she said in a rush of words.

'I see.' He paused for a moment and then said, 'All right. Today you rest. No swamp duty.'

'*Vielen Dank*, Herr Commandant!'

One of the SS officers with the Commandant obediently wrote the instructions and the prisoner's number in a book. The SS woman with the whip moved off as though nothing had happened. The Commandant had decided. Just like that. There was nothing good-natured in his judgment. Every day just as easily he sent hundreds of women to their death. That day, however, Hortense Daman lived.

It seemed to Hortense that everything they were made to do took its toll of human life. Women fell out and died on marches to work, or even on the way back to the big camp to report sick. They died in the latrines. They died in the blocks at night. Some gave up the fight and could not wait for death in such ways. Hortense saw two French-women throw themselves on the electrified wire where they died instantly and hung like strips of yellow rag until the current was switched off and they could be removed.

Reports of the advancing Allied armies reached SS and inmates alike. The prisoners were delighted with every German reverse. The SS speeded up their programme of death, encouraged by their leader, Heinrich Himmler.

A week or so later Hortense and her mother were being marched back from the factory in the morning after a twelve-hour night shift when she noticed the guards becoming very agitated. The SS shouted at the prisoners to keep in line, five to a row, and as they approached the camp gate prisoners inside the compound waved their hands behind the wire in panic. Without drawing attention to herself Hortense peered round the women in front of her and could see a large entourage of SS officers by the

Commandant's office.

'Eyes left,' the guards shouted. 'Halt!'

Hortense stood in the middle of the group, her neck twisted round and found herself looking directly at a small man in SS uniform with heavy silver braid epaulettes and oak leaves in a circular wreath on his left collar. His face was round, he wore a thin clipped moustache and round steel-rimmed spectacles under a high peaked cap. Commandant SS Sturmbannführer Fritz Suhren, Assistant Commandant SS Hauptsturmführer Johann Schwartzhuber and all the other SS hung on his every word and movement. Hortense had no difficulty in recognising Heinrich Himmler, Reichsführer of the SS.

She stared at the man whose organisation was responsible for so much misery throughout occupied Europe and which had destroyed her own family. She became aware that the camp SS were making a selection in front of Himmler, perhaps to impress him. She heard prisoners' numbers being read out and allocated to go on a transport to a convalescent camp at Mittelwerde. Hortense had never heard of Mittelwerde. As always she listened for her own number.

A woman near her began to sob quietly so the guards could not hear. Hortense saw it was Madame Semoin, whose husband ran a large tobacco factory south of Brussels.

'*Nommer vier, sieben, sieben, acht, sieben, Nommer . . .*' the SS continued working down their list.

47787. Stephanie Daman. Her mother's number.

Hortense felt as though she had been struck in the stomach. In the instant she felt sick, strangely detached, unmindful of standing awkwardly with her head twisted round towards Himmler and the other SS officers who were smiling and chatting by the small garden she had cleaned up.

When the SS stopped reading out numbers, Hortense was hardly aware hers had not been called. The guards told the prisoners who had been selected to be ready to move later that morning on the transport, marched the squad of prisoners through the wire and dismissed them. By the time Hortense turned round to see what had happened outside, Himmler had moved off to a chorus of 'Heil Hitler!' and stiff arm salutes flung up from his staff and the camp officers. She stared out through the fatal strands of electrified barbed wire at Schwartzhuber and five SS in peaked hats with the death's head emblem who were standing in a group talking about their leader's visit.

Hortense turned to Yvonne Baseden (Dee or 'Fanny'), the French girl who had arrived with Mary Lindell and had become a close friend.

'What's this convalescent camp they're talking about?'

Fanny and the others with her looked at Hortense a moment and then she said gently, 'It's just another lie. We all know what really happens. All transports're the same. There's only one way out of Ravensbrück.'

Hortense thought of the trucks that went to the Jugendlager packed with the sick and old. They always came back empty. She looked round at the prisoners in the compound, at the pathetic skeletons inside their grey-blue dresses, at the huts and the barbed wire which penned them in. She saw Madame Semoin again, in tears but comforting her daughter who was sitting on the ground exhausted and very sick, loving her as best she could in the miserable conditions of their lives. At least, Hortense thought, they are alive. It is always better to be alive, to fight to stay alive. Hortense made up her mind. She turned around and walked back to the Little Camp gate. Schwartzhuber was still talking with the other SS outside his office.

'Herr Commandant,' Hortense called out.

The prisoners inside near the gate stopped talking. They stared in silence at the slender form of the young Belgian girl standing at the wire, and feared for her.

Out of the corner of her eye Fanny noticed Stephanie Daman walking terribly slowly towards the gate, her face drained of colour, staring at her daughter.

'Get lost,' the SS guard at the gate snapped at Hortense.

She ignored him and called out again, louder.

'Herr Commandant, Number 42742 reporting!'

The guard lost his temper and began to shout abuse at Hortense but quickly stopped when he heard Schwartzhuber behind him.

'Open the gate.'

'*Jawohl*, Herr Kommandant.' The SS unlocked and dragged open the wooden gate covered in wire.

'*Komm her*!' Schwartzhuber said expressionlessly.

Hortense mustered herself, shook off the tiredness of the long night's workshift and marched smartly across the road as best as her bad leg would allow towards the group of SS officers. She stopped in front of Schwartzhuber and stood rigidly to attention, feet together in the regulation style with her hands pulled down straight at her sides.

'Number 42742 reporting, Herr Commandant.'

'Ah, Hortensia,' Schwartzhuber said, recognising her. 'What d'you want this time?'

'I want to know why they took my mother's number just now.'

'Oh, that? Don't worry, Hortensia,' Schwartzhuber said smiling. 'Just as they explained. She's going to another camp. Mittelwerde Convalescent Camp. Most of them are elderly and I've arranged for trucks to take them there, so they don't have to walk, you understand.'

'But my mother's not elderly, Herr Commandant. She's only fifty and she works hard every day stoking furnaces at the Siemens factory. If she has to go, then take my number too. I'll go with her.'

'But you're young,' Schwartzhuber replied in some surprise.

'Well, I still want to go with her.'

'I see. I'll think about it.' Schwartzhuber waved his hand to dismiss her. She was escorted back across the road into the camp by the SS trooper who shoved the gate closed after her.

Stephanie Daman came up and grabbed her daughter as soon as she was back in the compound.

'What've you done? Hortense, what madness!' Completely uncaring of her own fate, Stephanie was desperate with worry about her daughter and the awful risk she had run. She wrung her hands together and was inconsolable, gripped with the fear that the SS would punish her daughter with a beating and then put her on the transport as well. The other prisoners who had been watching agreed. They knew full well the meaning of the selection. All but one, a mother, thought Hortense was mad to volunteer. The women who had been selected waited patiently, resigned to their fate. Hortense and Stephanie sat together holding hands, their fingers twisting and curling and patting each other. They said little although they both knew these minutes were the last they would have and there was so much to say. For Hortense the time passed very slowly and seemed longer than the two hours before the SS marched back. They shouted for everyone to form up in ranks again. The trucks had arrived.

Schwartzhuber and his officers came out of the office. One of the officers issued papers to each of the SS Block Leaders who marched back to the squads of women prisoners. The compound rang with shouts as they bellowed out the numbers of the selected women.

Hortense listened for her mother's number, or for her own. The selected prisoners fell out of the ranks and made their way, painfully for the most part, to the waiting trucks. Most were old, as Schwartzhuber had said, but among them were a few sick younger women.

Madame Semoin's daughter suddenly broke ranks and walked forward. Hortense was saddened but not surprised to see she had been selected, for she was exhausted. All her hair had fallen out and she was very ill indeed. She was however astonished and filled with foreboding when suddenly Madame Semoin gave a little cry and broke ranks herself to join her daughter. The SS made no move to stop her, though she was fit for her age and her number had not been called.

Still the Block Leader had not called out Number 47787. It hardly seemed possible. Hortense wished she could look round to see if her mother was still there. Madame Semoin and her daughter had reached the back of a truck and were waiting for an older woman to clamber in.

One by one the Block Leaders stopped calling out numbers. In a daze, Hortense realised number 47787 had not been called out. She and her mother had been given another chance.

Madame Semoin lifted the light frame of her daughter into the truck, looked round once more at the women and the life she had left, and climbed in too. The parade was dismissed. Life in the camp went on.

The SS did not stop their 'games' in the latrines, and usually punished the entire hut. On these occasions Hortense and her mother frequently found themselves marched up with the others to the high ground in the compound overlooking the swamp and the flat lands of the river Havel. Here they had to stand for two hours or more in the full force of the cold Siberian east winds. One of these punishments occurred after they returned from a full twelve-hour shift in the factory and Hortense noticed her mother swaying in the freezing winds, almost unconscious, her face grey with cold. All the women had only their camp dresses but Hortense saw her mother's shoes were terribly worn. The leather uppers had almost come apart and her feet were exposed to the biting wind and snow. Ice had formed on her toes. Stout shoes were essential for survival in the camps, especially in the winter months and Hortense realised the simple truth that unless her mother could find another pair of shoes she would die. If she did not collapse then, the SS would notice her weakening and select her soon enough for a transfer from which there would be no escape.

When she returned to her billet she asked the Blockälteste where she could find another pair of shoes for Stephanie.

'No chance at all,' was the curt response.

The Blockälteste was a Belgian and generally treated the women in her hut fairly, but obtaining another pair of shoes was an absurd idea. There were no stores in the Little Camp and Hortense saw that she would have to go back to the main camp. Then she thought of 'Aunty' Sophia Meyer, the German Kapo she had helped in Block 9. Meyer had made a great fuss over being looked after and had sworn she would do anything to return the favour. Was this the time to ask? Hortense wondered whether Meyer could be trusted. Would she even remember?

Typically Hortense made up her mind very quickly. She had to go to the main camp, find Meyer in the stores and exchange her mother's shoes for a new pair. This simple plan was filled with dangers, which Hortense understood full well. Her own recovery was by no means complete but her ignorance of human character had evaporated in the harsh realities of camp life. For an eighteen-year-old girl, she knew much about the business of survival, and the cost of failure. Death was the camp's way of saying a person had failed.

The only way to leave the Little Camp with a chance of coming back was to report sick. This was more dangerous than ever as the elimination programmes of Suhren and Schwartzhuber gained momentum. Supplied with a continuous influx of prisoners from camps cleared out in the East, the doctors in the hospital were less fussy about selecting those they considered useless to the German war effort. She decided she must avoid drawing attention to her leg or she might end up being sent to the isolation blocks. She would pretend to have toothache.

Once in the main camp she would have to escape from the Revier, then walk down the Lagerstrasse to the camp administrative buildings on the side where prisoners never dared to go, find which hut Meyer worked in, always assuming she was still there and had not died or been transported somewhere, and persuade her to change the shoes. She would have to risk meeting Dorothea Binz.

She told her mother she had terrible toothache. There was nothing for it but to go to the main camp to see Dr Hellinger, the dentist. Stephanie Daman did not like the idea, even though Hortense convinced her she was really in pain. Everyone knew Hellinger had a reputation for callousness and cruelty. She knew he sent women on transports when he could not be bothered to treat them. But neither of them realised the extent of his crimes. Hellinger's personal responsability was to extract gold teeth and fillings from victims to be killed in the extermination programmes, and he attended most of the executions, waiting while Sergeant Schulte carried out his expert task of shooting women in the back of the head, before he pulled gold from the mouths of their shattered skulls. His job was presumably less gory when the victims were gassed. He sent the gold to the SS account which had been specially opened by Walther Funk, the Reichsbank President, on the orders of Himmler.

'Let me see if I can try and change your shoes while I'm over there,' Hortense said as an afterthought.

'How will you do that in the hospital?' Stephanie asked.

'I don't know, but those shoes are really useless, Maman, and I might as well try if I'm going. We know you can't change them here.'

'But where will you find a better pair?'

'Anything's better than the pair you've got,' Hortense replied drily. 'I might find someone I know in the Revier who will help.'

'That's so,' Stephanie said uncertainly, knowing Hortense had made a lot of contacts in the hospital. She had no suspicion of Hortense's real plans but the logic of her argument was unassailable. Her shoes were in tatters and she knew as well as her daughter that she must do something or she would die. Only when she was convinced about Hortense's 'toothache' did she agree to swap shoes.

Hortense reported sick and shuffled back to the main camp with a large group of other sick women. They were made to sing as usual.

As they neared the big gate, they passed the large private house rumoured to belong to Himmler.

'Eyes left!' the SS guards screamed.

Prisoners saluted the Reichsführer's residence whether he was inside or not.

The squad turned through the main gate in the sombre concrete walls into the courtyard and shambled to a stop in front of the Revier.

'Undress! Hurry, hurry,' the guards shouted.

Hortense took her clothes off and one of the nurses came to take her temperature, in her anus as usual. A woman near Hortense fainted with the cold. A guard strode off and returned with a fire bucket full of water which he threw over her until she woke screaming. He dragged her to her feet again.

Hortense was told to put her clothes on. She stood at attention and thought of all the things that could go wrong. After an interminable wait she was ordered into the office by a Kapo and came face to face with Doctor Hellinger, the 'Butcher'.

'Well, what's wrong with you?'

'Number 42742 reporting, Herr Doktor,' said Hortense smartly, being as polite as she could. 'There's nothing wrong with me.'

'What!'

Hortense had trusted again to her instinct and plunged on with her impromptu story. Hellinger stared at her.

'You see, Herr Doktor, I'm wearing these shoes which are falling apart and it's very cold now and there're no stores to change them in the Little Camp, so I thought I could see my aunty in the stores here in the main camp to see if she could help me.'

'How d'you expect to get into the stores?' Hellinger interrupted sharply. Prisoners were not allowed on the administrative side of the Lagerstrasse.

'She's German,' Hortense said, supposing that this qualified her completely and desperately hoping Hellinger did not pursue the matter of 'Aunty' Sophia's exact relationship with the Daman family.

'I think this is very interesting,' mused Hellinger, obviously intrigued by the audacity of the young prisoner in front of him and fascinated by the story she spun so convincingly. 'I want to see this. You can go now to the stores, but you will report back here with a new pair of shoes.'

Hellinger laughed suddenly as he dismissed her, slapping his hand on the desk, '*Jawohl*, report to me with a new pair, or I will pull out all your teeth.'

Hortense looked at his face as she turned to go. He was enjoying himself, but deadly serious.

In a daze she left the Revier and walked down the wide sandy expanse of the Lagerstrasse feeling very vulnerable and small. The accommodation huts stretched away into the distance on the right and the out of bounds administrative blocks filled her horizon on the left, squatting behind fences thickened out with rolls of barbed wire. They were the exclusive province of the Kapos and SS guards. No one volunteered to cross the Lagerstrasse. Hortense wondered where Binz was.

A guard shouted at her. 'Come here, you! What're you doing here?'

'Number 42742 reporting, I'm going to see Sophia Meyer in the stores,' Hortense replied, committed by now and following the simplest strategy in the hope that the guards knew of Meyer. She hoped that Meyer's being German would help again.

The SS guard swore at her but he let her pass. Twice she was stopped and twice she managed to escape with the same excuses before she reached the stores. The building was surrounded by the usual barbed wire and protected by a wooden wall. She approached the gate and gave her story again.

The Kapos on duty were surly and disagreeable. Hortense thought they would beat her up. Instead they marched her in, took her number and told her to wait by a window.

Hortense waited quietly, unable to think. She saw several Germans working there who all looked very well-fed compared with the women prisoners on the other side of the Lagerstrasse. The seconds and minutes passed. Hortense looked about the stores compound, frightened that Meyer might not be there at all. She looked down at her shoes, her mother's shoes.

'Sophia Meyer!' Hortense began to shout suddenly, feeling better for the effort.

Almost immediately she regretted it. Dorothea Binz appeared at the other end of the compound, immaculately dressed in her grey uniform. She screamed in a fury at the shouting and began to advance towards Hortense, flicking her heavy whip against her high black boots.

Hortense stood rigid. She stared as Binz moved slowly towards her along the side of the stores hut. There was no chance of escape. Just as Binz reached her, the window opened and Meyer put out her head.

'It's all right. Don't worry,' she said to Binz. 'This girl's mine. She's all right.' She turned to Hortense. 'I'm glad you've come to see me like I said. So what is it, my dear? What can old Aunty Sophia do for you?'

'My shoes are bad,' Hortense explained and when Meyer leaned further out of the window to see for herself she appeared quite shocked.

'Yes indeed! Those really won't do. Fetch them off and I'll see what I can find.'

Binz glared as Hortense unlaced what remained of the leather uppers of her mother's shoes and handed them to Meyer through the window. She watched Sophia Meyer take them down a passage in the stores and disappear round a corner. Hortense stood barefoot on the freezing ground hardly daring to breath in case she upset Binz by the slightest movement. It seemed an age before Meyer reappeared.

'Here you are, my dear,' Meyer said leaning out of the stores window with a brand new pair of shoes. Hortense stared. Even Binz looked surprised. The shoes were in perfect condition with new leather which laced up with eyes and hooks well above the ankles, and thick wooden soles to keep the feet well off the ground.

'Well, try them on, and tell me whether they fit,' Meyer urged Hortense in a motherly way.

'Yes, yes! Thank you. They're wonderful!' Hortense could not find the words to describe her feelings. Binz gave her no time.

'Now get out! And don't ever come back!' Her shouts echoed after Hortense as she quickly retraced her steps up the broad Lagerstrasse towards the main gate and the Revier.

'Number 42742 reporting, Herr Doktor, with a new pair of shoes,' said Hortense when she entered Hellinger's office later that afternoon.

'I don't believe it,' the dentist exclaimed, standing up to peer over his desk at the footwear of the young girl in front of him. 'You managed to get away with these without a beating?' He was genuinely amazed.

'Yes, Herr Doktor.' Then fired by her success, she added, 'You lost your bet.'

Hellinger shrugged and laughed.

The return to the Little Camp was as time-consuming as the journey out, with endless waiting outside the

Revier, counting and recounting the prisoners in the squad and then singing on the way back. Burdened by none of the fears she had felt in the morning, Hortense did not mind. She was thrilled with every step in the new shoes and impatient to see her mother's face when she handed over her prize.

As soon as the guards dismissed the prisoners in the Little Camp she went to find her mother. Stephanie Daman had watched her daughter stand with the others on sick parade that morning and set her mind to the possibility that she would not see her again. Her pleasure turned to astonishment when Hortense gave her the new shoes. She tried to persuade Hortense to keep them but Hortense would have none of it. She watched her mother put on the strong new shoes and lace them up and was filled with intense personal satisfaction. Her feelings were multiplied by the knowledge that all the risks she had taken and the full measure of her success were entirely for the one person in the world who mattered to her. Stephanie loved her so well that she had given her own food to save her daughter's life, and now Hortense had run risks in her turn to strengthen her mother's chances of survival.

After so much walking Hortense's leg was burning and she found it impossible to avoid reporting sick again, this time for real. The following day she joined the squad to march back to the main camp and was sent to recuperate for two days in Block 9.

In January 1945 the camp held 40,000 prisoners, nearly seven times the number it had been built to hold, the weather was brutally cold and the isolation barrack was badly overcrowded with sick and haggard women. Hortense looked about the hut for a place to sleep but there was no room. She was beginning to despair and resign herself to sleeping on the floor when she met Violette Szabo who offered her a space on her own bed.

Hortense had first come across Violette in Block 15

when she had finally come out of the hospital blocks and before moving to the Little Camp. Violette wore the red triangle of a political prisoner with the letter 'E' which denoted 'Engländerin'. Hortense knew she had been in the Resistance fighting the Germans but Violette never told anyone the details. She had been trained by SOE in England and worked in Rouen and Limoges before being captured after a two hour fire-fight, when she held off 400 troops of the SS Division Das Reich while her partner Jacques Dufour escaped. Like Hortense, she had been marched from her prison cell to interrogation by the Gestapo in their office nearby.

Violette had a rich head of hair similar to Hortense's, which was beginning to grow back after her typhus attack, and she was strikingly beautiful. She was six years older than Hortense and came from an ordinary background, unlike many of the women in SOE, having been brought up by her father in a working-class area in Brixton in South London. Her father was a British soldier who had married a French girl he met on active service in the Great War. Violette spoke fluent French, English and German and was in demand to translate between the guards and prisoners. They had much in common. Hortense had arrived in the camp less than a week before Violette though the two did not meet and make friends until the autumn.

Hortense stayed her two days in Block 9 and was saddened to find Violette depressed and uninterested. She seemed to have lost some of her will to live. None the less this exceptional woman gave up her bed space for her friend and slept on the floor although she had been sent to the isolation block to recover from a mass of open sores which had erupted all over her legs. It was the last time they met. Orders arrived from the RSHA in Berlin. Only a few days later, on 26 January, Violette was taken with two others, Denise Bloch and Lillian Rolfe, to the crematorium, shot in the back of the neck by Schulte, and cremated. Commandant Suhren, Schwartzhuber, and Doctor Hellinger were present at the murders.

By the end of February the Red Army had consolidated its front line on the river Oder, at places only eighty miles from Berlin. Budapest had fallen with a loss to the Wehrmacht of another 110,000 German soldiers and Hitler ordered the recruitment of more young men and boys as desperately needed reinforcements. He thought the British and Americans were still recovering from the German Christmas offensive in the Ardennes and moved his reserves to the East, to protect Berlin. He was wrong. While his troops temporarily stabilised the Oder-Neisse line, the Allies in the West built up a massive superiority in men and *matériel* for the final attack across the river Rhine. However grand strategy was not Hitler's only concern. The Communist menace in the East was always National Socialism's greatest enemy. The Russian front had absorbed more German divisions than any other since the invasion of Russia in 1941. At the last Hitler was determined to defend what was left of Germany and Berlin against the Russians.

To help muster German morale in this ideological struggle, Goebbels continued to issue a stream of convincing propaganda. Surprisingly most Germans still believed him, although cities in the heartland of the Reich lay devastated by British and American bombing and most families had lost sons or husbands in the fighting. Goebbels broadcast on the radio that Berlin would always remain German, and made propaganda films in typically racist style about the Russian 'sub-humans' who would rape German women, loot and murder the population. These claims were supported by explicit footage of dead civilians lying in the ruins of their homes. For years the Germans had murdered millions of the civilian populations of the East but now that the Russians were fighting back inside Germany it is possible that for once the victims shown on Goebbels's film actually were Germans.

The propaganda was believed by the SS, and filtered through to the camp inmates at Ravensbrück. True or not, the women knew how helpless they were, locked inside the camp until the guards left. They all hoped the English and American troops would liberate them before the Russians, and fear of what would happen to them if the Red Army reached the camp first grew in proportion to the obvious nervousness of the SS.

SS forebodings about their future took a simple course. While the Russians in the East and the British and Americans in the West prepared their final assaults on Germany, the SS increased the pace of death in the camps. The new gas chambers and the crematorium were flat out with their task, and all the time numbers in Ravensbrück rose steadily as trains arrived from prisons evacuated on all fronts.

Schwartzhuber redoubled his efforts to select the weak and old for special handling and in the meantime, presumably oblivious to the inevitable fate of Germany, he was having a villa built for himself in the woods off the road which led to the factory. Occasionally Hortense was detailed to join work parties carrying out the construction. In the middle of March she had been sent with a group of women on a work detail with some of the few men imprisoned at Ravensbrück and they were constructing a path to the villa. Three Slavs with her dug out the clay with shovels and filled a heavy wheelbarrow, which she then had to push up a steep path to the top of the hill. In the middle of the day, when she was already exhausted and moving slowly to conserve her strength and protect her leg, she started up the path again with another load of clay.

Suddenly round the corner on the path above her came Commandant Schwartzhuber on his bicycle. Hortense stopped helpless in the centre of the path quite unable to shift the heavy barrow in either direction in time to let him pass.

'*Verdammt! Scheisser*!' Schwartzhuber screamed and shot off the side of the path into the trees. He fell off as the bicycle bounced on the rough slope and rolled head over heels with the machine to the bottom, swearing fiercely, cut and bruised.

Desperate at this sheer bad luck, Hortense peered over the edge and watched Schwartzhuber clamber back up the slope, leaving his twisted bicycle at the bottom.

'You damned maniac!' He began to shout and curse as he approached her and Hortense backed away from the inevitable beating. When he reached the path he dusted himself off and turned on Hortense, his face bloodshot with rage. Then he noticed the three Slavs standing beyond Hortense. They had seen the whole incident. They had seen also that the five of them were in the wood, hidden from view of the SS guarding the work detail. As Schwartzhuber advanced on the young Belgian girl, they all took a different grip on their long shovels, silently grouped together like the tattered remnants of a peasant uprising and shuffled towards Hortense, their eyes fixed on their final enemy the Commandant.

Schwartzhuber was livid, but like an animal he at once spotted the bleak, almost fatalistic expression in the eyes of the men. He stopped. There was nothing overtly aggressive in the Slavs' attitude, and yet there was something subtly different about the way they held their shovels. He measured the few paces between them, judging how long he would take to pull his revolver and cursed that he was for once without support of the SS. The guards further up the slope were unaware of the deadly little scene on the steep path in the trees.

Hortense turned to see the three men gazing intently at Schwartzhuber. She caught the same look in their faces and was horrified to see what they intended to do if the Commandant attacked her.

She watched, feeling her fate suspended for an age in time, while Schwartzhuber glared at the Slavs. Then he spun round and stamped off up the path, swearing terribly. When he was out of sight the three men relaxed, dropped their shovels and leaned on them, prisoners and workmen once again. They grinned at Hortense but it did not help. She was in a state for the rest of the day wondering whether Schwartzhuber would arrange some other punishment for her when she returned to the Little Camp. At the end of the day, her work detail was taken back along the track and they were dismissed after the inevitable roll-call. Nothing happened. She waited in dreadful anticipation for her number to be called out on the loudspeakers. Still nothing, and no comment was made at evening Appel. Even after knocking the Commandant off his bicycle, some caprice of good fortune had intervened and she had escaped the fate of thousands.

On 23 March the British opened their final offensive to cross the river Rhine with a barrage of 3000 guns, a quarter of a million tons of ammunition and twenty-five divisions, against five weak German divisions. But they were still 250 miles from Berlin. In the East the Russians had crossed the river Oder and were building up massive reserves for the final battle assault on Berlin itself. They were poised to give the body blow to Hitler's Thousand Year Reich. And only sixty miles from Ravensbrück.

Towards the end of March and into April, the work duties in the factory began to slacken off. When the squads formed up in the morning or evening to march to work, the guards sometimes read out numbers of women who were not required and could go back to the blocks. Generally Hortense and her mother were selected to work.

In the early hours of 16 April, the seventy-fifth anniversary of Lenin's birthday, the Russian onslaught on Berlin began in a roar of 8000 guns. Two and a half million men in nine Soviet armies were launched in two great sweeping pincers to envelop and destroy the German capital. By this time the British armies had been ordered to stop their advance to Berlin. They halted on the banks of the river Elbe, still fifty miles from the outskirts and the same distance from Ravensbrück.

The same day, Hortense was working on her loom in the factory when she saw the SS Aufseherin Marguerete walking down the line of machines. She had obviously been crying and without really thinking Hortense remarked on it.

'Aren't you well?'

'Trust you to notice, Hortensia,' the SS woman replied with some humanity but others were watching them and she added sharply, 'Anyhow, just carry on working.'

Hortense turned back to making the coils on her loom but suddenly a commotion started at the entrance to the long hall where they worked. Ten or so SS officers barged in accompanied by a platoon of SS troops pushing trolleys. All the prisoners were ordered to stop working and gather at one end of the room. The SS troops began to dismantle the machinery, load it on to the trolleys and take it all outside where they put it on waiting trucks.

Meanwhile the two civilians engaged in a heated argument with several of the SS officers. Finally one officer and the thin civilian set up a table by the door on which they stacked bags of Reichsmarks neatly to one side. They opened ledgers, consulted lists of prisoners and began shouting for the women to step forward.

Much to Hortense's amazement they called out names not numbers. To add to her confusion, they wanted to pay the prisoners. Everyone was astonished. No one had ever been paid before. They did not know of the Russian attack, nor of the SS cost analysis to work certain prisoners to death at a fixed rate per day, to be paid by Siemens. It is likely that a combination of these factors, principally the first, motivated the civilians and SS to pay the women, rather than an enthusiasm to balance the books.

All the women in the Little Camp were political prisoners, with red triangles, and some declared they had no intention of taking the money.

'Daman, Hortensia,' screamed a guard and Hortense stepped up to the impromptu pay desk.

'Here's your pay,' the thin-lipped civilian said without looking up. 'Sign here.'

'I don't want it,' Hortense replied, without even looking to see how much he was offering.

'You must take it,' he shouted, furious with her. 'You've worked for it. You have to take it.'

'Well I'm not taking it.'

'Get back in line,' he bellowed hoarsely. 'Next!'

Stephanie also refused her pay. The civilian screamed at her in exasperation to fall back at once. She stood next to Hortense waiting to see what would happen next. Something had upset the dangerous but predictable balance of camp life. Far from giving them confidence that they would shortly regain their freedom, the bizarre pay parade convinced them the SS would soon kill them all.

The two Siemens managers again started arguing with the SS. It seemed the thin civilian was unimpressed by military reports that the Russian armies were launched in massed formations against Berlin, and were within forty miles of Ravensbrück as their troops fought in an arc to crush the north of the capital. He insisted that the SS make the prisoners clean up the factory.

He turned to Hortense and her mother and surprised them by shouting, 'Madame Daman!' Numbers, it seemed, were an embarrassment of the past. 'I want you to polish this machine.' He gestured at one of the looms and the fat manager took them over and showed them what to do.

# The Russians are Coming

'The war is nearly over,' he whispered to Hortense as he bent across to demonstrate what to polish.

It was their last time in the factory. Later that day the SS marched them all back to the Little Camp where they were left for two days. They were still fed but they had done their last work detail. The women, sat about, tired and worried, on the inside of the wire while the SS guards marched restlessly about outside.

On the second day the SS mustered all the women in the Little Camp and hustled them along the road to the main camp. Hortense felt an ominous sense of oppression as they marched once more through the grey walls of the big camp. Her feeling of foreboding was matched by the reports they heard there that the Russians were very close.

Hortense, her mother and the other Belgians were housed in Block 2. This block had always been occupied before by better favoured prisoners who received extra food. This was no longer the case. Rationing had broken down completely and all they ate during the next two days was camp 'coffee' slopped out into their bowls. Hortense and Stephanie rested as much as they could on their bunk, grateful for not having to work. With the breakdown of camp life, there was no structure to their fight for survival and all they could do was wait, hoping that the SS would not get around to gassing or shooting them. They could see large numbers went daily to the crematorium. The chimney was always furiously belching smoke over the roof of the punishment block close by. And they hoped that when the Russians arrived they would not be raped. There was survival in hope, but none of the women was optimistic.

Hortense was very hungry and unsure of the passage of time but on the third day the SS came for the Belgians.

'*Raus! Raus!* All Belgians out!'

About eighty women moved slowly out of Block 2 and were taken down the broad, sandy length of the

341

Lagerstrasse to the other end of the camp. The place appeared deserted. Most prisoners were lying in their blocks. Hortense thought they were being taken to a place of execution.

At the far end of the Lagerstrasse the SS officer led them through a small wicket gate in the electrified fence which separated the camp from an area of SS workshops. They walked down a narrow corridor between live barbed-wire fencing and Hortense was terrified in case she staggered on her bad leg and touched the wire. Beyond this wire perimeter they found themselves in a large open area with a few wooden barrack huts.

They passed four prisoners lying silently on the ground, propped up back to back facing the four points of the compass. They were too weak to move, too weak even to close their eyelids which hung slightly apart in sunken owl-like sockets. Their skin was drawn tight and fleshless over their noses, like beaks. Hortense was shocked to hear some of the women in her group laugh at them. The sight was not incongruous, for death was commonplace, but there seemed to be no reason for them to be dying like that in the middle of a wide open area.

The SS officer showed them a barrack hut. 'You're going back to Belgium,' he announced.

This surprising declaration cut no ice. The women assumed it was another deception on the lines of the Mittelwerde transports. None of them believed the SS had the slightest intention of releasing their prisoners.

The officer left them in charge of two older and shabbily dressed SS guards. At once some of the stronger prisoners, such as Dr Marie-Claude, who had helped Hortense in the Revier, and Yvonne, demanded food. The two guards shrugged and said food was no longer available.

Cries of panic came from the hut, 'Gas! Gas! They're trying to gas us!'

Several of the women had been into the barrack hut

and came running out waving their arms in warning. There was a powerful smell of gas inside the whole of the hut, permeating everything, clinging to the bunks, the thin straw mattresses and even the rough wood of the boards.

Everyone was convinced the Germans had intended some trick to kill them. No one would go inside until they had knocked out the boarding which covered the windows, removed the bunks and contaminated bedding and let a through-draught clear the air. Some still refused to go in and spent the cold April night outside. Stephanie persuaded Hortense to go in and they found a place reasonably free of the smell of gas, and rested. Hortense slipped into a state of half-walking and half-sleeping, tired out and exhausted, in pain from her leg injury, which had become inflamed again, and weak from lack of food. The camp kitchens had stopped providing even the repulsive ersatz coffee. All they had during these three days was water.

At the same time, the Russians were fighting on the outskirts of Berlin. General Zhukov's armies had fought every metre of the way to encircle the shattered capital against German troops, who were desperate in the belief that all prisoners would be killed by the Communist soldiers. General Rokossovski's armies to the north were closing on Ravensbrück in their path to Rostock on the Baltic Sea.

In lucid moments during the hours of waiting, Hortense talked to her mother. They were both sure the authorities were going to leave them there to die, like the four they had passed in the compound outside. No one came to visit their hut, except the two elderly guards, and the compound was silent and empty. Even if their two guards disappeared, they would still be prisoners as long as the current was on in the fence.

Stephanie and Hortense were rag and bone, but it was Hortense who needed most help now. Months of camp life and long hours of work on so little food were no way to recover from the illnesses she had suffered. Her energies were utterly sapped. Their combined survival was in the hands of Stephanie who found a little strength to carry on for both of them. Apart from finding water to drink, she hardly left Hortense and they both waited to see what would happen.

On Monday, 23 April, the third day in the strangely quiet block outside the main camp, an SS officer arrived at their hut.

'Follow me,' he ordered. 'You'll all come with me.'

It was a simple statement of what they had to do, no shouting, no blows. This must be the end, Hortense thought, a new subtlety to make them come voluntarily towards the gas chambers until it was too late to object. Anyway, in their condition, how could they object?

They walked, not in the usual squad, five abreast and singing, but in a motley group. They shuffled slowly through the narrow corridor of barbed wire, back the full length of the Lagerstrasse, where no sign remained of the tens of thousands of women who had mustered there on Appels every day, stamping their feet against the cold. The two guards and the officer marched alongside them. At the end of the Lagerstrasse, Hortense could see the main gate. If they turned left in front of the Kommandantur, opposite the Revier, they would go to the crematorium.

The officer did not turn left. They walked out of the gate. The SS men wandered off to talk to some others standing further away. For once none of them took any interest in worrying the prisoners.

The iron grip of the SS was lifted. There was a growing feeling of nervousness. Some women began to bicker. They had begun a new battle to survive, aware that their physical weakness made them depend on others but dreadfully unsure what would happen next. There was talk that they were going to be saved, to be taken away, and they were terrified of being left behind. In the distance they could hear the sound of artillery. Hortense and her mother found a place on the grass bank, and there were prisoners as far as she could see along the road. Further down they saw a group of men in strange uniforms walking towards them, wearing peaked hats and side flaps over their ears. Russians! Behind them came a convoy of lorries. A rush of frightened chatter swept the women. Russians! But the women were in any case too feeble to run away.

The soldiers drew nearer. Then someone said, 'It's the Red Cross!' but the big six-wheel trucks had huge white, not red, crosses painted on top of the canvas canopies. This was their salvation.

The Red Cross had begun their attempt to reach the concentration camps four months earlier. In January, after the failure of the Ardennes offensive, Hermann Goering had suggested to Himmler that Count Folke Bernadotte in Sweden might help the Germans sue for peace. Bernadotte was Vice-President of the Swedish Red Cross and nephew to the king of Sweden, and the contact arose through Goering's first wife, Carin von Kantzow, a Swedish aristocrat he had met in Sweden before the war. Himmler did not take up the idea until February, when he arranged for Bernadotte to fly into Berlin, on the advice of Walter Schellenberg who was on his staff and had been trying to find ways of making peace since 1942. Himmler dared not tell Hitler.

Bernadotte flew to Berlin in February and then again in the beginning of April, knowing full well he was not so much entering the lion's den as sticking his head in the very mouth of the lion. He told Himmler the Allies would settle for nothing less than unconditional surrender but proposed a deal for the release of the concentration camp prisoners. He was not alone in thinking the Nazis would try to kill as many as they could before their eventual and inevitable defeat. Himmler finally agreed to release one prisoner for four German soldiers captured in the fighting.

This remarkably brave piece of negotiation was put into practice by Danish and Swedish members of the Red Cross who equally bravely volunteered to drive trucks, the easiest possible military targets, across Germany in the middle of a battlefield.

Hortense and her mother sat with their group on the bank for the rest of the day and through the night. Trucks came and went full of prisoners from further along and occasionally Red Cross officials could be seen having earnest discussions with groups of SS officers. The women were not convinced and during the night hardly slept for thinking that this was one last and awful charade thought up by the SS to eliminate them before the Russians arrived. The convoys continued to come and go in the morning and Hortense began to think they would never be taken. All the time the sound of warfare grew in the distance. Finally a group of lorries drew up near the Belgian women. It was their turn.

A young Swedish truck driver with typical Scandinavian blond hair stopped his vehicle at a grassy bank near the main gate of Ravensbrück. He got out of his cab and stretched. Then he walked quickly round to the back to help the prisoners on board. In the last part of the two day journey from Denmark, the noise of gunfire had suddenly come much closer and he was keen to be away. The Red Cross had no agreement with the Russians.

He stopped in his tracks, looking at the group of women like skeletons in filthy, matted grey and blue striped dresses. They tottered and stumbled towards him, their voices reedy with panic, their hair in wisps round their heads.

'Jesus!' whispered his co-driver, coming up behind him. They had both heard stories from drivers who had been to Neuengamme concentration camp near Hamburg, but this was their first trip.

'Come on,' the driver said as another barrage of guns could be heard not far south of the river Havel. He hoped the shock did not show on his face or in his eyes. 'Let's get on with it. Help them in.'

He unhooked the tailgate and the women wasted no time in clambering up and jostling each other for space inside. The driver reached over to help two women who seemed to be close together, mother and daughter, perhaps. The older woman climbed in with remarkable vigour, considering how emaciated she was, and they both helped to lift up the younger woman. He was amazed how feather-light she was.

Hortense was grateful for the driver's help. In the scramble someone had kicked her left leg which began to bleed. She found it extremely difficult to walk and when she looked up into the back of the truck she had had no idea how she would be able to climb in. Inside there was a good deal of pushing and once more the mother and daughter team worked together. Stephanie was the fitter. She warned the other women in no uncertain terms to keep their distance, stop shoving her daughter and behave.

As the trucks pulled away, Hortense looked back at the camp with its grey concrete walls and the SS offices nearby. A movement in one of the windows caught her eye and she recognised the SS Aufseherin Marguerete who was watching the convoys leave. The SS woman saw Hortense looking back, lifted her hand and gave an imperceptible wave. Hortense did not wave back. Though the SS woman had not been brutal there was nothing to be grateful for in Ravensbrück. The truck lurched forward and they left the camp behind in the trees.

Astonishing as Count Bernadotte's arrangement with Himmler had been, there were certain major practical drawbacks. The agreement stated that the convoys had to travel in daylight, on the main roads, on a certain route and be escorted by Germans. The agreement did not envisage the convoys driving through the last and most vicious battle in Europe during the war, when neither artillery nor aeroplanes of either side would take any notice of or understand the white crosses hurriedly painted on the roofs of ordinary khaki military transport. Hortense and her mother began to move through this vast battlefield to flee the hordes from the East, just as they had right at the start of the war four and a half years before. This time they were helpless, exhausted, in the hands of others and could not escape the destruction around them.

# 13

# The Last Journeys

'Geteilte freud' ist doppelt freude.' 'Joy shared is joy doubled.' Goethe of Weimar.

Nearly two weeks before the Red Cross arrived in Ravensbrück, during the night of 10 to 11 April, Hortense's father Jacques was lying in his bunk in Buchenwald dreaming of hundreds of planes flying over the camp. Suddenly he was shaken awake by his friend Victor Bezemans.

'The Americans are nearly here! Those are American planes,' he said excitedly.

Bezemans was weaker even than Jacques, but they moved as quickly as they could outside the wooden hut and stood in the camp street to see the evidence of their rescue with their own eyes.

Later that morning they saw a large column of the SS guards marching away with packs on their backs. But there were still sentries in the guard towers and the current in the barbed wire fence remained on. Later, whatever their orders, the guards abandoned their posts and disappeared as soon as they saw the American tanks moving through the village, about two kilometres away, beyond some trees. Jacques Daman and the prisoners could see the tanks too, through the wire, and relished the sound of machine-gun fire.

At once, a commando of inmates of all nationalities rose up, brought out weapons they had stolen and concealed ready for this moment, and took over the camp. They shorted the current, forced several holes in the barbed wire fence and occupied the administrative offices of the camp Kommandantur and the telephone exchange. They hoisted a white flag on the top of the squat tower over the archway which joined the solidly built brick buildings standing either side of the main gate.

The telephone rang in the exchange. The Chief of Police in Weimar, Schmidt, wanted to speak to the Camp Commandant.

'He's not here at present,' one of the German prisoners replied with a crowd of others listening at his shoulders. 'We're hoping he'll come back soon.'

'How's it going at Buchenwald?' Schmidt demanded.

*'Comme ci, comme ça.'*

'Are all the prisoners dead yet?'

'Not quite all.'

'And the sentries're still at the posts?'

'Yes.'

'Good. It'd be a disaster if the prisoners managed to escape. There'd be a bloodbath in Weimar.'

Schmidt was lucky. Troops of the 6th Armoured division in General Patton's 3rd US Army took Weimar that day, arrested Schmidt and put him beyond the reach of rough justice.

The Americans arrived in Buchenwald shortly afterwards. The first men into the camp were Sergeant Herb Gottschalk and Captain Keffer, later Professor of Physics at Pittsburgh University. They found 21,000 men in the camp and an open trench filled with more than 15,000 rotting skeletal corpses. They never forgot the smell, or the sight of the crowds of prisoners coming to welcome them, some shuffling so slowly they seemed hardly to move. Their skinny bodies had run out of strength to move faster.

Jacques joined the others crowding the square by the main gate. Men with some strength left were dancing and laughing, singing national anthems of every sort, and even those about expire somehow pulled themselves out of their huts to witness what they had hoped for so long to see.

The Americans troops were still fighting the retreating SS but more soldiers arrived in the camp and set up an organisation to cope until the Red Cross could take over. They started field kitchens and began making a list of everyone alive in the camp. Jacques gave his name and home address. Three days later two Americans brought fresh food into his hut. Jacques had become so used to the emaciated shapes of his fellows in the camp that he was amazed at the striking health and fitness of the red-cheeked American soldiers framed in the doorway. For their part, the two soldiers were incredulous and embarrassed by the sight of so many devastated and filthy men crammed inside the wooden hut and lying on the bare boards. Jacques made certain he refused to eat more than a very little of the delicious food they offered. He knew full well that rich food would cause havoc in stomachs used to camp slop, and had no intention of dying from dysentery after they had been liberated.

In Louvain François and the family were still sitting round the radio at night, listening to the seemingly endless lists of names obtained by the British and American troops in camps in Germany: Neuengamme, Natzweiler, Bergen–Belsen, Dachau. François, perhaps more than the others, knew what misery attached to each name.

However it was by telegram that they learned their father was alive. Bertha received the news on 14 April and immediately came round to Mussenstraat to tell François. It was a weekend but he wasted no time. At General Headquarters in Brussels, he used his position as Adjutant in the Belgian army to rustle the paperwork through and obtained an indefinite pass which allowed him to join the American troops at the front. He was not a man to allow a small problem like the lack of transport to get in his way and persuaded a British army corporal who was a despatch rider to give him his uniform, boots and motor bicycle. Within the day François set off on his own to drive across Germany to find Jacques. At last he could do something to help his father. Germany had only recently been invaded by the Americans, the towns and villages were in ruins, the people bitter and reluctant to admit defeat and he knew the journey would not be easy. He pressed on recklessly over roads pockmarked with shell holes and covered with rubble from bombing, praying he would be in time, before his father either died or was moved. François's sense of guilt that he had been responsible for sending his father to Buchenwald made him savagely determined to bring him back himself.

In the camp, Jacques was unwell and had had to visit the invalid block for treatment. He was very weak. Wearing his shabby grey and blue striped coat, which fell to his ankles, he spent much of the day sitting with his Belgian friends admiring the brazen good health of the American troops. Watching their youth and strength, he felt and looked eighty years old, though he had passed his fifty-fifth birthday four days after the camp was liberated, on 15 April.

'I'm sure François will come for me,' Jacques said suddenly, staring at the main gate.

'Nonsense!' his friend Adolphe Malherbe laughed. 'All the way over here in Germany? I doubt it.'

'If he's still alive, he'll come,' Jacques Daman replied with simple conviction.

'I'll bet you he doesn't,' Adolphe smiled. He was a small man with glasses and came from Kortrijk-Duitsel near Louvain. Jacques had no doubt about his son and took him up on the bet. They settled on a crate of the best champagne as the wager.

Three days later, on 18 April, the Americans called the Belgians together and told them they were going home. They mustered at the main gate and were driven to Weimar airfield in US Army 'deuce-and-a-half' trucks. They were told Dakotas would take them back to Belgium.

'Where's your son now?' Adolphe asked good-naturedly as they sat by the few airfield huts, waiting for the planes.

'I don't know,' Jacques replied, despondent but still sure. 'But I know he's coming.'

François had been badly held up by the condition of the roads, by three punctures and by endless roadblocks of American Military Police, who were taking no chance that Nazis might slip through their extended lines in disguise, a trick they had tried with considerable success at the start of the Ardennes offensive. After three gruelling days and nights on the road, François was moving up through the 2nd echelon support troops of the 6th Armoured division, not many miles short of the front which had liberated Buchenwald a week before. He was closing in on Weimar, while his father waited on the airfield for the Dakotas to take him home.

The Belgians with Jacques were used to waiting, and to disappointment. The American planes never turned up at Weimar. After a whole day spent by the runway, the trucks took them back to Buchenwald and they slept another night in the hut they had hoped that morning never to see again.

The next day they reassembled as instructed near the main gate to await new developments. Jacques and Adolphe sat together on a couple of boxes and talked of home.

'Any Belgians here yet?' Jacques asked.

'No,' Adolphe replied, laughing. 'You've lost your bet. But we'll drink the stuff together back home, don't you worry about that.'

Jacques did not notice Adolphe wander off with one or two others, chatting busily. He was watching the American soldiers near the gate. He could not get over how very healthy they looked. A number of his friends walked slowly back to him and stood in a group, among them Adolphe and another man from Louvain, Louis Somers.

'Have you got your bottles of champagne?' Adolphe said, grinning.

'There's still time,' Jacques replied firmly, smiling himself. 'I haven't lost my bet yet.'

Several more joined them and Jacques remarked, 'Any more of you and we'll have enough for a game of cards.'

They gathered round him and Jacques said, 'What happening? What's going on?'

No one spoke except Adolphe, who said, 'Jacques, old friend, I've lost my bet.'

Jacques looked back at the soldiers at the gate. One of them with his back to him caught his eye. He was wearing different combat clothing to the Americans. He had on a thick leather jerkin tied at the waist with a wide belt, riding trousers and high boots. His back was spattered with mud and dust. Something about that back was familiar, his head too. Jacques suddenly concentrated on the figure, which slowly turned.

'My son!' Jacques burst out, as François turned to face him. 'My son!' Tears began to stream down his face as he struggled to his feet, pushing his hands on his knees, oblivious of his smiling friends. His son! He had known his son would come.

'Father!' François walked quickly towards him, hands outstretched and they fell in each other's arms. Jacques's face was unashamedly streaked with tears, his mind filled with the joy of seeing his son again, and his skinny hands moved feebly over François head to prove by touch what was almost too much happiness for his eyes to see.

'My child, my child!'

François held his father close, but so carefully. He was appalled to find his father so changed, so grey, thin and aged. He could not prevent his tears but the expression on his thin face told a different story, of relief at having found his father at last after such a journey across Germany, of grief at his beloved father's terrible condition, and of crucifying guilt that it had all come about because of his own persistence in the Underground.

Behind them Adolphe was still grinning, and Louis Somers was congratulating François on his epic, and unique, drive to find them in the camp.

Having come so far, François was not going to allow his father and the other Belgians out of his hands. After a while he left them to hustle round the American officers and the Red Cross. Impressed with his determination, they were only too pleased to help. They provided a truck and driver and François arranged for Jacques and twenty others to be driven across Germany straight to Louvain.

'Aren't you coming too?' Jacques asked when they were all safely installed in the truck.

'No, father,' François replied, his face serious and in control again. 'I'm going to use the bike and stay in Germany for a while to see if I can find Hortense and mother.' They had been seen in Ravensbrück but there was a possibility that they had been moved from there. Transport between camps were common. 'I'll see you back home in Louvain.'

'Good luck.' Jacques understood his son's feelings too well to try to dissuade him.

The truck lurched off homeward bound and took three days and nights to reach Louvain. Jacques and his friends were unsympathetic about the destruction they saw on the road. They had no trouble with the Military Police.

'We've come from Buchenwald!' they called out and one look in the back of the truck at the emaciated men

355

in dirty grey and blue coats was enough for the amazed policemen to stop all the other traffic and wave them on. Finally the truck stopped in Tiensepoort, not far from Pleinstraat. No one knew they were coming. Jacques and Louis Somers were picked up by an only too willing man in a car and taken home. Jacques told the driver to go to Frederik Lintstraat where his eldest daughter Bertha and her husband Guillaume lived, with Michel their little son. Of all the family, Bertha was most sure to be at home. The driver dropped him outside the house and Jacques stood for a moment by himself looking round, weak and thin inside his dirty camp clothes but triumphant that he had come back. He savoured the familiarity of the terraced street and the atmosphere of his own home town. Then he knocked on the door.

It was opened by his youngest daughter Julia, who stood for a moment staring at the strange-looking person outside. She was fourteen years old. Suddenly recognition dawned.

'Father! Father!' she shouted and flung herself into his arms.

He was back with his family.

Behind Julia he saw Michel, his little grandson, toddling along the passage to see him, calling, 'Granpa! Granpa!'

He weighed 5 stone 12 pounds. He had to go through official medical examinations but the doctor who took most care of him was Viktor Janssens, Bertha's brother-in-law, who had stayed with her for much of the Occupation.

Jacques lost no time in going to see his house in Pleinstraat and then took an interest in the repair work François had already begun. There was nowhere to sit in the house so he spent a good deal of time in the bar opposite, run by Léon. There he met Syd Clews, who with other British soldiers used the bar because it was the nearest to their depot in the factory.

Syd was a thoughtful person with a fine sense of humour and he could not help noticing how gaunt the elderly Belgian was, and sad. He offered Jacques a drink, for company. Then they began to chat and soon got on rather well. Syd had picked up a smattering of Flemish buying stores locally and they had no difficulty understanding each other.

'I'll get you some extra bits and pieces,' he said in a low tone to Jacques one day. The Belgians were very short of rations and he hated the idea that a man who had been through so much should be left without the food necessary to his recovery. Running the stores put him in the perfect position to help. He gave his Belgian friend cigarettes, though Jacques was not particularly keen on English brands, and extra food. In the rank of Staff Sergeant he was entitled every month to a bottle of gin and a bottle of whisky, at seven shillings each, which he shared with Jacques although he could take only a very little.

In time Syd learnt why Jacques looked a man who had lost part of his life. The older man told him something of his family's history in the Occupation and that his wife was lost somewhere in the Nazi camps. And he told Syd about Hortense too.

In Germany François used the motor bicycle to look for his mother and sister. He spent a grim two weeks driving from camp to camp looking at thousands upon thousands of skeletal survivors and going through lists of names in the temporary offices set up in each camp by the Red Cross. There was no sign or record of them.

On 23 April as François began his search for them, Hortense and Stephanie had just left Ravensbrück and were moving into the middle of the Nazis' last stand against the massed Soviet divisions from the East.

The convoy of trucks left Ravensbrück escorted by German staff cars and was immediately held up on roads jammed with a mixture of Wehrmacht vehicles. Hortense and Stephanie were in the last of ten trucks and could see the countryside through the canvas hooped over the back, a dirty green frame to their first sight of the world outside the camp. Neither of them felt free. All around were Germans and some of the women were sure the move was just another skilful lie, a cover up for death transports. Hortense shared these general suspicions, but the further they drove away from Ravensbrück, the better she felt. They passed through the small town of Furstenberg going north and then turned westwards towards the port of Lübeck 150 miles away on the coast. They kept to the main roads in accordance with Bernadotte's agreement.

Hortense noticed the sound of artillery fire getting nearer and nearer as the hours passed, the deep note of the big guns and a sharper, sometimes continuous hissing roar, of the multi-barrel rockets known as Stalin's Organs. These vast 240 mm rockets pulverised whole areas of enemy positions and terrified the soldiers with their noise. The Germans were making their last stand against General Rokossovski's 2nd White Russian front, with no chance of success but with great determination. The fighting was as bitter and vicious round Berlin at the end as it had been throughout the German occupation of Poland and the Russias.

The pace was extremely slow. They were held up by Wehrmacht traffic withdrawing westwards to new positions or simply in headlong retreat to avoid capture by the Russians. Huge Tiger tanks, Panzer tanks, lorries filled with exhausted troops hardly more than boys, half-tracks and staff cars, and motorbike despatch riders surrounded them. Hortense watched a hurrying procession of men in field grey uniforms with the winged eagle badge on their chests above the swastika which had spread fear and misery across Europe. Their faces were grimed with dirt, drawn with endless fighting and their uniforms shabby. Their days of success, lording it over the occupied territories, were gone and they were now fighting with their last breath of life round the capital of their Thousand Year Reich.

After a couple of hours the convoy stopped in a village, near a water pump. Some of the women got out to drink, but Hortense had no strength to climb out and knew she would be unable to climb back. Stephanie was prepared to fetch them both water when the tall, blond driver came and looked inside over the tailgate.

'Would you like a drink?' he asked Hortense, using sign language and smiling.

She enjoyed the young man's attention, not simply because he was tall and good looking but because he was the first man who had been genuinely pleasant to her for a very long time.

'Yes, please,' Hortense replied gratefully, nodding. She was pleased her mother did not have to leave her.

'Pass your mug, if you've got one?' he said in gestures.

'I have,' Hortense said but hesitated. 'I've had typhus. I don't know. It may be infected still.' As she spoke she wiped the mug doubtfully on her filthy camp dress.

The young Swedish driver shrugged and smiled. He reached out and took the beaker. In a moment he had filled it and drank from it himself, just to set her mind at rest and prove she had his full support. Guessing at the treatment she had received, he felt she had lost confidence in mankind. Then he refilled the beaker and passed it up to her in the lorry, making a special show of wiping the lip where he had been drinking.

The convoy restarted and continued its snail-like progress through the battlefield. The noise of gunfire was louder and the Germans with them on the road more frantic.

The Bernadotte-Himmler agreement stipulated conditions which did not make the race to escape the Russian advance any easier. They were surrounded by Germans. They were escorted by them and had to remain on main roads which were also used by the Wehrmacht. When

Hortense and her family had tried to walk out of the German grasp in 1940 they had been able to avoid the conflict. Now she and her mother were in the middle and had no option but to take their chance. Freedom and their home lay in the West. Their trucks were vulnerable enough as military soft-skinned vehicles but the white crosses on the tops made them more obvious than ever. There was no way of telling that the lorries belonged to the Red Cross. Finally the convoy had to travel in broad daylight. Count Bernadotte had little option when he sat opposite Himmler in Berlin. He was not in any position to force his arguments. The Swedish Red Cross were unable to change the rules when they left the camp and the result was cruelly expensive.

Not more than half an hour after their stop for water, Russian planes began attacking the packed road. It seemed to Hortense that the sky was full of fighter aircraft screaming round the vehicles like hornets, bombing and machine-gunning at will.

Panic was immediate. Everyone on the road, prisoners and Germans, fell out of their vehicles into the deep ditches at the side of the road. Hortense could not move fast enough, partly because of her stiff leg, which was in agony, and partly because she seemed to seize up inside.

'Hortenseke! Come on!' Stephanie shouted. She saw at once her daughter had lost her power of action. Since they had moved out of the Little Camp the force of their relationship had been with Stephanie. She did not hesitate. With bombs exploding on the road either side of them, there was no time for niceties. She reached back for Hortense, grabbed her by the hair, which was growing back, and pulled her out of the truck. Hortense hung on tightly to her mother's hand wrapped in her hair and tumbled after her into the ditch on the right of the truck. Most of the other women had moved more quickly and chosen the other ditch as far from the truck as possible. Only the slow ones went for the ditch near the lorries and almost as Stephanie and Hortense reached the ditch, their lorry was hit and burst into flames above them on the road.

Stephanie pulled Hortense as far away as she could, wriggling down the ditch. They lay face down on the bank at the bottom, blocking their ears to the shattering noise of planes diving on the road and shaken with the groundwaves of the explosions. Hortense heard hysterical screaming right beside her and looked up. A German officer and a woman in uniform had leaped off a motorbike and fallen in the ditch next to them. The two were quite oblivious of sharing the nearest useful cover with two dirty emaciated camp prisoners in striped blue and grey dresses. They lay side by side in abject terror, both shrieking with fear, tears pouring down their cheeks. They were so close Hortense almost reached out to touch the officer. She took a quick look at the road. Every vehicle seemed to be on fire, a tank, staff cars; blazing petrol fires had engulfed all the Red Cross lorries.

The planes left as quickly as they had come, leaving devastation on the road. Hortense and her mother got slowly out of the ditch and joined the other prisoners. They had been lucky. The ditch on the other side had received a direct hit and several of the women were killed outright, and some more were injured. Hortense looked at their lorry. It was burning fiercely. She was shocked to see the tall Swedish driver lying quite still in the road beside his cab, his blond hair filthy and matted with blood. The Swedes had suffered badly. All but a few of the drivers had been killed or seriously wounded. The convoy had been destroyed.

The remaining drivers managed to save one lorry. The wounded were put inside and the rest followed it very slowly through the chaos of broken vehicles until they could turn off the road. The Swedes made for a wood and told the women to hide there and wait for them.

They said they were going to find some more vehicles and come back.

Hortense felt no sense of outrage at the attack on their column. She and all the other women understood that they were caught up in the middle of a fierce battle and could not claim special privileges when they all wanted the Germans to be defeated. Clearly the pilots had no way of knowing there were camp prisoners among the Wehrmacht military vehicles, and it was doubtful whether it would have made any difference had they known the significance of the white crosses on the roofs of the trucks.

They had plenty of time to consider all this for the Swedes did not return until the third day. For two nights the women lay hiding in dense bracken deep inside the wood. The distant noise of the battle had gradually caught them up, like a huge destructive thunderstorm, until the crash and thunder of its greatest elements filled the air around them.

Confidence returned with the Swedes who brought new lorries and the convoy started again on the third day. Once more the pace was slow. The planes again dived on to the road, bombing the vehicles and machine-gunning the figures they could see running for cover. Once more Stephanie seized her daughter and dragged her out of their lorry, across a ditch and under a hedge, and they hid in a field beside the road with a group of other women.

For the first time since hearing the Stukas dive-bomb her home in Pleinstraat in 1940, Hortense was terrified. Waves of nausea filled her to the exclusion of everything else. All she could think of was being helplessly torn apart by the terror which rained upon them from the sky. She clung to her mother's breast like a little child, trying to curl into a tight ball as small as possible so the pilots could not see her or the bombs seek her out on the ground.

The bravest men and women will testify to being frightened under air attack but there is more to Hortense's reaction than this. In 1940 she was a young girl just in her teens, with a child's callous ignorance of suffering and death. Like all children she faced life day by day with simple honesty, unburdened with the fear of future grief. She accepted events as they occurred, including danger and its consequences. This uncluttered attitude had hardened during the Occupation, when the excitements and risk of the underground life demanded tough decisions and allowed no sentimentality; and it carried her through the camp. There, prisoners who pummelled their brains for the logic of their misery soon lost heart and died. However she was now eighteen, not a child, and the tall, good looking driver had given her confidence that there was a real chance of survival, if they escaped the battlefield. She was weak from lack of food and sick with her leg wound, but she could see a growing light at the end of a long tunnel and she desperately wanted to be there.

There were a lot of dead. A number of prisoners had been machine-gunned and the cries of the wounded could be heard long after the noise of the aircraft had faded away. After some minutes Hortense recovered enough to take notice of what was going on and walked back to the road with her mother. 'Hortenseke! Help me,' a woman called out. Hortense looked and recognised a woman she knew well from Louvain, lying behind some tufts of grass. She had been in the camp for months. Hortense went over and stared in amazement. 'Please help me.' Quite conscious, the woman seemed unaware she was going to die. Her stomach was open from chest to pelvis and her guts were heaving inside.

'Come on,' Stephanie said firmly and pulled her daughter away. There was nothing anyone could do.

A smaller number of women gathered on the road: after months or years in the camp, some had died in the last race to freedom. They helped the Swedes pile the dead in one lorry and the wounded in another and once more they hid in a wood. The drivers returned with more lorries. There were many less women to bring out.

The drivers had a conference in the wood. Their German escort had vanished and it was decided to ignore the rules of the Bernadotte-Himmler agreement. If they continued to move by day they would all be killed. The pilots clearly had no idea what the white crosses meant, and travelling on the busy main roads was asking for more trouble. They waited for nightfall, and the small line of lorries continued westwards on the side roads. The noise of battle could be heard on all sides but their progress was no faster. They dared not show any lights and quite often volunteers had to walk in front of the trucks to make sure the vehicles did not drive into the ditches. They hid in woods during the day and arrived in the port of Lübeck two days later.

Hortense saw at once there was nothing for them in Lübeck. The town was in ruins, with hardly a building neither damaged nor completely destroyed. Fires burned everywhere in the rubble which had fallen out of collapsing houses and blocked many of the roads. The Swedes drove them to the port. They hoped to find a boat to take them to Denmark or Sweden, but every ship was in flames or burnt out. They wasted no time and turned back from the dock areas, *en route* north to Kiel. There was no rejoicing in the scene of destruction, but Hortense was not alone in feeling some satisfaction that the Germans had had their share of the war.

The drivers pressed on in the dark as fast as they dared. After Lübeck the sound of guns faded. Kiel had suffered the same beating as Lübeck so they headed for Denmark, keeping to the small roads and forest tracks. Without the incessant fear of air attack or being overtaken by the

Russian advance the atmosphere began to lighten and spirits rose.

The drivers decided to travel by day now. The countryside was quiet, the only sound the steady grind of the diesel engines and squeak of springs on the potholed roads.

Finally on Sunday, 29 April in the early evening sun, the half dozen battered trucks entered the woods in the flat lands west of Flensburg. They trundled slowly up a long ride in the forest. They came to a single white pole spanning the track between the tall pine trees. A group of Red Cross officials were waiting. The trucks pulled up in a clearing on the other side of the pole and switched off their engines. A great peace descended on the clearing. Only the soft sound of steps rustling the fallen pine-needles could be heard. The Red Cross men and nurses came to the back of Hortense's lorry.

'You're in Denmark,' they said, smiling.

Hortense and Stephanie had heard that Denmark had not been liberated but there was no fighting and they were out of Germany. Maybe, just maybe, they might live to go home.

They helped each other out of the lorry and shuffled painfully back to the white pole which marked the border. All the others who had survived so far had the same thought. The evening air was still sunlit, warm with the promise of spring as the women gathered at the barrier. They looked down the avenue of pines back the way they had come, towards Germany. There was nothing to see except the forest ride which disappeared southwards into a point between the swaying trees under the pale blue sky. Like school children, they all jeered and shook their fists at the 'Third Reich'.

And they began to laugh.

The following day, Monday, 30 April, Adolf Hitler committed suicide in his bunker beneath the Imperial

Chancellery in Berlin and was cremated. A week later, on 8 May, the European war officially ended.

In Louvain there was no news of Hortense and Stephanie. The family sat every night and listened to the broadcasts of names. Every night they went to bed depressed. They could not believe they would continue to hear nothing once the fighting was over. François came back from his search round the concentration camps in the British and American zones of occupied Germany. He had found nothing. They were disheartened thinking of the speed with which Jacques's name had been sent back to Bertha in Louvain.

The days passed and turned into weeks, still with no report. François was not alone in thinking the worst. Never a person to waste words, he needed no more than a glance at his father's face to know neither of them expected to see Hortense and Stephanie again.

As May slipped into June and the weather turned fine after the deepest winter of the war, the family began to accept the real possibility of their loss. But no one spoke of their fears. None of them would quite give up hope. Bertha continued to visit the Red Cross and the Ministry of Health and Social Welfare to lodge requests for news of Hortense and Stephanie, while François made his own extensive inquiries through official military channels. Many of his old comrades in the Partisans helped including Pierre van Goitsenhoeven. All they discovered was that Ravensbrück had been sucked under the Russian advance on 29 April. The Russians had discovered there 2000 sick and dying women, out of the tens of thousands who had been imprisoned in the camp. In the last weeks the SS had simultaneously allowed the Red Cross to take away truckloads of the women, because their commander Himmler had agreed to it, and killed all but a handful of the rest. Most of the former died of hunger and exhaustion on forced marches to the West to escape the Russians.

'We'll never see them again,' Jacques voiced all their feelings one night as they sat round the kitchen table in Bertha's house.

François and Bertha dared not speak. In the soft light of the lamp they watched the tears roll silently down their father's cheeks.

The voice of the broadcaster droned on with the list of names, one after the other, each a terrible indictment on the misery of Hitler's regime. Bertha's husband Guillaume sat quietly in the corner with Julia. Half hoping, half listening, they were all sunk in their own thoughts, staring at the floor.

'Daman, Hortense,' said the voice.

Everyone in the little kitchen looked up at once staring at the radio in disbelief.

'Daman, Hortense,' repeated the voice and continued down the alphabetical list.

Jacques's tears of unhappiness turned to joy. 'She's alive,' he muttered thickly. 'My Hortenseke's alive!'

Everyone was crying, but silently keeping their questions till the end. A deep pit of sorrow remained in their thoughts, ready to engulf them in spite of the good news. There was no news of Stephanie.

'Van den Eynde, Stephanie,' intoned the voice after taking so long to reach to the last letters of the alphabet, 'Van den Eynde, Stephanie.'

They went wild, talking, shouting, laughing, and crying. The tears could not be stopped. Even François cried, knowing the full penalty of his sense of guilt would not have to be paid. Against all the odds they had survived. All three of them.

'Where are they?' Bertha asked, wiping her cheeks.

'In a hostel in Sweden, it said,' replied François who had not missed a single detail. 'A place called St Margaret, in Malmö.'

Minutes later there was a knock at the door. Guillaume went to see who it was.

'Have you heard? Did you hear, Hortense and Stephanie are in Sweden!' Neighbours also listening had come at once. They were not the last. The street was busy for hours as people came round to Bertha's house, sometimes from quite far away, to pass on the wonderful news.

Hortense and Stephanie had arrived in Malmö in the first days of May. They were safe once they had reached the Red Cross in the forest at the Danish border. There they had rested, taken off all their clothes and had a really good wash without anyone laughing at them. They enjoyed a warm milk drink and slept for hours. The Red Cross nurses would give them no solid food and controlled their diet carefully. They were taken to Copenhagen, where they picked new clothes and had a trip round the city, after which they had a short but frightening boat-train journey on the ferry to Sweden and Malmö.

From Malmö they were moved to St Margaret, to a chapel which was used as a place of quarantine. Like Hortense, so many of the women had had contagious diseases such as typhus, typhoid, scarlet fever, gastro-enteritis and others, and the Red Cross wanted to keep them under observation for a while. Apart from these additional problems, all the women were seriously under-weight and needed good nursing on the path back to health. Hortense weighed just on five stones and her leg wound was still not healed. Not only their bodies needed rest and attention. It would take a long time for their minds to recover balance among people who had no idea of what they had experienced. They felt quite different from the millions in Europe who went mad with excitement on Victory day.

They had been in Malmö only a day or so when a girl came in to the chapel and said, 'The war is over.'

There was no reaction, no cheering, nothing. Hortense, Stephanie and all the other women looked at her in utter silence. For a long time no one spoke and then a voice said flatly, 'Hoorah.'

It was over. There was nothing more to be said.

Hortense and Stephanie spent the days resting and soaking up the summer sun, thinking about going home. They were allowed to write one postcard, and this arrived in Louvain after the radio broadcast which the family had heard. The postal service was run by the military and was unable to cope with the volume of distressing mail between families spread all over Europe, let alone the celebrations of victory. There was so much to do in the aftermath of war and information about people took a long time to come through.

Finally in late June the two received word that the Belgians were to be repatriated. On the morning of Friday, 29 June they were taken to the airfield at Malmö and boarded a Royal Canadian Air Force Lancaster bomber. The crew had been told who they were to carry and went out of their way to assist the slower women into the belly of the aircraft and gently lead them to seats in the bomb bay. Hortense was very excited at going home, but even more so by the prospect of her first flight in an aeroplane. The big four-engined plane took off, gained altitude and wheeled south-west on a course over Denmark and Holland towards Belgium. Hortense found the noise inside deafening, but she was so keyed up she sat and chatted to one of the crew in the middle of the aircraft or peered through an observation bubble at the view of the landscape below her.

The Lancaster turned and made its finals to land at Evere military airfield at Brussels just over two hours later, in the early afternoon. Hortense could hardly control her excitement as the bomber lumbered along the taxiway towards the control tower. She could see a number of cars parked beside the airfield buildings at the side of the runway and she pointed out to her mother the little figures she could see, men women and children, waving at the plane. The families had come to welcome them home.

The Lancaster stopped and the pilot cut power to the engines which quickly wound down. One by one the propellers stopped moving leaving the women with a moment's peace and quiet. The silence was broken by the door in the aircraft flapping open and a rush of happy voices filled the inside of the plane. In a moment, Hortense and Stephanie were standing on the ground, back in their own country once more.

Hortense looked round for the family. 'There's no one here,' she said in astonishment. Stephanie nodded, trying to keep her face from showing her disappointment.

Suddenly they heard a familiar voice. 'Over here! Hortenseke, Stephanie!'

Auguste Geyssens and his son Jacques ran across the tarmac towards them. They all embraced each other warmly. Auguste was Hortense's godfather and her uncle.

'We didn't hear of this plane till only just a short time ago,' explained Auguste. 'We were the only ones with a car and I said I'd go at once with Jacques to meet you here. Come with us,' he urged smiling happily and leading them without delay to his car. 'I've something to show you both. We're going to Bertha's house.'

Fussing over Hortense and Stephanie, Auguste and his son settled them both in the car and took the road back to Louvain. In between the endless talk, Hortense looked out of the window. This was her country. Much of it would have been unappealing to a stranger's eye, for so many places were spoiled by the debris of war, but this was where she belonged. These were her roots. She recognised places and savoured them as the finest wine. She thrilled at a group of trees, a café, a square, all things which are taken for granted in more peaceful times when separation is voluntary and the return to enjoy them is assumed without question. There had been so many times when she had thought never to see these familiar and well-loved sights again. But she had never lost her confidence in the outcome of the war. She felt an almost savage pleasure overwhelm her at the thought that she could enjoy them without fear of being arrested, interrogated and imprisoned.

The Germans were gone.

Auguste Geyssens pulled up in Frederik Lintstraat, at Bertha's house. There was no one in the street. For a brief moment Hortense and Stephanie stood on the doorstep together, rather as they had done throughout the endless months in the camp. The power of the relationship they had forged between them had brought them through, giving one the strength to lift the other when she was down. This force had proved indestructible. Strong as it was however it had its origins in a deeper and wider base which was the whole family. In that moment of reunion this family love filled them both, swelling and bursting inside them, and became tangible when the door opened and they found themselves wrapped in the arms of their father and husband, Jacques, Bertha and Julia beside him, François behind her with little Michel, Lisa and her son Jacques. Behind them were Pierre van Goitsenhoeven with his mother and father, Auguste Geyssens's wife Julia and Marie-Louise's husband Dr Viktor Janssens.

All those who had made that first long and utterly fruitless journey as refugees in May 1940 were back together, against all the odds. All except Stephanie's father and mother. Barbara had died soon after returning in 1940 and 'Bompa' died two weeks before Jacques had returned from Buchenwald, sadly without knowing any of the three had survived. He had prayed every day to see his beloved daughter and granddaughter again. He never forgot Hortense's face as he saw her last, standing on the pile of rubble in the Little Prison in Louvain after the bombing, framed by the gap in the prison wall. He remembered shouting, 'Courage!' to her and he had always been sure that even if he never saw her again she would have died with the sound ringing in her ears.

The tears continued to flow long after the first emotional embrace, as one or other in the crowd of family and friends would suddenly succumb to the sheer pleasure of their return or be reminded of the horrors they had suffered. The story-telling went on through the afternoon, into the evening and past midnight until Hortense and Stephanie were exhausted.

'Let me take you home,' Jacques smiled.

'Pleinstraat?' Stephanie asked, surprised. 'I thought someone said the house was damaged.'

'It was. François has done all the repairs and this will be the first night anyone's slept in it since the Germans wrecked it. We won and we're going back.'

Hortense was extremely tired by the time they were driven round to Pleinstraat and hardly able to concentrate on the new decorations to the house. It was enough to be in her own home again. She fell asleep at once, content that her parents were together again on one side of her and her little sister Julia on the other. She was back in her own bed, without fear of a midnight knock on the door. She was eighteen and the war was over.

# 14

# The New Generations

'Live all you can; it's a mistake not to.' Henry
James in *The Ambassadors* (1903).

Peace started with a party. Hortense was woken
the following morning by the sound of a band
in the street, right outside the house. When she
looked out she saw Pleinstraat was full of people. All
their friends had turned out to welcome them home
and were determined to celebrate. They had been up
early and decorated the street with branches of foliage.
A large notice hung over the front door of the shop
which declared 'Welkom' and was surrounded by hanging
garlands, evergreens, masses of flowers and the flags of
Belgium, Great Britain and the United States.

Jacques and Stephanie declared open house, and
friends came in to see them one after the other all
day and long into the night. Groups gathered in the
street outside and Léon's café opposite never closed.
Those from Pleinstraat who came to see them included
Hortense's great friend Anna Storckel, Josephine de
Roost who had had hidden explosives in her house,
Gustaaf Legrande the prison verger and Marcel Van
den Borght the gendarme. Hortense met her old contacts
and friends in the Resistance, among them her close
cousin Pierre Hermans, Jommeke Vanderstappen, Josef

Homblet, Joan and Philemon de Witt, and others who had run safe houses including the nuns from the Groot Begijnhof. They talked of the Occupation and mourned the ones who had not survived. François's contacts from the Légion Belge or Secret Army came from Brussels, headed by General van Overstraten.

Jan Sprengers was one of the first to see Hortense, and brought his wife. They had met on the farm where he had spent the rest of the war in hiding. He was in tears of happiness to find Hortense was alive and well, and overwhelmed with gratitude for the risk she ran to warn him; and he cried some more thinking of her ordeal in the camp. Hortense was taken by surprise to find he was married, but discovered she was not broken-hearted in the event. So much had changed since she had been fond of Jan. They were both changed in different ways and it did not seem to matter any more. But beyond that, he was still a close friend.

The British soldiers from the depot joined in. Her father and François introduced her to Staff Sergeant Syd Clews. François had met Syd with his father in the café and the two got on easily. They often sat and talked about the family before François heard his mother and sister were still alive. By the time they came home Syd knew quite a lot about the Damans. When he heard about the welcoming celebrations he did what he could to manipulate the depot stores for food and drink, using all the tricks, as only the best quartermaster sergeants in the British army know how. His Flemish was improving all the time and in the weeks that followed he always came over to join in when he had some spare time. Hortense was attracted by his cheerful enthusiasm and uncomplicated pleasure in life and people. Syd found himself fascinated by her.

The next day the visits started again and the festivities continued without a rest for four days. Hortense had recovered some weight in Sweden and she loved a good party, but she was tired out every evening. She found it impossible to stay up talking into the small hours although she wanted to pick up all the threads which had been destroyed when they were arrested.

There was talk of the Germans. She learned of the fate of the Military Governor, General von Falkenhausen. He had supported the group of officers who tried to kill Hitler with a bomb in July 1944, and was arrested himself by Himmler's SS and sent to a concentration camp. Others had had more luck. Max Gunter, who had tortured both Hortense and her mother, and countless others in Breendonk, fled from Louvain to Germany in September 1944 before the Allies liberated Belgium. He had not been seen since. Like many other SS, Gunter was sentenced to death *in absentia* on 9 July 1949, and all efforts to locate him since have failed. His counterpart Robert Verbelen, also a Belgian by birth, succeeded in escaping justice too. He fled to Germany and then to Austria where he took out Austrian citizenship. He was sentenced to death by a Belgian court and steps were taken to extradite him from Vienna where he lived. The attempt was long-winded and unsuccessful: in December 1965 Verbelen was acquitted by the Austrian court and allowed to remain free in Austria. He still lives openly in Vienna and can be found in the telephone book. Other Belgians in the SS whom Hortense had had the misfortune to meet during her captivity were given the fate they deserved: Lambert Janssens, Fernand Faignaert, the brothers René and Albrecht van Avondt, Frederik Dirickx, Marcel Engelen and other young men – most were in their early twenties at the beginning of the war – were tried at a court in Louvain in November 1945, found guilty of war crimes including torture and murder and sentenced to death.

Victory brought a great swing of popular feeling against those who had assisted the Germans. More than 87,000 were brought to trial for collaboration in varying degrees.

By November 1945 only 914 had been tried, 300 were sentenced to death, and 58 received prison sentences of less than five years. Eventually 10,000 were acquitted. Sentences of death were passed on 4170 but only 230 were actually executed.

The SS in the camps were also tried in due course. Professor Karl Gebhardt and Viktor Brack, the SS doctors who pursued experiments in gangrene and X-ray sterilisation on humans, were hanged. Their assistant doctor Hertha Oberheuser received twenty years in prison. Others like Dorothea Binz, doctors Percy Treite and Rolf Rosenthal, the dentist Hellinger, the matron Elisabeth Marschall, Carmen Mory and many others were captured in the aftermath of German defeat, were tried and received judgment at the Nuremberg trials, which ranged from death by hanging to long prison sentences. Hortense was asked to testify but her mother and father did not want her to be subjected to a humiliating cross examination by defence counsel. She had suffered enough. She was still a legal minor and they would not let her go. Many who did appear as witnesses at the trials never recovered from being made to feel it was themselves who were the guilty ones.

The accusations of collaboration and the process of these trials may have been necessary but they kept alive the bitterness of the wartime years. Worse, the political ambitions of the Communists had spoilt the reputation of the Partisans. Hortense was shocked to find people suspicious of anyone who had been in the Belgian Army of Partisans. She learned also that a good many were cashing in on the safety of peace to paint their own wartime experiences in exceptionally colourful and imaginative terms. The result was that Hortense, her family and other Partisans like Hermans and van Goitsenhoeven, who had fought the Germans during the war preferred not to say anything about it, rather than be associated with the bar-fly story-tellers. The time would come for them to speak out and tell the truth, when the bitter feelings of the war years had grown less acute.

Today those who survive now believe that each small fragment of their history during that momentous period must be recorded or the new generations will never know what really happened, the sacrifices of ordinary men and women will be forgotten, and freedom will again die under the oppression of another 'New Order'.

Whatever the atmosphere immediately after the war, their exploits were officially recognised. Hortense was awarded various decorations, among them the prestigious Belgian appointment of Knight of the Order of King Leopold II and bar, the Croix de Guerre and bar, and the Medal of Resistance. She was finally rewarded twenty-five years after the end of the war, somewhat late in the day, for helping the Russians, when the general in Moscow sent her the Distinguished Badge of the Soviet Committee of War Veterans. In addition to Belgian awards, her brother François, Pierre Hermans and Pierre van Goitsenhoeven received a British honour, the King's Medal for Courage in the Cause of Freedom, in recognition of their excellent and brave work in the Resistance all through the Occupation. The presentation was made at the British Embassy in Brussels by the Ambassador Sir Christopher Warner and Squadron Leader Peter Townsend was among those who attended the ceremony.

After the welcome home party was over Hortense set to recovering her health. Viktor Janssens was very helpful and chiefly responsible for her treatment, although she and her parents were examined by other doctors to complete the official records. Under Viktor's care, which was all the more effective because he was 'family', her leg slowly healed, but she was left with an awful scar and a slight limp. Her mental rehabilitation was important too, though far less well understood then than it would be today. For years she grappled to come to terms with what she had been through while the rest of the world forgot the Occupation and turned to rebuilding their lives in the post-war era.

Still a teenager in 1945, she had experienced more in the five years of war than most people would expect in a lifetime. Her activities in the Underground had been unusual enough but as the truth of the concentration camps emerged she found she was regarded as something of a freak. People were astonished that anyone could have survived. Instead of understanding or sympathy, most of them revealed a barely concealed and prurient fascination in whether or not the women had been raped, sterilised or otherwise abused by the Nazis. In retrospect, thinking of the camps, Hortense and her parents were surprised at their own survival, but they did not talk much about it.

No one outside the family knew of her injuries and not even Viktor was able to tell at first why she had suffered so much in the camp Revier as the result of a single injection, although he may have had his suspicions. The truth dawned on her in the most bizarre way. In the first September after she came home, she went to a big fair in Louvain where she saw a large tent advertising an exhibition of waxwork models showing unusual medical diseases. She was torn between trying to forget what had happened, and a natural curiosity. She paid her money and went in. The exhibits had nothing specifically to do with the war but simply pandered to a morbid interest in sickness and death. The waxworks were accurately made to demonstrate the effects of extreme medical conditions. Hortense recognised in the lifelike models symptoms of diseases such as typhus and typhoid, which she had seen in her bare little corridor in Ravensbrück. Then she saw a wax model with a terribly swollen black leg. Deeply shocked, she found herself looking back in time at her own leg, when Elisabeth Marschall lifted it up to show her what had become of it the short time since being given the injection. A notice under the display told her these were the symptoms of a severe case of gangrene.

During those first difficult months she saw a lot of Syd Clews. He told her he had been in Louvain at the start of the war and he spent more and more time with the family, always helping in this and that. He was good company, thoughtful and kind, and Hortense soon realised his attentions were not simply because he was sorry for her. He was genuinely fond of her and his feelings were truly honest, unaffected by the implications or influences of her past. While still in the protection of her family, and happily with her mother and father still alive, she realised something new and special had emerged with him which was quite apart from the disasters of the previous years. As the weeks passed she cherished his affection more and more until, simply, they came to love each other.

Syd stayed in the depot at the Philips factory until his discharge from the army on 4 December 1945. He had to return to England but hurried back to Louvain in January and they were married there on Saturday, 23 February 1946.

Hortense and Syd made a new life for themselves in England, and he went back to his job on the management of a large pottery works in Staffordshire. They are retired now. Hortense had one last important battle to fight, which had started in the war and which demanded more than her full measure of courage. As a girl she had fought for freedom for her family, as the men had fought, and she had retained her femininity throughout, even in the camp. In peacetime she had the freedom, and she wanted her own family. She wanted children. For some time she did not realise what had happened to her in Ravensbrück. The enormity of the crime committed by the SS only became apparent as the facts of the X-ray experiments emerged at Nuremberg and were linked to the diagnoses of her doctors in England. She was not deterred. Happily, the SS had not done the job properly. But she took years to recover, with Syd's help. She was a well-known patient at her local hospital, where she now works for a hospital charity. Eventually she gave birth to a daughter, Julie, on 4 April 1961, a night the young doctor on emergency call has never forgotten. Typically not satisfied, she gave Syd a son, Christopher, seven years later on 28 June 1968. Now she has a granddaughter named after her mother Stephanie, with whom she suffered so much and who was so very close to her.

Syd's support has been invaluable, for Hortense soon found that victory did not necessarily qualify everything done in the war as a success. The Resistance had fought the Occupation but had opened some deep divisions in the community. All sides had suffered considerable losses. One day Hortense and François were discussing the war in the kitchen of the house in Pleinstraat when Bertha, exasperated by the endless talk of the past, put into words the most important question of all: 'Was it all really worth it?'

François and Hortense sat in silence while she pointed out that their father and mother had aged terribly, Hortense was sick and many of their friends had lost their lives.

In fact Jacques Daman too was very ill, debilitated by his ordeal, and died only five years after the war. He was buried in the cemetery opposite his house in a lovely plot which has been set aside for people who fought in the Underground in Louvain. Stephanie outlived him by a few years but she was never well again and died on 30 August 1954, when visiting Hortense and Syd in England. She was buried in Tunstall cemetery in Staffordshire. Hortense has always believed her mother should rest in peace beside her husband Jacques, in the cemetery where she placed flowers on the graves for so many years. François too suffered from the intense pressures he had survived on the run and only lived to the relatively young age of sixty. He died of cancer on 28 December 1973.

Was it all really worth it?

The question was hard to answer in the immediate aftermath of the war, and Hortense has taken a long time to see her experiences more objectively. Certainly the cost of resistance was high, much more than it has been since for others in different circumstances and places, for the Nazis were exceptional in their treatment of all who opposed them.

Perhaps François should have answered the question, for he was a man of twenty-seven when the Germans invaded his country. Is it fair to ask a girl of thirteen to marshal her arguments in the same way? Clearly not. The voting age has come down to eighteen in some countries, but there is no legal system in the world which places full responsibility on the shoulders of a child of thirteen. By the time Hortense was eighteen the war was over. For Hortense the question should have been put the other way around: could she have stopped herself being involved?

Her views and attitudes to life were forged by circumstances, by her parents and the society in which they all lived. Like all thirteen-year-olds she had a mind of her own by which she measured the invasion of her country. Perhaps her opinion was immature, maybe she reached the wrong conclusions. At seventeen the Germans called her a terrorist. At thirteen she had no grasp of the wider political or strategic implications, but she had eyes to see the brutalities of war and the oppression in her country. And she hated it. Her conclusions may have been simple but they were honestly held. From her point of view, she believed she had to fight.

The argument is surely unassailable. Critics cannot point to a child and say, 'You should have known better!' If criticism is to be made the adults must bear responsibility: her brother François and her parents were old enough to 'know better'.

Hortense's character makes it doubtful that she would have taken much notice even if her parents and family had tried to stop her. It is unlikely that any child so determined would have listened. Every parent knows the problems of controlling their teenage sons and daughters. She was certainly too young to judge the absolute rights and wrongs. It is equally certain she was old enough to act. Perhaps the reason why her parents and François gave their advice and support was precisely because they saw there was nothing they could do to stop her. They saw that her first enthusiasm to resist did not fade away as she grew up, that she became more aware of the dangers, that she had the courage and the commitment to fight on; so they quietly led and encouraged her. Her mother and father must have been worried out of their minds every time they saw her leave the house, knowing what risks she ran. None the less they gave her the full benefit of their family strength, which proved the bedrock force that pulled them all through the camps. Far from preventing Hortense, they supported her. What else could they have done?

Children everywhere in the world would benefit from the same encouragement. We cannot expect the same objectivity from a child as from his elders, so how can we insist the child with courage and commitment stands quietly on the sidelines? Should we condemn a child to a lifetime of regrets? Good judgement is born of experience in youth and reflection with age. If this is the quality which is important in the adult, then the child must act. By accident of birthplace there have been, and still are, young people, some younger than thirteen, fighting all over the world, in Afghanistan, Beirut, Belfast, El Salvador, Cambodia, Laos, Nicaragua, Vietnam, Somalia and many other places. From the child's perspective, who can honestly say they are wrong? Some may find a comparison of Hortense's case with these examples less than palatable, but grand objectivity is in rather short supply in the harsh realities of war, particularly in a young person. Then, perceptions are narrow and in the end only the victor is the judge, jury and executioner. We none of us choose our birthplace, so perhaps the most important thing is that young people fight their corner, whatever their colour or creed. We should only hope that we have the courage to react like Hortense.

# Bibliography

Baudhuin, Fernand, *L'économie Belge sous l'occupation 1940–1944*, Emile Bruylant, Brussels, 1945.

Bernard, Henri, *Un Maquis dans la ville*, Brussels, 1970.
*Guerre totale et guerre révolutionnaire*, Brussels, 1962–5.
*La Résistance Belge, 1940–1945*, La Renaissance du Livre, Brussels, 1969.
*Histoire de la Résistance Européenne 1940–1945*, Marabout Université, Verviers, Belgium, Gerard, 1968.

Boom, Corrie ten, *The Hiding Place*, Hodder & Stoughton, London, 1972.

Braddon, Russell, *Nancy Wake*, Cassell, London, 1956.

Brussel, Louis van, *Partizanen in Vlanderen, met actieverslag van Korps 034-Leuven*, Frans Masereel, Brussels, 1971.

Brusselmans, Anne, *Rendezvous 127: the diary of Anne Brusselmans*, Benn, London, 1954.

Bullock, Alan, *Hitler, a study in tyranny*, Pelican, London, 1962.

Calvocoressi, Peter, and Wint, Guy, *Total War*, Allen Lane, Penguin, London, 1980.

Champlain, Hélène de, *The Secret War of Hélène de Champlain*, W. H. Allen, London, 1980.

Charles, Jean-Léon, *Les Forces Armées Belges 1940–1945*, La Renaissance du Livre, Brussels, 1970.

Charles, Jean-Léon and Dasnoy, Philippe, *Les dossiers secrets*

# Bibliography

*de la Police allemande en Belgique 1940–1944*, L'Imprimerie Van In, Lier, Belgium, 1972.

Cookridge, E. H., *Inside SOE*, Arthur Barker, London, 1966.

Cosgrove, E., *The Evaders*, Clarke Irwin, Ontario, 1970.

Cowan, Lore, *Children of the Resistance*, Frewin, London, 1968.

Cruikshank, Charles, *Deception in World War II*, Oxford University Press, 1981.

Daman, Jaak, *Van Breendonk naar Buchenwald*, Drukkerij van Linthout, Brussels, 1947.

Delandsheere, Paul, and Ooms, Alphonse, *La Belgique sous les Nazis*, L'Edition Universelle SA, Brussels.

Derry, Sam, *The Rome Escape Line*, Harrap, London, 1960.

Dufournier, Denise, *Ravensbrück: the women's camp*, Allen & Unwin, London, 1948.

Dupuy, Trevor N., *European Resistance Movements*, Watts, New York, 1965.

Ed. collection, *Escape from the Swastika*, Marshall Cavendish, London, 1975.

Elliot-Bateman, Michael (ed.), *The Fourth Dimension of Warfare*, vol. I, *Intelligence Subversion Resistance*, Manchester University Press, 1970.

Foot, M. R. D., *Resistance*, Granada, London, 1978.
SOE *1940–1946*, BBC, London, 1984.
SOE *in France*, HMSO, London, 1966.

Foot, M. R. D., and J. M. Langley, *MI9 Escape and Evasion*, Little, Brown, Boston, USA, 1979.

Gleeson, James, *They feared no Evil*, Robert Hale, London, 1976.

Gotovitch, J., *Les rapports de la Sicherheitspolizei sur la Résistance Belge en 1943*, *Cahiers d'Histoire de la Deuxième Guerre Mondiale*, Pierre de Meyere, Brussels, 1967.

Gotovitch, J. *Réflexions sur la définition et la répression du terrorisme*, Editions de l'Université de Bruxelles, Brussels.

Gotovitch, J. (ed.), *Archives des partisans armés (Louis van Brussel, der Bundesarchiv, Foundation Jacquemotte)*, Brussels, 1974.

Govis, Johannes A. (ed.), *Belgium in Bondage*, Fischer, New York, 1943.

d'Harcourt, Pierre, *The Real Enemy*, Longmans, London, 1967.

Hohne, Heinz, *Codeword Direktor*, Secker & Warburg, London, 1971.

Hoste, Charles, and van Brussel, Louis (eds.), *Verbelen et ses consorts*, Centre de Documentation du Musée National de la Résistance, Brussels, 1984.

Howell, Edward, *Escape to Live*, Longmans, London, 1978.

Jouan, Cécile, *Comète*, Thomas, Brussels, 1948.

Julitte, Pierre, *Block 26*, Harrap, London, 1972.

Kirschen, Gilbert Sadi, *Six amis viendront ce soir*, Presse de Belgique, Brussels, 1983.

Koestler, Arthur, *Scum of the Earth*, Cape, London, 1941.
*Darkness at Noon*, Cape, London, 1940.

Kogon, Eugen, *The Theory and Practice of Hell*, Secker & Warburg, London, 1950.

Langley, J. *Fight Another Day*, Collins, London, 1974.

Laqueur, Walter, *Terrorism*, Weidenfeld & Nicholson, London, 1977.

Liddell Hart, B. H., *History of the Second World War*, Cassell, London, 1970.

Littlejohn, David, *The Patriotic Traitors*, Heinemann, London, 1972.

Long, Helen, *Safe Houses are Dangerous*, Kimber, London, 1985.

Lorain, Pierre, *Secret Warfare*, adapted by David Kaln, Orbis, London, 1984.

Lorinfosse, Guy de, *Au service de Leurs Majestés*, Brussels, 1974.

Macksey, Kenneth, *Partisans of Europe*, Hart-Davis, Mac-Gibbon, London, 1975.

Michel, Henri, *The Shadow War*, Deutsch, London, 1972.

Miksche, F. O., *Secret Forces, the techniques of Underground movements*, Faber, London, 1950.

Mitscherlich, A., and Mielke, F., *The Death Doctors*, Elek, London, 1962.

# Bibliography

Mountfield, David, *Partisans: the secret armies of World War II*, Hamlyn, London, 1979.

Munson, Kenneth, *Fighters and Bombers of World War II*, Peerage Books, London, 1969.

Murphy, Brendan, *Turncoat*, Macdonald, London, 1987.

Neave, Airey, *Saturday at MI9*, Hodder & Stoughton, London, 1969.

Poller, Walther, *Medical Block Buchenwald*, Souvenir Press, 1961.

Reitlinger, Gerald, *The SS: alibi of a nation 1922–1945*, Arms and Armour, London, 1981.

Rémy, Col., *Réseau Comète*, Librairie Académique Perrin, Paris, 1966.

*The Eighteenth Day*, Gateway, Los Angeles, 1978.

Rich, Norman, *Hitler's War Aims*, vols I, II, Deutsch, London, 1973.

Russell, 2nd Baron of Liverpool, *The Scourge of the Swastika*, Cassell, London, 1954.

Sim, Kevin, *Women of Courage*, Corgi, London, 1983.

Tanham, George K., *Contribution à l'histoire de la Résistance Belge 1940–1944*, Presse Universitaire de Bruxelles, Brussels, 1971.

Taylor, James, and Warren Shaw, *A Dictionary of the Third Reich*, Grafton, London, 1988.

Tickell, Gerard, *Odette*, (Chapman and Hall), Pan, London, 1955.

Villiers, José, *Granny was a Spy*, Quartet, London, 1988.

de Wilde, Maurice, *Belgium in the 2nd World War*, de Nederlandsche Boekhandd, Antwerp, 1985.

Wilkinson, James D., *The Intellectual Resistance in Europe*, Harvard University Press, Cambridge, Mass. and London, 1981.

Wolf, Jules, *Le Procès de Breendonk*, Larcier SA, Brussels, 1973.

Research was also carried out with a large number of people who were good enough to give their recollections of the times;

and a great deal of information was obtained from the following sources where the staff were always most helpful: the Public Record Office, Kew; Centre des Recherches et des Etudes Historiques de la Seconde Guerre Mondiale, Brussels; Swedish and Belgian Red Cross, through Amicales of the Belgian Prisoners of Ravensbrück and of Buchenwald; Ministère de la Santé Publique et de la Famille, and the Palais de Justice, Brussels; Special Archives Division, United States National Archives and Records Service, Washington DC; Imperial War Museum, London; RAF Escaping Society; and the Special Forces Club, London.